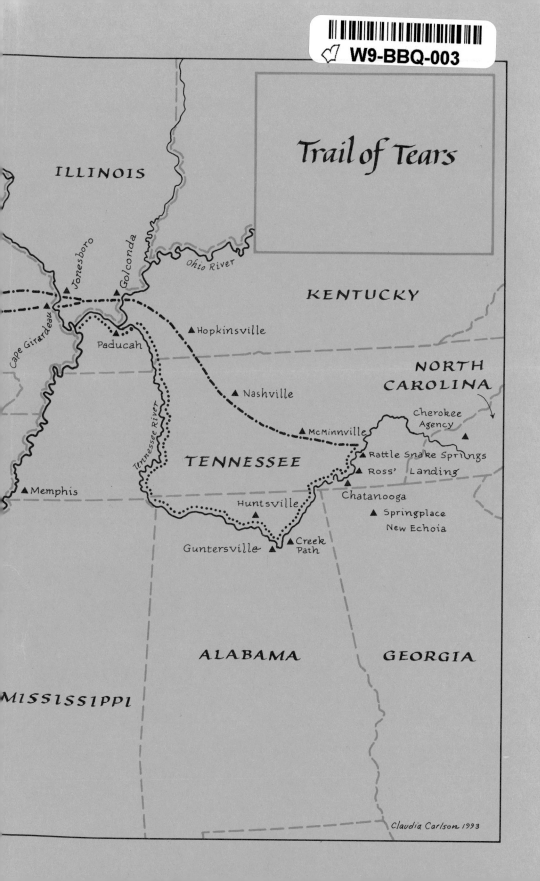

Trail of Tears

ILLINOIS

Jonesboro

Golconda

Ohio River

Cape Girardeau

KENTUCKY

Paducah

Hopkinsville

NORTH CAROLINA

Nashville

Cherokee Agency

Tennessee River

McMinnville

TENNESSEE

Rattle Snake Springs

Ross' Landing

Memphis

Chatanooga

Huntsville

Springplace
New Echoia

Guntersville

Creek Path

ALABAMA

GEORGIA

MISSISSIPPI

Claudia Carlson 1993

MANKILLER

MANKILLER

A CHIEF AND HER PEOPLE

WILMA MANKILLER

and

MICHAEL WALLIS

ST. MARTIN'S PRESS NEW YORK

DESIGN BY JUDITH A. STAGNITTO

Library of Congress Cataloging-in-Publication Data

Mankiller, Wilma Pearl.
     Mankiller : a chief and her people / Wilma Mankiller and Michael Wallis.
          p.   cm.
     ISBN 0-312-09868-5
     1. Mankiller, Wilma Pearl. 2. Cherokee Indians—Biography.   3. Cherokee Indians—Women.   4. Cherokee Indians—Kings and rulers.   I. Wallis, Michael.   II. Title.
E99.C5M335   1993
973'.04975'0092—dc20
     [B]   93-25698
                                                                     CIP

First Edition: November 1993
10 9 8 7 6 5 4 3 2 1

*T*his book is dedicated to my brother Louis Donald Mankiller, who gave up much of his youth to feed and clothe his siblings. Then in 1990, he donated a kidney to me, enabling me to continue with my life and work in good health.

CONTENTS

Contents

ACKNOWLEDGMENTS

My acknowledgment goes to all Cherokee people past, present, and future, especially the women, who have always tried to keep harmony and balance in our world.

There are many people who need to be recognized for helping with this book. It was a team effort. I will start with Charlie Soap, without whose support I would never have been elected chief, and without whose love my life would have taken a very different path.

My appreciation goes to Robert Conley for helping me to conceptualize a book that would include aspects of my life as well as Cherokee history. I want to thank my family, all of whom provided information for the book, but especially my mother, Clara Irene Sitton Mankiller, and my daughter Gina. She typed all the transcripts from the sessions with Michael Wallis, as well as countless pages of stories, commentary, and editorial notes. Special accolades also to my sister Frieda Mankiller Mullins, Lee Fleming, and Linda Vann for their help with genealogical research; to Bob Friedman and Kristina Kiehl for the equipment to do this work; and to Lynn Howard, Lisa Finley, Sammy Still, and Nita Cochran for help with photos.

Finally, I want to thank my co-writer, Michael Wallis, for his great work on this book; St. Martin's editor Robert Weil for his wisdom and unequivocal support of this project; Hazel Rowena Mills, a stellar copy editor and unsung hero of this book project; and Dr. Duane H. King, of the National Museum of the American Indian, Smithsonian Institution, for his review and comments. And lastly, my love and appreciation to Gloria Steinem for suggesting the format for this book.

—WILMA MANKILLER

I will be forever grateful to Wilma Mankiller for asking me to share in the telling of her life story and the story of the Cherokee people. I first met Wilma in 1982, and since then, she and her husband, Charlie Soap, have become friends with my wife, Suzanne Fitzgerald Wallis, and me. I was honored and pleased when Wilma met with Robert Weil, our superb editor at St. Martin's Press, and suggested that I act as her collaborator for this important book.

From the very beginning—long before the first word was written—Wilma and I were in complete agreement with Robert that this book should be not only the story of Wilma's life to date, but also should convey at least part of the story of her people and their rich history and heritage. The writing of the work was a true collaboration in every sense of the word. I will always cherish the memory of those long sessions spent at Wilma's home as we wove the fabric and fiber that make up the story of this remarkable woman's life.

Many people and many sources of information were of great help during the researching and writing. My appreciation goes to all those sources who preferred to remain anonymous. Countless friends and family members, librarians, researchers, and others also deserve my everlasting gratitude for contributions to this book's development.

I am thankful that despite the many blunders I have made during the course of my life, I had enough good sense to connect with Suzanne, my wife and best friend. Suzanne's continued belief in me and in my work as a writer sustains me through all the moments of doubt and despair that seem to go with the job.

Many thanks also go to Dixie Haas Dooley for her diligent research and administrative assistance, as well as her encouragement and suggestions. Dixie's early and enthusiastic support for this book, along with her creative contributions, did not go unnoticed. Appreciation goes to Dr. Lydia Wyckoff for her consistent insight, invaluable guidance, and her lasting friendship. Special thanks to Allen Strider, Oklahoma's consummate native son, for always being there.

Hazel Rowena Mills is undoubtedly the best copy editor drawing breath. That is the opinion of Wilma Mankiller and Michael Wallis or anyone else who has had the pleasure of working with Rowena. This book benefits from Rowena's deft touch. Her superior editorial prints are throughout the pages. A standing ovation to you, Rowena.

Robert Weil, our hardworking editor at St. Martin's Press, has guided this project since its inception in Chief Mankiller's office. From the start, he did his level best to see that the book we all hoped for became a reality. Our heartfelt thanks to you, Bob. As an editorial architect, you are without equal.

Kudos as well to Becky Koh, the assistant editor, who never failed to respond to cries for help and to provide answers and counsel. Thanks to others at St. Martin's Press, including Twisne Fan, Stephanie Schwartz, Henry Yee, Judy Stagnitto, Claudia Riemer, Karen Burke, and Barbara Andrews.

Finally, my gratitude to the feline duo of Beatrice and Molly, who clocked in long hours of pleasure and pain with me at the word processor.

—MICHAEL WALLIS

This book is more than the story of Wilma Mankiller. It is also the extraordinary story of the Cherokee people and their indomitable courage. The chapters of this book weave together the story of one Cherokee woman with the history of all the people of the Cherokee Nation, much as traditional Cherokee stories weave together the unbroken threads of tribal history, wisdom, and culture preserved by each generation.

To honor the eternal voices of all Cherokee storytellers and oral historians, we have used a traditional Cherokee story to begin each of the thirteen chapters in this book. We feel that the untarnished power and wisdom of these stories speak directly from the heart of all that is Cherokee.

INTRODUCTION

Dawn arrives in the countryside of northeastern Oklahoma, warm and familiar like an old pal who's come calling. Sunlight seeps through stands of oak, sycamore, and dogwood, then melts as slowly as country butter over thickets of sumac, sassafras, and persimmon. Stalks of soft light reach the weeds and vines clinging to the sagging wire fences. The rays inch across the garden, and finally the frame house in the clearing is streaked with gold. Inside, the aroma of coffee and biscuits mixes with radio news and morning murmurs.

Before too long the front door slowly opens and Wilma Mankiller— the woman of the house—emerges. She is barefoot and wears a brightly colored dress. Her dark hair is still damp from a morning shampoo. She sits on a kitchen chair on the narrow porch and sips a mug of coffee. A murder of mischievous crows, dancing like ebony marionettes, scolds from the nearby trees. In the distance the voices of jays, mockingbirds, and wrens deliver a chorus. Soon hawks will begin patrolling the sky.

Walkingsticks appear, seemingly from nowhere, to dine on tender leaves. The spindly insects resemble twigs as they slowly creep over the porch and the railing. Some crawl up the chair. One moves across Mankiller's legs, but she doesn't appear to notice or care. Another moves across her shoulders and starts up her hair, but Mankiller gently shakes the creature free. She knows the walkingsticks are not interested in her, but merely want to reach the redbud tree growing next to the porch.

The surrounding forests and hills conceal the animal life native to this eastern region of Oklahoma. There are a few mountain lions and bobcats, and an abundance of coyotes, foxes, and many breeds of smaller animals. There are also deer. Plenty of deer. Often they appear near Mankiller's house and take their share from the garden. Every hunting season, she gets requests from sportsmen who want to stalk the land. She always tells them the same thing. They may hunt all they wish, but they may not shoot anything.

This is the place on earth that Wilma Mankiller loves best. She is surrounded by 160 acres of ancestral property, allotted to her paternal grandfather, John Mankiller, when Oklahoma became a state in 1907. The land is located in Adair County, within hollerin' distance of the Cherokee County line. Named for a prominent Cherokee family, Adair County is the heart of the area first settled by Cherokees in the late 1830s. The county still claims a higher percentage of Native American population than any other in the United States.

With the Cherokee Hills on the north and the Cookson Hills on the south, the county has a natural beauty that at least partially masks its very real poverty. Small farms and ranches, fruit orchards, and lumbering are the economic mainstays. But the people derive only modest incomes from their hard labor. Here, a person's wealth and worth are measured in other ways besides bank accounts and worldly goods.

In generations past, the Cherokee people came to this area to rebuild their nation after the westward trek from their beloved homelands in the mountainous South. Herded by federal soldiers, the Cherokees took a path in 1838–39 that became known as the Trail of Tears.

At Tahlequah, the seat of Cherokee County in the eastern foothills of the Ozarks, where their bitter journey ended, the Cherokees built new homes and some of the first schools west of the Mississippi for the education of both men and women. They also reestablished an intricate government in Indian Territory, including a system of courts of law. Although oral historians assert that the tribe possessed a written language long before, the Cherokees put to good use the eighty-five-character syllabary developed by Sequoyah over a twelve-year period prior to the Trail of Tears, to publish Oklahoma's first newspaper in both Cherokee and English.

Many Cherokees continue to live on the hardscrabble farms dotting the region—a land of streams, cliffs, forests, and meadows that is still much the same as it was years ago when outlaw gangs fled to the dark hills to find refuge from the law in the Cherokee Nation. Colorful place names given to favorite natural haunts persist, such as Wildcat Point, Whiskey Holler, and Six-shooter Camp. It is country where conversation centers on farming, hunting, weather, football and, forever and always, politics. Not just mainstream party politics, such as candidates for county commissioner or sheriff or the U.S. Senate, but also tribal politics—the critical issue of Cherokee leadership.

Much of the talk at the gas stations, bait shops, and convenience stores scattered along the country roads is about Wilma Mankiller. This is only natural, since she serves as the principal chief of the Cherokee Nation of Oklahoma. The Cherokees represent the second-largest tribe in the United States, after the Dine (Navajo) Nation. Mankiller is the first female to lead a major Native American tribe. With an enrolled tribal population worldwide of more than 140,000, an annual budget of more than $75 million, and more than 1,200 employees spread across 7,000 square miles, her responsibilities as chief are the same as a head of state and the chief executive officer of a major corporation.

Although it is the land of rugged males who, for the most part, prefer to see fellow "good ol' boys" run for political office, it is difficult to find anyone from the Cherokee ranks, including some of Mankiller's former political foes, who can find fault with the performance of her administration. It was not always that way. In the beginning, there were many problems and obstacles. Often, those were mean times. There were some Cherokees who didn't wish to be governed by a female. Wilma Mankiller had her share of enemies. Her automobile tires were slashed. There were death threats. Chief Mankiller was admittedly an unlikely politician. But gradually she won acceptance. In time, most of her constituents became quite comfortable with her. Now when disagreements occur, they are based on issues rather than gender.

Wilma Mankiller shares her home and life with her husband, Charlie Soap, and Winterhawk, his son from a former marriage. Her two daughters, Felicia and Gina, and their children often stop by to visit, as do other family members and friends. Mankiller's widowed mother lives just down the road.

In the winter, Mankiller's house is warmed by a stove fed by the constant supply of firewood cut from the surrounding forest. Native American art, including masks, baskets, and pottery as well as Cherokee, Kiowa, and Sioux paintings, adorns the shelves and walls. Colorful blankets drape the chair backs and couches. Framed family photographs are scattered about tabletops. On a living room shelf is a small bust of Sam Houston, the revered Texas statesman and folk hero called "the Raven" by the Cherokees who adopted him. Cases hold Mankiller's beloved books, mostly volumes of poetry, novels, biographies, and histories. The works of her favorite authors, including Gloria Steinem, Alex Haley, and Alice Walker, are mixed with the writings of Vine Deloria, Joy Harjo, Robert Conley, Chaucer, Tolstoy, and Milton.

As comfortable as the house is, Mankiller also loves being outside on the land. She tends to the garden and sometimes she walks, trailed by one or two of the family dogs, to a nearby spring where past generations of Mankillers fetched fresh water and gathered mint and watercress.

The nearest community—with just a small grocery–gas station and a school—is called Rocky Mountain. The land where Mankiller and her family reside is known as Mankiller Flats. Born at Hastings Indian Hospital in Tahlequah in 1945, she was raised at Mankiller Flats from her first days. She spent her early years there, with her parents and eight of her ten brothers and sisters. The land is important to Mankiller. It was allotted to her grandfather, and now she and her family maintain it. The land is an important part of their heritage, and they preserve it for future generations.

But of primary importance to Mankiller—the woman who overcame tremendous personal crises—are the thousands of people she serves and her mission to bring self-sufficiency to them. Mankiller felt honored to become her tribe's chosen leader, but she readily adds that she did not seek the responsibility. Indeed, she thought she had reached her pinnacle in tribal government in 1983, when she became her tribe's first female deputy chief.

"Prior to my election, young Cherokee girls would never have thought that they might grow up to be chief," she says. Mankiller had been asked to run as deputy chief by Ross Swimmer, a quarter-blood Indian lawyer and former bank president, who assumed leadership of the Cherokee Nation in 1975. Swimmer convinced Mankiller that, if elected, she could effect greater change in the rural Cherokee communities where she worked.

When Swimmer, a staunch Republican, resigned in 1985 to go to Washington to head the Bureau of Indian Affairs, it was his deputy, a liberal Democrat, who took over. Mankiller was left with a tribal council which more than likely would not have chosen her to take Swimmer's place had it not been for the Cherokee Constitution mandating that the deputy chief move to the higher post when the chief resigns.

In a historic tribal election in July 1987, Mankiller won the coveted post in her own right, and political success brought an unprecedented worldwide interest in both her and the Cherokee Nation. In 1991—winning with an 83 percent majority—she was reelected for four more years.

"We are a revitalized tribe," says Mankiller. "After every major upheaval, we have been able to gather together as a people and rebuild a community and a government. Individually and collectively, Cherokee people possess an extraordinary ability to face down adversity and continue moving forward. We are able to do that because our culture, though certainly diminished, has sustained us since time immemorial. The Cherokee culture is a well-kept secret."

Since becoming chief of her people, Mankiller has become a visible force in America. Named *Ms.* magazine's Woman of the Year in 1987, she has been awarded many honorary degrees and citations, and makes numerous national media appearances and public presentations on behalf of her tribe. But the hardworking chief is much the same unaffected person she always has been. She is at her best when in the halls of Congress quietly advocating better health care, improved housing, or more jobs for the Cherokee people.

Her father, the late Charley Mankiller, was a full-blooded Cherokee, and her mother, Irene, is of Dutch-Irish descent. "We traced our family name back to the eastern part of the country, where the Cherokees lived in great numbers," says Mankiller. "As best we can tell, our name is an old Cherokee military title. It was usually given to a person who was in a position of safeguarding a Cherokee village."

Cherokee culture thrived for hundreds of years in the southeastern United States until the tribe was pushed westward out of its homelands. Among those who survived the Trail of Tears were some of Mankiller's paternal ancestors. They were part of the tribe that regrouped to make Tahlequah its capital and embarked on what historians today call the Cherokees' "Golden Age." This was, in spite of the removal, a time of prosperity, marked by the development of businesses, schools, and a flourishing culture. In those days, people helped each other more and maintained a greater sense of interdependence.

Nonetheless, this prosperity did not last. The years of good fortune and revival after the shameful removal ended with tribal division over the Civil War. At the war's end in 1865, the Cherokees—many of whom had not taken a side—were treated like defeated southerners. Eventually, poverty replaced affluence as a predominant theme as more and more Cherokee land was taken to make room for other tribes who were also forced to leave their homes and move into Indian Territory.

By 1907, the federal government had dismantled the tribal government, ignored the Cherokee Constitution, and divided up the land in individual allotments. It was at that time that Wilma Mankiller's family received its share of property in the wooded hills. In that remote setting, where she and her siblings were raised, the family grew strawberries and other crops for a living. There was no indoor plumbing, so the Mankiller children hauled water about a quarter of a mile to their home.

"I remember when we bartered with neighbors and ate what we grew," she says. "Those days helped me so much. I was raised with a sense of community that extended beyond my family."

When she was ten years old, Mankiller's entire family was moved to California as participants in the federal government's relocation program. "It was part of the national Indian policy of the 1950s," she explains. "The government wanted to break up tribal communities and 'mainstream' Indians, so it relocated rural families to urban areas. One day I was living in a rural Cherokee community, and a few days later I was living in California and trying to deal with the mysteries of television, neon lights, and elevators. It was total culture shock."

The Mankiller family eventually became acclimated to California. Mankiller attended school and met her first husband, a well-to-do Ecuadoran. They had two daughters, Felicia in 1964 and Gina in 1966. It was during the turbulent 1960s, while starting her family, that Mankiller began to raise her political consciousness. Her concern for Native American issues was fully ignited by 1969 when a band of university students occupied the abandoned prison on Alcatraz Island in San Francisco Bay. They wanted to attract attention to issues affecting them and their tribes. Mankiller answered the call. Out of that historic experience, an activist was born.

"In most ways I was a typical housewife at that time," recalls Wilma, "but when Alcatraz occurred, I became aware of what needed to be done to let the rest of the world know that Indians had rights too. Alcatraz articulated my own feelings about being an Indian. It was a benchmark. After that, I became involved."

She attended sociology classes at San Francisco State College and took on Native American issues with a fervor. Mankiller worked as a volunteer for five grueling years with the Pit River Tribe in California on treaty-rights issues, helping to establish a legal defense fund for the battle to reclaim the tribe's ancestral lands. She also devoted much of her time to Native American preschool and adult education programs and directing a dropout prevention program for Native American youngsters.

In 1974, Mankiller divorced her husband of eleven years. "He wanted a traditional housewife. I had a stronger desire to do things in the community than at home." Two years later, she returned to Oklahoma with her daughters. "I was delighted to be back on our ancestral homelands," she recalls. "I wanted to come home and raise my kids and build a house on my land."

She managed all that and more. In 1979, after almost three years of helping to procure important grants and launch critical rural services for the tribe, Mankiller enrolled in graduate courses at the nearby University of Arkansas. Late one morning in the fall of 1979, while returning home from class on a two-lane country road, Mankiller was seriously injured in a freak automobile accident which resulted in a fatality. An oncoming car, which had pulled into her lane to pass, collided head-on with Mankiller's station wagon. Unbelievably, the young woman driving the other vehicle, who was killed, was Mankiller's close friend. When Mankiller regained consciousness in the hospital, her face was crushed and her ribs and legs were broken. It was one of several brushes with death. After avoiding the amputation of her right leg, she endured seventeen operations and was bedridden for months. During the long healing process, Mankiller never allowed herself to become discouraged or to sink into despair.

"That accident in 1979 changed my life," she says. "I came very close to death, felt its presence and the alluring call to complete the circle of life. I always think of myself as the woman who lived before and the woman who lives afterward. I was at home recovering for almost a year, and I had time to reevaluate." For Mankiller, it proved to be a deep spiritual awakening when she adopted what she referred to as "a very Cherokee approach to life—what our tribal elders call 'being of good mind.'"

Then in November 1980, just a year after the tragic accident, Mankiller was diagnosed with myasthenia gravis, a chronic neuromuscular disease that causes varying weakness in the voluntary muscles of the body. Treatment required surgery to remove the thymus gland and a program of drug therapy. In December 1980—just barely out of the hospital—she was back on the job. She needed only one month to recover from her illness. Although a regimen of drugs followed, work seemed to be the best medicine of all.

"I thought a lot about what I wanted to do with my life during that time," says Mankiller. "The reality of how precious life is enabled me to begin projects I couldn't have otherwise tackled."

In 1981, she spearheaded the tribe's most ambitious and lauded experiment to that date—the Bell Community Revitalization Project. With hundreds of thousands of dollars in federal and private funds and with their own labor, the residents of a poverty-stricken community named Bell in eastern Oklahoma remodeled dilapidated housing, constructed new homes, and laid a sixteen-mile pipeline that brought running water to many homes for the first time. Beyond the physical improvements, the volunteers from the Bell community did the work themselves, while developing a strong bond and gaining a sense of control over their own lives.

The national publicity that followed made the Bell Project a model for other Native American tribes eager for self-sufficiency. This work also established Mankiller as an expert in community development, and brought her to the attention of Cherokee Chief Ross Swimmer.

The election to deputy chief occurred two years later, and in 1985, when Swimmer resigned from office, Mankiller became principal chief. Still, she did not feel she had a mandate until 1987 when she was elected on her own, even though from the very start she never slowed down.

"In order to understand how I operate, it is necessary to remember that I come from an activist family," says Mankiller. "My father was involved in union organizing, community service, and liked to discuss political issues. With a background like that, you naturally get involved in the community."

Her terms of office have produced countless highlights: a dramatic increase in tribal revenue and services; the attraction of new businesses to eastern Oklahoma, where many Cherokees live; the garnering of more than $20 million in construction projects, including new clinics; the procurement of funding for innovative programs to help Cherokee women on welfare develop microenterprises; the establishment of an $8 million Job Corps training center; and dozens of other projects, ranging from an extensive array of services for children to revitalization of the Cherokee judicial system. Other initiatives Mankiller has spearheaded include a new tribal tax commission, an energy-consulting firm, a pilot self-government agreement with the federal government, and an agreement with the Environmental Protection Agency.

In October 1986, Wilma married her old friend Charlie Soap, a full-blooded Cherokee and the former director of the tribal development program. Mankiller and Soap met while working together on the Bell Project. Known as a quiet but effective "Cherokee powerhouse," Soap has focused his effort on development projects for several low-income Cherokee communities. He also directs a community-based program designed to assist needy children in rural areas. "Wilma's a hard worker and she is very sharp, but most of all she is a caring person," he says. "It's that quality of Wilma's that has made a real difference for the Cherokees."

When Soap recites his personal heroes, his wife tops the list. When Mankiller names her heroes, Soap is her first choice. "He is the most secure male I have ever met," says Mankiller. "He is not threatened by strong women. He is supportive of women, of women's causes, and of me and my work."

Mankiller's love of family and her people paid off in major dividends again, in 1990, when she was faced with yet another physical dilemma. Recurrent kidney problems resulted in the need for a kidney transplant. Her oldest brother, Don Mankiller, consented to serve as the donor, and the operation was a success. During her convalescence, she had many long talks with Charlie Soap and other members of her family before ultimately deciding to run for yet another term as chief.

"It was a big decision," says Mankiller, who admits that it finally came down to the fact that she believed too much unfinished work remained. Her mission was not completed. With her reelection in 1991, the Cherokee people returned Mankiller to office with a landslide vote.

But all the honorary degrees and successful tribal development projects do not begin to measure the influence that Mankiller has had in so many diverse circles of America. First and foremost are her stewardship of the Cherokees, and the pride she has instilled in thousands of Native American people. She has shown—in her typically ebullient and joyous way—not what Cherokees or other native people can learn from European Americans, but what whites can learn from native people. In fact, without the knowledge of the interconnectedness of all living things and the spirituality that Native American culture so powerfully possesses, many white Americans are beginning to understand that they have much to learn from native wisdom, culture, and spirituality.

Spirituality is then key to the public and private aura of Wilma Mankiller, a leader who has indeed become known as much for her able leadership of the Cherokee Nation as for her spiritual presence among all Americans. A woman rabbi who serves as the head of a large synagogue in New York City commented that Mankiller was a significant spiritual force in the nation. One would imagine that a rabbi in Manhattan and an Indian chief in Oklahoma would have little in common, but it is clearly Mankiller's way of life—her religion, so to speak—that has formed bonds with spiritual leaders throughout the country.

No less significant has been Mankiller's reputation among women and women's groups. A woman who proudly describes herself as a feminist, a leader who is concerned with women's issues worldwide, Mankiller is ironically a female leader who has been as comfortably embraced by men as by women. Most of the attacks directed against her in those early days of campaigning because of her gender, because she threatened the male Cherokee status quo, have subsided. She has become a leader who can play easily to a multitude of audiences—from the cover of *Ms.* to the cover of *Parade*—in an effortless way that few others have been able to duplicate. Perhaps it truly is her innate love of all people that breaks down so many doors.

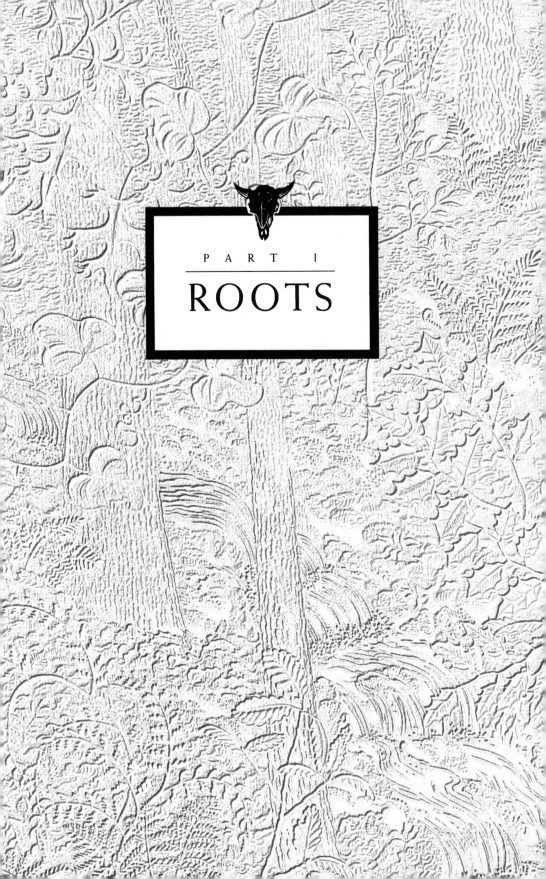

PART I

ROOTS

CHAPTER 1

ASGAYA-DIHI

Native Americans regard their names not as mere labels, but as essential parts of their personalities. A native person's name is as vital to his or her identity as the eyes or teeth. There is a common belief that when a person is injured, her name is maligned, just as she might be bruised when in an accident.

Throughout Native American history, there was often a need to conceal one's name. This is probably why Powhatan and Pocahontas are known in history under assumed identities, their true names having been hidden from whites so that their names could not be demeaned, defiled, or destroyed.

If prayers and medicine fail to heal a seriously ill person, the spiritual leader sometimes realizes that the patient's name itself may be diseased. The priest then goes to the water and, with the appropriate ceremony, bestows a new name on the sick person. The healer then begins anew, repeating sacred formulas with the patient's new name, in the hope that these measures will bring about restoration and recovery.

Asgaya-dihi. Mankiller. My Cherokee name in English is Mankiller.

Mankiller has survived in my own family as a surname for four generations before my own. It is an old Cherokee name, although it was originally not a name at all, but a rank or title used only after one had earned the right to it. To call someone Mankiller would have been like calling another person Major or Captain.

There were many titles in the early days of the Cherokees. Each Cherokee town, for example, had its own Water-goer (Ama-edohi) and its own Raven (Golana), and each town had its Asgaya-dihi.

My own people came from near Tellico, from the land now known as eastern Tennessee. My great-great-great-grandfather's name was written down as Ah-nee-ska-yah-di-hi. That translates literally into English as "Menkiller." No record exists of the names of his parents, and the only name recorded for his wife is Sally. The son of Ah-nee-ska-yah-di-hi and Sally was listed as Ka-skun-nee Mankiller. The first name, Ka-skun-nee, cannot be translated, but it is with this man, my great-great-grandfather, that the name Mankiller was established in the family line as a surname.

Jacob Mankiller, born in 1853, was a son of Ka-skun-nee Mankiller and Lucy Matoy. Jacob married Susan Teehee-Bearpaw and, in 1889, they had a son they named John. He was the oldest of eight children. John Mankiller was my grandfather. He married Bettie Bolin Bendabout Canoe. Her Cherokee name was Quatie. Born in 1878, she was nine years older than her husband. My father, Charley Mankiller, was their son.

I know that Lucy Matoy, my great-grandmother and the wife of Ka-skun-nee, came from what we call one of the Old Settler families. Sometime after 1817, these families immigrated of their own free will to what became the Cherokee Nation West, an area west of the Mississippi in the far reaches of Arkansas and beyond, in what would later become Indian Territory. This voluntary immigration occurred two decades before the federal government, anxious to seize native people's land, evicted Cherokees from their homes in Georgia, Tennessee, North Carolina, and Alabama, forcibly removing them on what was known as "the trail where they cried." As far as the name Matoy is concerned, our history tells us that in 1730, a Chief Moytoy was declared "emperor" of the Cherokees by Sir Alexander Cuming, an unofficial envoy representing the English Crown in America. I can't prove it, but I strongly suspect that the surname Matoy is but another form of the name or title Ama-edohi, which had been corrupted by the English into Moytoy. As far as I can determine, all of my ancestors on my father's side, other than this Matoy line, moved west later on, in the late 1830s, on the Trail of Tears.

At the turn of the century, there was another attempt to ravage our people through several legislative acts which in effect almost destroyed the Cherokee Nation and its ability to function as a sovereign entity. In 1907, Indian Territory was finally devoured and ceased to exist when

Oklahoma became a state. Land held in common by the Cherokee Nation was parceled out in individual allotments of 160 acres per family. The land we now call Mankiller Flats in Adair County was assigned to my paternal grandfather, John Mankiller. I never met my grandfather, although I often feel the connection between the two of us. I live on my grandfather's allotment. I have built my house several hundred yards from where his home once stood. Each spring, Easter lilies bloom in what used to be his yard. They remind me of him and of our ancestry.

My father, Charley Mankiller, was born in his father's frame house on November 15, 1914, just seven years after Oklahoma statehood. At the time of his birth, much of the land that had been allotted to the Cherokees was being taken away by unscrupulous businessmen with the cooperation of Oklahoma's judicial system. Unspeakably greedy people would arrange to be appointed guardians of Cherokee children, and then take control of their individually allotted Cherokee land. As documented in Angie Debo's impressive book, *And Still the Waters Run*, this was practiced most widely in the early 1900s when oil was discovered in Oklahoma and the boom years started.

My father's mother died in 1916 when her son was only two years old. She died in one of the dreaded influenza epidemics that tore through America during World War I. Jensie Hummingbird, my father's older half sister, helped raised him. I remember Aunt Jensie. She spoke no English at all. She did not own a car or get around very much. She tended to stay close to her home. We visited her quite a bit. She was a very kind woman who was sick most of her life. Aunt Jensie had only one son, Charley Hummingbird, who cared for her until she died in 1990.

My grandfather went off to join the army and took part in the Great War that became known as World War I. In fact, a large number of American Indian people served in World War I. This interests me. As a student of Native American history, I realize that the question of United States citizenship for native people was addressed in the Dawes Act, or the General Allotment Act, of 1887. This was the law that prepared native people for the eventual termination of tribal ownership of land by granting 160-acre allotments to each Indian family, or eighty acres to an individual. All of the allottees were to become United States citizens, subject to the same criminal and civil laws as other American citizens. Even though Theodore Roosevelt called the Dawes Act "a mighty pulverizing engine to break up the tribal mass," the act failed because Native Americans considered land not as a possession but as a physical and spiritual domain shared by all living things. Many of our people were reluctant to turn away from the traditional view of common ownership of land.

Despite these early measures, Native Americans were not considered official citizens of the United States until 1924. That was the year Congress passed the Indian Citizenship Act, bestowing voting rights and citizenship on all Indians "born within the territorial limits of the United States." Native people, however, were still considered to be outside the protection of the Bill of Rights. Among many native people, there is a feeling that citizenship was conferred uniformly in 1924 because so many American Indians, like my grandfather, had volunteered for military service during the war.

In 1936, twelve years after the Indian Citizenship Act became law and nine years before I was born, Grandpa Mankiller died. He was only forty-six years old. The official cause of death was pernicious anemia, but we now believe that his death resulted from kidney failure caused by polycystic kidney disease. Severe anemia is a common side effect of kidney failure. My father, in turn, inherited this disease from my grandfather, and it was passed on to several of his children, including me.

There were only two children to mourn their father's death, my father Charley and his only full sibling, his older sister Sally. She was a beautiful girl who liked to wear fine dresses with her black hair piled on her head. People who knew her as a girl say she was very dainty, always carrying a parasol when she walked in the sun. Sally later married a full-blooded Cherokee named Nelson Leach, and they lived near Rocky Mountain on a portion of the Mankiller family allotment.

Like my dad, Aunt Sally was forced to attend Sequoyah Training School near Tahlequah. This was very customary of the period. Sally began classes there in the 1920s when she was a little girl and stopped attending the school in the early 1930s when she became a young woman.

Sequoyah Training School started as an orphan asylum. The Cherokee National Council passed an act establishing the asylum in 1871 to provide housing for children orphaned by the Civil War. The war was fought partly in the Cherokee Nation, and Cherokees served in both the Union and Confederate armies. Later, the orphan facility became an asylum for Indian people who experienced mental or physical problems of such severity that they could not cope without assistance. Finally, it was turned into a boarding school for Indian children.

In 1914, our people authorized Cherokee Chief W. C. Rogers to sell the school and its forty acres to the United States. It then became a federal institution under the control of the secretary of the interior, and was maintained as an industrial school for "the Indian orphans of Oklahoma of the restricted class," meaning native people of one-half degree of Indian blood or more. Congress passed an act in 1925 changing the name of the school to Sequoyah Orphan Training School in honor of Sequoyah, the man credited with developing our Cherokee syllabary.

It is still a school for native people today, but now it is not an orphanage. Known simply as Sequoyah High School, it is one of five Native American educational facilities in Oklahoma. The school, including its residential program, is funded by the Bureau of Indian Affairs and operated by the Cherokee Nation of Oklahoma. Our people not only maintain Sequoyah School, but also oversee the policies that govern it, and the twelve campus buildings. Most of the students are Cherokee, but as many as sixteen other tribes are also represented, coming to Sequoyah from many Indian nations.

Back in the bad old days, the BIA representatives who maintained boarding schools such as Sequoyah would go hundreds of miles and return with native children. The philosophy, reflecting an errant missionary zeal, was to get native children away from their families, their elders, their tribes, their language, their heritage. They isolated native children so they would forget their culture. The boarding-school concept was simply another way for the federal government to deal with what its officials always called "the Indian problem." After first trying to wipe all of us off the face of the earth with violence, they attempted to isolate us on reservations or, in the case of many people such as the Cherokees, place us in an area that the government called Indian Territory. All the while, they systematically conjured up policies to kill our culture. So the federal government rounded up Indian youngsters and forced them to attend boarding schools whether they wanted to or not. This was true for most tribes, not just the Cherokees.

At Sequoyah School, south of Tahlequah, the capital of the Cherokee Nation, my father and his little sister were forbidden to speak their native language. They could not speak a word of English when they first went there, so they were whipped for speaking Cherokee. The whole idea behind those boarding schools, whether they were government operated like Sequoyah or a religious operation, was to acculturate native people into the mainstream white society and, at the same time, destroy their sense of self. The boarding-school officials hoped to make the "little Indians" into "ladies and gentlemen." So they cut their hair short and did not allow them to utter one word of their native language. Oftentimes, all visits to family and friends back home were denied. The idea was to "civilize" the children. There was even a popular expression about "killing the Indian and saving the man."

> *When I was about seven years old they took me to this damn Indian school of the government's and we had to stand in line and they cut my hair off. They just cut my braids off and threw them into a box with all the other children's braids. My old grandmother went over there and got them and my grandfolks stayed at the winter camp all winter to be near me. . . . It was hard being an Indian in them days. Later I learned to be proud.*
>
> Archie Blackowl, a Cheyenne
> The Indians in Oklahoma

All his life, my father had mixed emotions about the school named Sequoyah. He spoke of having been punished for only the slightest infractions, and of the many other problems he experienced there. On the other hand, he could get sentimental about the place. It had an orchard, a big garden, and a lot of farm animals. The students provided all the labor necessary to keep the operation going. One Sequoyah superintendent my father spoke well of was Jack Brown, who was part Cherokee and had a great interest in history and literature. Sequoyah was my father's home for twelve years. It was not a perfect home or even a loving place, but it was there that he developed lasting friendships with other Cherokee children and youths from other tribes. At Sequoyah, he also acquired his love of books, a gift he passed on to his children. Most people have mixed emotions about their home. My dad's feelings were perhaps a little more intense because of the acculturation program and what must have been a lonely life in a barren dormitory.

Still, the fact remains that the primary mission of Sequoyah and the other boarding schools was for the children to leave everything behind that related to their native culture, heritage, history, and language. In short, there was a full-scale attempt at deracination—the uprooting or destruction of a race and its culture. Consequently, many young Cherokees and other native people subjected to the boarding-school experience, including my father, came away from those years of indoctrination more than a little brainwashed.

At many of those schools scattered across this country and Canada, much mental and physical abuse occurred. I have a friend from a Canadian tribe who lived in a traditional community as a girl. It was very isolated. She can recall the young men coming home from religious boarding schools with all sorts of problems. Many of them never married, but stayed to themselves. They turned to alcohol and drank themselves to death before they reached their thirtieth birthdays. My friend and other concerned tribal members were puzzled by this phenomenon. When they examined the problem, they discovered that there had been widespread sexual abuse of the young men in the boarding schools. All of it was documented. And incredibly, some of those problems still exist at some of the boarding schools that remain in operation. In the late 1980s, a Senate select committee investigated sexual-abuse cases at Native American boarding schools. So this is not ancient history.

I am thankful that even though my father was raised in such a boarding-school environment, he did not buy into everything that was being taught. Fortunately, he came from a strong family, and because of his traditional upbringing, the school was not successful in alienating him from his culture. He was a confident man and, to my knowledge, he never felt intimidated in the non-Indian world—a world he came to know even better after he met my mother.

Her name is Clara Irene Sitton. She was born in Adair County on September 18, 1921, to Robert Bailey Sitton and Pearl Halady Sitton. My mother's family was made up primarily of the Sitton and Gillespie families, and their ethnic background was mostly Dutch and Irish. She does not have a drop of Indian blood in her veins, although she sometimes forgets she is white. From the day she married my father, her own life became centered around Cherokee family life.

My mother's ancestry goes back to North Carolina, where her kinfolk from the Sitton side were some of the first iron makers, while the Gillespies were craftsmen who turned out fine long rifles. It is an intriguing possibility that the Sittons were related somehow to Charles Arthur Floyd, the Dust Bowl–era bandit from rural Oklahoma who was better known as "Pretty Boy" Floyd. They came from the same county in northern Georgia as Floyd and his kinfolk. This family legend has never been proved, but it was always exciting for me to consider, because "Pretty Boy" was a Robin Hood—style bandit, the subject of much myth.

My mother's father was born in 1874. I have been told that Grandpa Sitton was tall and distinguished looking. He was a farmer all of his life. He died, like my father's father, at a relatively young age, in 1932, during the Great Depression when my mother was only eleven years old. A few years before his death, my grandfather had skinned some rabbits and then went to the barn to harness his mules to plow. The mules apparently smelled the rabbits' blood on his hands and became frightened. They wanted to get out of the barn and, in the panic, they pushed my grandfather up against the wall. He suffered serious internal injuries which probably shortened his life.

My mother's mother was born in 1884 and lived until 1973. Her mother died when she was very young, so my grandmother went to live with her half sister, Ida Mae Scism Jordan, in Washington County, Arkansas. In 1903, when she was nineteen years old, Grandma Sitton left her home in Arkansas to visit friends. She came to the Wauhillau community in Indian Territory. That's where she caught the eye of my grandfather. At twenty-nine, Robert Sitton was a confirmed bachelor, but the vivacious, diminutive young woman captured his heart. After a brief courtship, they were married that same year and soon started their family. My grandparents set up housekeeping near Wauhillau, where my grandfather's parents, William and Sarah Sitton, lived. Wauhillau was a thriving new settlement made up of Cherokee people and white pioneers, many of whom had come from Georgia about the same time as the Sittons in 1891.

After a few years, my grandparents packed their belongings in a wagon and a two-seated buggy and moved. They settled on a small farm they bought near the eastern Oklahoma town of Titanic, presumably named after the famous British transatlantic liner that had sunk on her maiden voyage in 1912. They cleared the land to make it suitable for farming. Except for their oldest daughter, Sadie, who stayed with her grandparents in Wauhillau, they sent their children to the one-room Titanic schoolhouse. My grandparents had seven children—three sons and four daughters—born between 1904 and 1921. My mother was their youngest child.

After a couple of other moves, including a stop at the town of

Foraker, Oklahoma, in the Osage country, where my grandfather worked for the railroad, they located in Adair County. Grandma Sitton was determined to raise her family in the fresh country air, so she was delighted when they found a farm for sale not far from the community of Rocky Mountain. That was where my mother was born.

I have heard it said that there was not a job on the farm my grandmother would not tackle, including plowing the fields. Folks described her as being spunky. Some years after my grandfather died and her children were raised, she sold her farm and moved into the town of Stilwell to run a boardinghouse.

My parents met when they were young. They had been around each other in the same area most of their lives. They would bump into each other at the general store in Rocky Mountain, a tiny settlement that attracted families from miles around. Mother can recall my dad teasing her when she was a girl. One time she even threw a pie at him. Even though he could make her as angry as a hornet, she was attracted by his good looks and quiet charm. They had a whirlwind courtship.

When they married, my mother was only fifteen years old. Dad was twenty-one. Of course, back in those days in the country, many folks married when they were quite young. My father was earning a rather precarious living by subsistence farming. He raised strawberries and peanuts for cash crops, picked berries and green beans for extra money, and traveled all the way to Colorado during the harvesttime to cut broomcorn.

My grandmother was dead set against the marriage. My dad was older and had been raised in an Indian boarding school. He had also worked here and there, and had generally "gotten around." Although her oldest daughter, Sadie, had married a mixed-blood Cherokee, Grandma Sitton did not approve of my father because he was Cherokee. He was different. She objected strenuously to their relationship. But my folks were in love. They simply did not listen. They got married anyway. They went to the Baptist church in the Adair County community of Mulberry, where a Reverend Acorn married them on March 6, 1937. The relationship between my grandmother and parents was strained for the next several years.

By the time I was born in November of 1945, my mother, Irene, had come to learn the culture of the Cherokees. The name Mankiller, which sounds strange to most white people, was not foreign to her because she had lived in Cherokee country all her life and had attended school with many Cherokee people. And even years later, when I grew up, the Cherokee last names were not at all odd sounding to a girl in rural Oklahoma. In fact, Cherokee names in my family were familiar and, quite often, revered. I know family and friends whose surnames are Thirsty, Hummingbird, Wolf, Beaver, Squirrel, Soap, Canoe, Fourkiller, Sixkiller, Walkingstick, and Gourd. Names such as those just are not unusual.

> *The name of honor was received after a person had attained some kind of special distinction in the tribe. This would occur through the performance of an act of great character, or it could be given by a secret society. The second name marked a moment of excellence in a person's life and was not a hereditary position. Hereditary names, such as that of an Iroquois chief, were passed down successively to whoever filled the position for as long as there were people to fill it.*
>
> Gerald Hausman
> Turtle Island Alphabet, *1992*

As I matured, I learned that *Mankiller* could be spelled different ways and was a coveted war name. One version is the literal *Asgaya*, meaning "man," combined with the personal name suffix *dihi*, or "killer." Another is *Outacity*—an honorary title that also means "Man-killer." Our Cherokee historians and genealogists have always told us that Mankiller was a military title, but we also heard that there was another kind of Mankiller in our past. We know that in the Cherokee medicinal and conjuring style, Mankillers were known to attack other people to avenge wrongs that had been perpetrated against themselves or others they served. This Mankiller could change things, often for the worse. This Mankiller was capable of changing minds to a different condition. This kind of Mankiller could make an illness more serious, and even shoot an invisible arrow into the body of an enemy.

Most of what I know about my family's heritage I did not learn until I was a young woman. That is when I discovered that many distinguished leaders from the past held the title of Mankiller throughout the various tribal towns. In the eighteenth century, for example, there was the Mankiller of Tellico, the Mankiller of Estatoe, and the Mankiller of Keowee. One prominent warrior and tribal leader, Outacity or "Man-killer," apparently joined a delegation of Cherokees visiting London in 1762, during the troubled reign of King George III, fourteen years before the Revolutionary War broke out.

Even though our family name has been honored for many centuries, during the years, I have had to endure occasional derision because of my surname. Some people are startled when I am introduced to them as Wilma Mankiller. They think it's a fierce-sounding name. Many find it amusing and make nervous jokes, and there are still those times when people display their ignorance. For example, I was invited in December of 1992 to attend President-elect Bill Clinton's historic economic summit meeting in Little Rock, Arkansas, just about a month prior to his inaugural. *The Wall Street Journal*, one of America's most respected newspapers, made a rather unfortunate remark about my surname that is best described as a cheap shot.

"Our favorite name on the summit list," stated the *Journal* editorial, "we have to admit, is Chief Wilma Mankiller, representing the Cherokee Nation, though we hope not a feminist economic priority."

Tim Giago, publisher of *Indian Country Today*, a Native American newspaper, quickly fired back at the *Journal*: "The fact that this powerful lady has been featured in several major magazines . . . has appeared on countless television shows, and has been given tons of coverage in major, national newspapers, appears to have escaped the closed minds at the *Journal*. One has to ask if they ever get out into the real world."

Fortunately, most people I come across in my travels, especially members of the media, are more sensitive and generally more aware than that editorial writer. When someone unknowingly or out of ignorance makes a snide comment about my name, I often resort to humor. I look the person in the eye and say with a straight face that Mankiller is actually a well-earned nickname. That usually shuts the person up.

There were times in my childhood when I put up with a lot of teasing about my name. I would want to disappear when roll call was taken in school and everyone would laugh when they heard my name. But my parents told me to be proud of my family name. Most people these days generally like my name, many of them saying that it is only appropriate and perhaps a bit ironic that a woman chief should be named Mankiller. The name Mankiller carries with it a lot of history. It is a strong name. I am proud of my name—very proud. And I am proud of the long line of men and women who have also been called Mankiller. I hope to honor my ancestors by keeping the name alive.

But I have started my story far too early. Especially in the context of a tribal people, no individual's life stands apart and alone from the rest. My own story has meaning only as long as it is a part of the overall story of my people. For above all else, I am a Cherokee woman.

CHAPTER 2

ORIGINS

*I*n the beginning, before Mother Earth was made, there was only a vast body
of water that was both salty and fresh. There were no human beings, only animals.
They lived in the heavens above the sea. They were secure in a solid rock sky vault
called Galunlati. As the animals, birds, and insects multiplied, the sky became more
crowded and there was a fear that some creatures would be pushed off the sky rock.
All the creatures called a council to decide what to do.

At last "Beaver's Grandchild," the little Water-beetle called Dayunisi, offered
to leave the sky and investigate the water below. Water-beetle darted in every direction
over the water's surface, but could not find any place to rest. So the beetle dived to the
bottom of the sea and returned with soft mud, which began to grow and spread until
it became known as earth.

The earth eventually became a great island floating in the sea of water. It was
suspended from the heavens at each of the four principal points by cords which hung
from the sky vault. The myth keepers claimed that when the earth grows old and wears
out, the cords will become weak and break and the earth will sink into the ocean and
everything will die. All will be water again.

After the Water-beetle returned to the sky rock and told the others about what
he had done, the creatures sent out the Great Buzzard, grandfather of all buzzards, to
find a place for them to live. The new earth was wet and soft and flat. The Buzzard
soared low, searching for a suitable place. He grew tired, and as his huge wings dipped
and struck the pliable earth, deep valleys were created. When the bird rose in the sky,

his flapping wings formed ridges and mighty mountains. This is what would become Cherokee country.

At last the earth dried and the creatures came down, but it was still dark, so they convinced the sun to move overhead every day from east to west. But the sun was so hot that Tsiskagili, the Crawfish, scorched his shell a bright red, and his meat was spoiled. Then the conjurers moved the sun higher in the sky, and at last they positioned it seven handbreadths high, just below the sky arch. This became what the soothsayers called "the seventh height," or the highest place. To this day the sun moves along below this arch, and then returns every night on the upper side to the starting point.

When all the animals and plants were created, they were told to stay awake and keep vigil for seven nights. They tried their best to do this, and nearly all of them remained awake the first night. But the next night several dropped off to sleep, and by the third night even more were asleep. This continued until the seventh night, when only the owl, the panther, and a few others were still awake. Because they did not succumb to sleep, they were given the power to see in the dark. Of the trees, only the pine, the spruce, the cedar, the holly, and the laurel remained awake seven nights. They were allowed to remain always green and were considered to be the best plants for medicine. Unlike the other trees, they were also allowed to keep their hair throughout the winter. This was their gift.

Human beings were created after the animals and plants. There were several versions of the story of how the first humans were made. It was said by some of the old Cherokees that in the beginning there were only a brother and sister, and that the man touched the woman with a fish and told her to multiply. In seven days she bore a child. She continued to do this every seven days until the earth became crowded. Then it was deemed that a woman should have only one child each year.

It is said that the first red man was called Kanati, or the Lucky Hunter. The first woman was named Selu, or Corn, and she was also red. So these red mortals— the first human beings—came to be called Yunwiya, the real people.

As with many other native peoples, we Cherokees have differing versions of our genesis story. Beyond the many theories of how we originated are debates about how we came to be called Cherokee.

When I studied or listened to the creation stories, I learned that the proper name by which we originally called ourselves is *Yunwiya* or *Ani-Yunwiya*, in the third person, which means "Real People" or "Principal People." The names by which many tribes are known today were given to them by white explorers and trappers. For example, *Nez Percé* is a French phrase meaning "those with pierced noses." But the Nez Percés called themselves *Nimipu*, meaning "the People." The Iroquois, the Delawares, and the Pawnees all called themselves by names that also meant "the People" or "Real People." And the people of the Dine (Navajo) Nation, when they refer to themselves, prefer the word *Dineh*, which means "the People."

Ancient Delawares in the Southeast called the Cherokee people *Allegans*. Cherokees were known to the Shawnees as the *Keetoowahs*. This was a variant spelling of *Kituhwa*, the name of an ancient Cherokee settlement on the Tuckasegee River in what is known today as North Carolina. According to our storytellers, it was one of the "seven mother towns" of our tribe. The inhabitants were called *Ani Kituhwagi*, or "people of *Kituhwa*," and they seemed to have exercised considerable influence on all the other towns along the Tuckasegee and the upper part of the Little Tennessee. Sometimes the name was used by other tribes as a synonym for *Cherokee*, most likely because the *Kituhwa* guarded the Cherokee northern frontier. Many years later, just before the start of the Civil War, the word resurfaced among our people residing in Indian Territory and was given as the name of a powerful secret society, commonly spelled *Keetoowah* in English.

Some scholars believe the word *Cherokee* is derived from the Muskogean word *tciloki*, which means "people of a different speech." Others claim that *Cherokee* means "cave people" or "cave dwellers" because several early tribes lived in an area full of caves. This derivation is from the Choctaw *chiluk ki*, or "cave people," alluding to the many caves in the mountain country where the Cherokees lived. The Iroquois called us *Oyata ge ronon*, "inhabitants of the cave country." Some of the other tribal people gave our people a name that meant "mountaineers" or "uplanders."

We have found that the name *Cherokee* has been spelled at least fifty ways throughout history. Most historians agree that the name is a corruption of *Tsa lagi*. It first appears as *Chalaque* in the Portuguese description of de Soto's expedition, published in 1557. Then our name shows up as *Cheraqui* in a 1699 French document, and in the English form as *Cherokee* in 1708.

As far back as anyone knows, our early people were, indeed, mountaineers, people who lived in the Allegheny region in what is now the southeastern United States. They made their homes in parts of the present states of North and South Carolina, Kentucky, Tennessee, Georgia, Alabama, Virginia, and West Virginia. They lived in this region so long that some of our origin stories have taken on a local character. For example, one of those early Cherokee stories is an explanation of the formation of the Great Smoky Mountains, a range of about eighty peaks more than five thousand feet high near the junction of the Carolinas, Georgia, and Tennessee. Our people hunted in these mountains and considered them sacred.

In spite of that tribal sense of our genesis in the Southeast, others believe that our Cherokee ancestors migrated south from somewhere around the Great Lakes. This theory is based largely on linguistic evidence, because we speak an Iroquoian tongue related to the languages of the Mohawks, Oneidas, Onondagas, Senecas, and Cayugas—all tribes that formed the Iroquois League. Others point to the tribal history of the Delawares, which describes a long, protracted war in which the Cherokees were ultimately driven south. Still other students of America before the Europeans came make a case for our people having come from South America, tracing a long migration trail north, then east, then south, finally stopping in the Great Smoky Mountain region. There is even one legend from our Cherokee oral tradition that seems to support that particular theory. This legend says the Cherokees originated on an island off the South American coast.

Little is certain except that when the Europeans arrived in the Americas, our people had been in their home in the Smoky Mountains for a great many years. Most likely our ancestors were mound builders.

> *As the long-forgotten peoples of the respective continents rise and begin to reclaim their ancient heritage, they will discover the meaning of the lands of their ancestors.*
>
> *Vine Victor Deloria, Jr.*
> God Is Red

A tale from our oral tradition suggests that there was once an ancient hereditary society called the *Ani-Kutani*. This society kept to itself a great deal of sacred knowledge, and controlled the spiritual functions of the tribe. This group eventually became too omnipotent and abused its sacred powers. Then, as the story goes, the people rebelled against its members and overthrew them. But for as long as we can tell, there was no central ruling clan or society. Our people lived in autonomous villages scattered over their southeastern domain. There is some evidence that each town had a war chief and a peace chief, sometimes called a Red Chief and a White Chief, charged respectively with the external and internal affairs of government. Each chief had a council of advisers.

Although many of the details of how our governments worked are not perfectly clear, it is certain that Cherokee women played an important and influential role in town government. Women shared in the responsibilities and rights of the tribal organization. Our Cherokee families were traditionally matrilineal clans. In general, women held the property, including the dwelling and garden. Women also maintained family life and farmed, while the men spent much of their time away on the hunt or in warfare. Early European observers made disparaging remarks such as, "Among the Cherokees, the woman rules the roost," and "The Cherokees have a petticoat government." It is said that when Ada Kulkula, or Little Carpenter, attended a meeting in Charleston, South Carolina, he was astonished to find no white women present. He even asked if it were true that "white men as well as Red were born of women."

There was also a very powerful woman who is alternately described as the *Ghigau* or Beloved Woman. The name may be a corruption of *giga*, or blood, and *agehya*, or woman. If so, the title might be phrased more accurately as "Red Woman" or "War Woman."

Whatever the case, prior to European contact and the influence of the whites on our culture, women played a prominent role in the social, political, and cultural life of the Cherokees. Nancy Ward, *Ghigau* of the Cherokees, participated in a May 1817 tribal council meeting at which she presented a statement signed by twelve other women pleading with the Cherokee people not to give up any more land.

Precious few non-Indian people are aware of the role native women played in ancient tribal societies. Written records of tribal people have been taken from the notes and journals of diplomats, missionaries, explorers, and soldiers—all men. They had a tendency to record observations of tribal women through their relationships to men. Therefore, tribal women have been inaccurately depicted, most often as drudges or ethereal Indian princesses.

In our tribal stories, we have heard of a Women's Council, which was headed by a very powerful woman, perhaps the *Ghigau*. This oral history is frequently discredited by Western historians as "merely myth."

I have always found their repudiation fascinating. An entire body of knowledge can be dismissed because it was not written, while material written by obviously biased men is readily accepted as reality. No wonder our written history speaks so often of war but rarely records descriptions of our songs, dances, and simple joys of living. The voices of our grandmothers are silenced by most of the written history of our people. How I long to hear their voices!

Because enemy tribes surrounded us, we found it necessary to be militaristic. Women even occasionally accompanied men to the battlefield as warriors. We were also profoundly religious, believing that the world existed in a precarious balance and that only right or correct actions kept it from tumbling. Wrong actions could disturb the balance.

Sometimes when our people were not careful or let down their guard, that balance was unsettled. That is just what occurred when the Cherokee people became more acculturated and adopted more of the values of the Europeans who invaded and infiltrated their country. Europeans brought with them the view that men were the absolute heads of households, and women were to be submissive to them. It was then that the role of women in Cherokee society began to decline. One of the new values Europeans brought to the Cherokees was a lack of balance and harmony between men and women. It was what we today call sexism. This was not a Cherokee concept. Sexism was borrowed from Europeans.

Probably the first Europeans our people ever saw were those in the company of Hernando de Soto, the Spanish conquistador who landed in Florida in 1539. Flush from conquests of native tribes in Peru, he and his men wandered northward through our highland villages and other Indian communities, kidnapping tribal leaders to ensure safe passage. In 1542, de Soto died, presumably of fever, in his camp on the banks of the Mississippi River. The following year, the remainder of de Soto's exhausted party, led by Luis de Moscoso, limped back to Mexico. Twenty-six years later, the Spaniards of the expedition led by Captain Juan Pardo arrived in Cherokee country.

The European intruders might as well have been from a different planet. Long before those white men made contact with our tribe, the Cherokees had developed a complex culture and society. The Spanish narratives from that period are unclear and sometimes contradictory.

Either we somehow managed to fare better with the Spanish than other tribes did, or else all of that experience was suppressed by the Cherokee wisdom keepers and not included in the oral recitations of our history.

What is known is that the Spanish "explorers," as many of us as schoolchildren were taught to call these invaders, were some of the most brutal and barbaric of the Europeans who invaded the "New World," as the whites called it. In their fruitless quest for gold and mineral riches, these enforcers of the notorious Spanish Inquisition mistreated and antagonized all the native people they happened upon in a zealous attempt to convert them to Christianity.

The lands that these Europeans invaded was hardly a "New World." Yet even today, there are people who believe that this vast domain called America was nothing but a wild and virgin land just waiting for the advent of the wise and superior Europeans to tame and domesticate it. In 1492, there were *more than seventy-five million native people* in the Western Hemisphere, with six million of those residing in what is now the United States. They spoke two thousand languages, and had been part of thriving civilizations long before the coming of Columbus. This rich culture of the native people nonetheless was demolished methodically and ruthlessly within a historically short period. The time for suffering had begun.

> *[Columbus] makes Hitler look like a juvenile delinquent.*
>
> *Indian activist Russell Means, 1991*

> *The Spanish conquest must be repudiated. Celebrating it would be shameful and the justification of a massacre.*
>
> *Ecuador Indian leader Manuel Castro, 1991*

That is why I thought it was very sad, in 1992, when so many people wished to *celebrate* the five hundredth anniversary of Columbus's arrival in the Americas. There were festivals, parades, seminars, motion pictures, and many attempts to summarize the monumental changes North America has undergone since 1492. It is doubtful that many Americans even paused to reflect on the true history of the continent—that of indigenous people who have lived on this land since time immemorial. The so-called Columbus discovery, which is indeed a myth, launched an era of cultural decimation and murder. Columbus and those who followed him are responsible for genocide, slavery, colonialism, cultural plunder, and environmental destruction. There was no "discovery." Nor was it an "encounter." That is also wrong. The "discovery" was, in fact, wholesale rape, theft, and murder.

> *From the moment we realized 1992 would be the 500th anniversary of Columbus's voyage to the Americas, we knew we couldn't overlook it. We live in a state with the largest concentration of both Native Americans and Native American tribes in the country. We would have to ignore, literally, the history of more than 250,000 Oklahomans not to know there was an America before Columbus.*
>
> Jeanne M. Devlin, editor
> Oklahoma Today, May–June 1992

But who can blame most Americans for forgetting or never knowing about native people? Who can fault them for not knowing about the high degree of organization and democracy many tribal cultures had attained prior to the invasion of Europeans? There is such a woeful absence of accurate information about native people, either historical or contemporary, that it is little wonder this void has been filled with negative stereotypes from old western movies and romanticized paintings. One friend of mine, a Seneca scholar, once remarked that many people have a mental snapshot of native people taken three hundred years ago, and they want to retain that image.

In the quarter century following the arrival of Columbus on Hispaniola, the island's native population plummeted from five hundred thousand to only five hundred. Contemporary historians estimate that North America aside, the Spanish conquerors slaughtered twelve million to nineteen million native people in the Caribbean, Central America, and South America in the first four decades of the sixteenth century. The invaders proved to be just as lethal on this continent. Since these purportedly God-fearing men—whose forebears in the name of God had been responsible for the Crusades and the expulsion of the Jews from Spain— could find no biblical reference to any people with red-toned skin, they believed that the natives were not human beings at all, but savages or merely some sort of animal. It was open season. Killing and maiming

Indians with lances, crossbows, and packs of the terrifying *perros de guerra*, or war dogs, were considered great sport.

> *The Almighty seems to have inspired these people [Indians] with a weakness and softness of humor like that of lambs, and the Spanish who have given them so much trouble, and fallen upon them so fiercely, resemble savage tigers, wolves and lions when enraged with pressing hunger.*
>
> *They laid wagers with one another, who should cleave a man down with his sword most dexterously at one blow; or who should take his head from his shoulders most cleverly; or who should run a man through after the most artificial manner: they tore away children from their mothers' arms and dashed out their brains against the rocks. . . . They set up gibbets, and hanged up 13 of these poor creatures in honor of Jesus Christ and his 12 apostles. They kindled a great fire under those gibbets to burn those they had hanged upon them.*
>
> Bishop Bartoleme de las Casas, 1552

Just as the Spanish conquistadores, bearing sword and cross, wreaked havoc amongst the Pueblo people to the west, their comrades in arms committed unspeakable atrocities against the various tribes they came upon in the Appalachian woodlands. Besides the extreme and intentional physical abuse that the Spanish dealt the native people they met during their quest, they also devastated the native population by spreading diseases such as measles, smallpox, and bubonic plague.

Our medicine men and women were correct in believing that all pestilence was the result of the world being out of balance. The violence and deadly diseases brought by the invaders most assuredly spun our world out of balance. Fortunately for our people, the Spanish did not remain long. But the time they did spend with the various tribes took its toll. The eventual arrival of French and English explorers in North America did little to change that aggressive behavior or to change for the better the native people's predicament. Neither our medicine nor our sacred rites could alter that.

For the Cherokees, one of the largest and culturally richest tribes in the Southeast, major change in lifestyle and custom did not occur after our fleeting encounters with the Spaniards. Cherokee culture shock occurred more than a century later when we came face to face with the English. Although not as overtly cruel as the Spanish, they were at best an imperialistic people capable of destroying entire villages of Cherokees, including women and children.

In 1654, some native people established a new village, as our forebears were wont to do from time to time, at the falls of the James River near where Richmond, Virginia, is now located. The English of the Virginia colony, who had just concluded a bloody war with the Powhatan tribes, were alarmed by the sudden arrival of the native people. The English did not want any more Indian people to live anywhere near them. So the colony sent forth one hundred Virginians and one hundred allied Pamunkey Indians to attack the village and drive out or exterminate the inhabitants. Neither goal was accomplished. The plan backfired. The resulting battle proved disastrous for the whites and the Pamunkeys, who lost their chief and most of their fighting men in combat. The village warriors were victorious. That episode—a humiliating defeat for the British—marked the beginning of a bitter, often murderous, relationship between the native people and the English colonies.

The relationship between the British and the native people continued to be fraught with violence. For example, we know that in July of 1673, James Needham and Gabriel Arthur of the Virginia colony made contact with Cherokees in eastern Tennessee. During a quarrel on a return trip to Virginia to procure trade goods, Needham was killed by his native guide, known as Indian John. After much heated discussion, the Cherokees determined that Arthur, who remained behind to learn the Cherokee language, would be spared. Arthur lived with our people for almost a year. Disguised as a Cherokee, he even went on a few war parties against the Shawnees and other enemies before he was allowed to return to his home.

Other white men soon followed. Ever mindful of our valuable stores of pelts, bears' oil, and beeswax, they were most anxious to negotiate trade routes between their colonial homes and the Cherokee domain. In 1674, Henry Woodward journeyed from Charleston to Virginia over a route that brought him to what he called "Chorakae" settlements on the headwaters of the Savannah River. Records are scant, but it is believed that by the late 1600s, despite occasional conflicts, more and more English traders from Virginia and South Carolina, lured by the prospects of great financial gain, began to visit the Cherokee Nation on a regular basis.

In 1684, a decade after Woodward first traded with our tribe, a treaty was drawn up at Charleston between some of the Cherokee chiefs and the colony of South Carolina. Presumably this document, signed in picture writing, was meant to guard our people against enemy tribes that had captured a number of Cherokees and sold them into slavery. But like so many other treaties to come, the agreement was abrogated quickly. Less than nine years later, another Cherokee delegation went to Charleston to complain that other tribes still were selling many of our people to the English for slaves. More promises were made and, as was frequently the rule throughout our tribal history, those promises too were unkept.

From that time until the American Revolution, our people were variously military allies, trading partners, or enemies of the English colonists. Now and then we were a combination, or even all three at the same time. We also engaged in on-and-off warfare with neighboring Indian tribes. The confusion of this period of our history resulted in large part because we did not have one person who was responsible for military decisions for all the Cherokee towns, or any person who could make unilateral decisions for all the Cherokees. The English colonies functioned in much the same manner. South Carolina, for instance, was not obligated in any way to honor pledges made by, say, Virginia. Different colonies were allied at different times with various Indian tribes, or with individual towns within the tribes, and those tribes might have been at war with one another.

Although some historians have argued otherwise, it is generally held that the first white trader to marry a Cherokee was Cornelius Dougherty (sometimes called Alexander Dougherty), a stalwart Irishman from Virginia who apparently settled among our people and spent the rest of his life with the tribe. Eleazar Wiggan, known to the Cherokees as "Old Rabbit," and Ludovic Grant were also early traders who took Cherokee wives. These traders established what were undoubtedly some of the first of the many old Cherokee mixed-blood families. Mingling and intermarriage with the whites had a critical effect on tribal development. The consequences would be felt for generations to come.

By marrying native women, the white traders found they were accepted in the Cherokee community. There were many practical rewards. White husbands learned their wives' customs and language; the women served as interpreters in matters of commerce. All of the offspring would be considered Cherokee, since the matrilineal kinship system, like that of the Jews, maintains that the children of our women are always Cherokee despite the race of their fathers. Nonetheless, there were negative effects. Marrying white traders, for example, disturbed the traditional Cherokee social organization because many of the wives went to live with their husbands. This was contrary to our custom of husbands residing in their wives' domiciles. Cherokee women who married whites tended to be submissive, and often acquiesced to their husbands. The spiritual leaders fought against the marrying of white men to Cherokee women unless the men accepted our way of life and came to live with their wives in the Cherokee community.

There were problems for the children, as well. They took their fathers' surnames along with the clan affiliation of their mothers, and became heirs to their fathers' houses and possessions. This caused much confusion and infighting. For the first time in our tribe's history, there was great inequality of wealth.

Other quandaries had to be faced. Oftentimes, the children of mixed marriages spoke both Cherokee and English, attended school, and embraced some of their fathers' customs and beliefs. They also picked up much of their mothers' wisdom about the natural world, plants, animals, and mountain living. However, Cherokee society began to erode as many of the mixed-blood youths, swayed by their fathers' religion, decided the old ways were heathen and bad. Mixed-bloods exerted tremendous influence on the tribe. Eventually, they would ascend to the ruling class in Cherokee society, replacing the old form of government. The purebloods and traditionalists tried to hold on, aware that the balance of our world was going awry.

As more white caravans moved into Cherokee country in the 1700s, elements of our tribe gradually became dependent on the various trade goods the whites brought with them, particularly tools such as knife blades and hoes fashioned of metal, which proved to be far superior to traditional stone implements. The old tribal customs and native attire still prevailed, although some Cherokees yearned to own more of the traders' utensils and trinkets. Those of our people who experienced significant contact with the English came to believe that they could not live without those things. In those instances, some Cherokees increased their dependency on the whites, swapping deerskins and other staples for hatchets, kettles, bolts of cloth, rum, firearms, and ammunition. Instead of luxuries, the white men's trade goods came to be regarded by some Cherokees as necessities. Native handicrafts gradually became scarce.

Increased associations with white settlers and traders brought other changes to the Cherokee way of life. Some of the old tribal customs and native dress persisted, but little by little, there were subtle adjustments to the surge of white dominance. Log cabins with several rooms began to take the place of traditional one-room dwellings. Native people developed a taste for white cuisine and strong drink. Domesticated animals such as horses, hogs, and poultry made life easier. So did the white men's ordnance. Guns became the primary weapons for hunting and warfare. Soon, some of the native people lost their prowess with the bow and arrow or the blowgun made from hollowed cane. They often put aside their knives made of stone, preferring the white man's blades of forged steel.

Sometimes even the act of hunting game took on a different meaning. Traditional attitudes about killing the animals of the forests and the tribe's ageless concern for keeping the world in balance were altered. Instead of relying on deer and other fur-bearing creatures for sustenance, a need was created to take more animals than were necessary, to supply skins and pelts for trading purposes. The deerskin trade comprised a vast infrastructure of commerce linking the leather industry in Europe with Indian tribes throughout the Appalachians.

White traders also came to the Cherokees to purchase Indian captives taken during battles. In the tribe's earlier history, most prisoners of war were tortured or slain. Slavery did not exist among our tribe before the coming of the Europeans. That changed with the traders. The shackled Indians delivered by the Cherokees were sent off to market. There they were sold on the block as slaves, like the Africans who were forced to work on the many plantations of the mainland colonies and the West Indies.

Spanish conquistadores had begun the importation of misery when they brought the first African captives to the Americas in 1505. Because the indigenous people of the Caribbean perished so quickly from maltreatment and disease, enslaved Africans were imported to perform manual labor. During the following four centuries, before the last black slaves in Brazil were finally freed in 1888, about ten million fettered slaves made the difficult journey from Africa. Virtually none of them ever again touched their native soil. It is believed that at least two million died at sea on squalid slave ships. Much of the human cargo went to sugarcane fields in the Caribbean or to Brazil. Although the Portuguese originally monopolized the slave trade, Dutch, British, and French sailors later dominated the trafficking, which peaked in the 1700s. Without regard for the individual lives of African slaves, the white Europeans viewed them only as a profitable commodity for all of the traders.

During the 1700s, if not before, our people also came to value the possession of slaves and to participate in the terrible commerce, introduced into the tribe by English traders who intermarried with our women. The Cherokees' black slaves were taken as the spoils of war or were captured runaways. The British government also presented slaves to influential tribal leaders, calling them "king's gifts." During the late eighteenth century, a growing number of the Cherokee elite—mimicking the English colonists—bought and sold slaves for their own use as field workers and servants. By 1790, the Cherokee elite had definitely adopted black slavery, although the practice never permeated the entire Cherokee Nation.

In 1738, a deadly smallpox epidemic, brought to South Carolina by slave ships, broke out among our tribe. Nearly half of our people died within a year. Another outbreak of smallpox occurred in 1739, probably brought by Cherokees who had contracted the disease after helping the British battle the Spanish in Florida settlements where smallpox was rampant. Smallpox struck our people again in 1759, and at various times throughout the rest of the century. Deadly epidemics of measles and influenza contributed to our misery.

As the smallpox scourge spread unchecked throughout the Cherokee communities, a veil of anguish fell on the Cherokee Nation. Many of our spiritual leaders believed the disease was a punishment for having broken ancient tribal laws. They discarded sacred objects, thinking they had lost their protecting power. Hundreds of our warriors committed suicide after seeing the mutilation and disfigurement that the disease caused to their bodies. Some shot themselves, others cut their throats or stabbed themselves with knives or pointed cane spears. Many sought relief through death by leaping into huge bonfires.

In time, alcohol became even more ruinous than smallpox. When rum was introduced into the Appalachian Mountains, it was swapped to the Indian tribes for deerskins. The impact of "demon rum" on Native American societies brought catastrophic changes to the world of the Choctaws, Cherokees, and other southern tribes.

Many factors conspired to weaken our tribe and to increase stress. Continual warfare with other tribes and with whites took an intolerable toll, and so did infectious diseases and alcoholism. Cherokees and other native people no longer thought of themselves as partners in any sort of compatible liaison with the world around them. Many Native Americans felt utterly violated and compromised. It seemed as if the spiritual and social tapestry they had created for centuries was unraveling. Everything lost that sacred balance. And ever since, we have been striving to return to the harmony we once had. It has been a difficult task. The odds against us have been formidable. But despite everything that has happened to us, we have never given up and will never give up. There is an old Cherokee prophecy which instructs us that as long as the Cherokees continue traditional dances, the world will remain as it is, but when the dances stop, the world will come to an end. Everyone should hope that the Cherokees will continue to dance.

M A N K I L L E R   F L A T S

The little Wren is the messenger of the birds, and she pries into everything. She gets up early in the morning and goes around to every house in the settlement to get news for the bird council. When a baby is born, she finds out whether it is a boy or girl and reports to the council. If it is a boy, she sings in mournful chorus, "Alas! the whistle of the arrow! my shins will burn," because the birds know that when the boy grows older, he will hunt them with his blowgun and arrows and roast them on a stick.

But if the baby is a girl, the birds are glad and sing, "Thanks! the sound of the pestle! At her home I shall surely be able to scratch where she sweeps," because they know that after a while, they will be able to pick up stray grains where she beats the corn into meal.

When the Cricket hears that a girl is born, it is also glad, and says, "Thanks, I shall sing in the house where she lives." But if it is a boy, the Cricket laments, "Gwe-he! he will shoot me! He will shoot me! He will shoot me!" because boys make little bows to shoot crickets and grasshoppers.

I was born into the Mankiller household on November 18, 1945, the sixth child of eleven in our family. It was a Sunday. My birth took place at the W. W. Hastings Indian Hospital, in Tahlequah, Oklahoma. I arrived at the tail end of autumn, a few months after the surrender of the Japanese and the conclusion of World War II. I suppose if my father had not fallen off a log while cutting trees for railroad ties, I would not have been born. But his leg injuries prevented him from enlisting in the military service and going off to war. So instead of fighting, he stayed around home, and three of us were born in or around that time.

I had three brothers and two sisters who were born before me. Louis Donald was born in 1937, Frieda Marie in 1938, Robert Charles in 1940, Frances Kay in 1942, and John David in 1943. Following me came Linda Jean in 1949, Richard Colson in 1951, Vanessa Lou in 1953, James Ray in 1956, and finally William Edward in 1961, the two youngest being born in California. So of the eleven children born to my parents, the wrens and crickets, as the old tale goes, were happy on five occasions.

When I was a little girl, everyone mostly called me by my middle name, Pearl. I was named Wilma after my father's uncle's wife, and Pearl after my mother's mother. Wilma is a short form of the Dutch name Wilhelmina. The name Pearl comes, of course, from the speck of sand inside the oyster that becomes an aggravation to the mollusk, and is covered with smooth layers of shell material that may develop into an object of gem quality. The simple story of how the pearl evolves has always appealed to me—not that I consider myself a precious treasure. I don't mean to say that. But the whole notion of an irritant developing into something of worth is appealing to me.

My earliest memory is of sitting on a trunk in our family house at Mankiller Flats in the Rocky Mountain community. We had just moved into the house, and I was as happy as could be. I was just a little girl, but I can recall that moment very clearly. My folks had rented from other people until 1948, when we settled there on the family land. That house was built by Charley, my father. He built it himself. His uncle, Looney Gourd, helped him with the construction. So did my oldest brother, Don. My mother now lives on the site of that house. We eventually rented that original family house to some of our cousins. After that, other people lived there. Then there was a fire and the house burned down. But back when I was just a small girl, that house was the first real family home I can recall. Thinking back to those times, I remember it as a little bitty house with too many people living there—and more still to come.

That house had been built of rough lumber and had four rooms, all with bare plank floors and walls. It was covered by a tin roof. In the winter, our only heat came from a wood stove. That is also how we cooked. There was no electricity, and we used coal-oil lamps to light the rooms.

We had a few pieces of furniture. There was an outhouse for a toilet. Mom used a wringer washer with a gasoline motor, and she had a clothing iron which was operated with natural gas. For washing and cooking, we had to haul water from the spring a quarter mile from the house. The spring also served as a refrigerator for some of our food. We kept a box in the cold water to hold milk and other perishables.

To this day, I prefer to use wood for heating my home. The smell of the fire is familiar. And I still love the sound of rain. When I hear it, I remember the sound it made when it fell on our old tin roof. That's a pleasant memory for me.

But other memories are not very sweet. We were not well off, at least when it came to money. Like many of the people in Adair County, we were really poor—"dirt poor" is how they say it in Oklahoma. I suppose there are degrees of poverty just as there are degrees of wealth. If so, we were on the bottom rung of the poverty ladder.

In the late 1940s and the 1950s, the Cherokee population had been predominantly mixed-blood for some time, and the mixed-blood element included many well-to-do people and some prominent individuals. Because of this, a faulty belief arose that all Cherokees had become happily assimilated into the mainstream of American society. That was not the case. In reality, there were many full-bloods, half bloods, or other mixed-blood Cherokees with more traditional lifeways. These people lived in extreme poverty in Cherokee communities such as ours, scattered throughout the hills. Those settlements that did not appear on any maps. Many of them were not visible from the road to travelers passing through the area. Each community was made up of families living on their individual allotments of land.

People tended to congregate for various events at a community center or a church or school, or at one of the tribal ceremonial grounds where dances were held. Sometimes our family attended services at Echota Baptist Church. On other occasions, we went to the Baptist church in Rocky Mountain. But we were never what might be called regular church-goers, and we did not go to Sunday school or learn a great deal about Christianity.

Sometimes we attended ceremonial dances. I remember all the food and people. There were always lots of children to run and play with, and laughter and no set bedtime for anyone. The dances were held outside. They lasted all night. It gave me such a good feeling to go to the ceremonial dances. We had such a great time. But I also recall that we were always secretive about going to the ceremonial dance grounds or even about going to some other Cherokees' houses for parties with fiddles and poker games. My sister told me we had to keep it a secret because some folks thought such things were sinful. I thought that was odd. Later, I figured maybe she was right. Perhaps some of our non-Indian neighbors would not approve of music making or especially of a ceremonial dance.

Most people we knew spoke Cherokee in their homes and as their first language. There were Cherokee-language Baptist churches. A significant number of folks spoke only Cherokee and no English. In our home, both languages were used, often interchangeably. Cherokee was spoken almost exclusively whenever we visited other native people or when they came to see us. My mother, even though she is white, learned to speak passable conversational Cherokee. When it was just the family, we mostly used English except for simple phrases such as the Cherokee for "Pass the salt" or "I need some water." As children, we certainly understood Cherokee, but because we had a white mother, we never became as fluent in the language as our father and other kinfolk.

In the small communities of eastern Oklahoma, native people raised large vegetable gardens and harvested plant foods from the woods, such as wild onions, greens, mushrooms, and berries. Hunting and fishing helped fill our plates, and when folks could afford it, they raised cattle and hogs. We were such a large family that our diet had to be supplemented by game. Occasionally my father or my big brother Don would kill a groundhog or a wild pig. The younger boys also went hunting. In those early days, we ate a lot of squirrel. Squirrels are small, so you have to have several to make a meal for a family. My mother would bread the squirrels lightly and fry them like chicken. They tasted a little like chicken. She made gravy from the drippings. Sometimes we had squirrel soup and dumplings, or soup made from quail or other birds. We gathered greens such as dandelions and poke. There were walnuts and hickory nuts, as well as blackberries, mulberries, and wild grapes. We fished and ate our fill of perch, crawfish, catfish, and frogs. Mom canned jars of tomatoes, beans, and corn from our vegetable garden, and stored food underground or in the shed. In some years, we also grew strawberries or peanuts which we sold for cash. Even though we were poor, I cannot remember ever being hungry as a little girl. Somehow, we always had food on our table.

Employment for the rural Cherokee population was generally sporadic and seasonal. Life was certainly not charmed in Adair County. Many traditional people cut wood to sell, and some worked on seasonal migrant harvest crews. It was a hard life and a constant struggle to acquire enough money to meet the family's bare-minimal cash needs. My older brothers, sisters, and parents had to scrape a living out of stony soil known more for flint rock than fertility. Don, being the oldest son, quit school after the eighth grade so he could help my folks support the family.

Often, the older kids used to go out with Mom and Dad to cut and peel timber to be used for railroad ties and as utility poles. Most of the time, I didn't go out on the timber expeditions, but once I did go along to cut ties. I picked up a soda-pop bottle that I found and I took a swig. What I expected to be sweet pop turned out to be kerosene. My folks had to rush me to the hospital in Tahlequah. Another time, my sister Frances sliced her knee badly while the family was cutting ties. She had to be transported over bad roads about thirty miles to the hospital for emergency treatment.

Most folks did not have dependable transportation. That meant regular jobs were few and far between. Besides cutting railroad ties, my father and Don went to Colorado each year to help bring in the broomcorn and generate enough money to buy shoes and some other basics for all the kids. Broomcorn was obviously important material for making brooms, but it was also used in shipbuilding enterprises. The corn was harvested and put into a machine that crushed it and made it into bales. The bales were hauled by truck from the farms around Campo, Colorado, in the southeastern corner of the state.

The Cherokee workers often traveled to Campo together, by car or on buses provided by the farm owners. There were Hispanics and some whites, but most of the field workers were native people. My dad and brother worked nearly every day of the week. They began at dawn, along with a crew of more than twenty other men. The work was backbreaking, and they paused only to swig dippers of water and wring out their sweaty neckerchiefs. The crews worked straight through until noon, then took a break for lunch. Women from the farms carried lunch out to the fields and set it on tables. The workers ate the big meals quickly to make time for a brief rest in the shade before going back to the fields, where they remained until sunset. They were paid nine, sometimes ten dollars per day.

It always seemed to me that the timing of the broomcorn harvest was off just a bit. Our school classes in Oklahoma began in early August so we could be finished in May to help with the local harvest. When school started, my father and brother were still in Colorado, so we had to begin classes without shoes for the new year. But before too long, Dad and Don would come home with some money in their pockets. Then they bought everyone shoes and warm coats before the cold weather set in. It was a very exciting time for all of us. Getting new leather shoes was pretty special. Most of our clothing was hand-me-downs or was made of flour sacks. Our flour came in huge sacks, so my mother used that cloth to make our clothes—both underwear and some of our outerwear. I recall that those sacks had roses or other floral prints on them. Even though, as the old saying goes, it is hard to make a silk purse from a sow's ear, the designs made our clothes look a little better.

There were no school buses in that area in those days. Every day, we walked three miles each way, to and from Rocky Mountain School. We made that walk in the extreme cold of winter and the heat of late spring. Occasionally, my brother Bob would sneak off to hunt or just to roam around in the woods all day. He would join us on the way back home and pretend he had been to school. Once when Bob skipped school to hunt in the hills near our home, he was bitten on the hand by a rattlesnake. By the time he returned home, his entire arm and shoulder were profoundly swollen. Fortunately, he was succesfully treated for the bite.

I attended classes at the school from first through fifth grades. It was just a little rural schoolhouse—a frame building painted white. My dad helped to roof it. It had one large general room, a kitchen, and two other classrooms. It was big enough to accommodate sixty students comfortably, but it was not fancy.

The teachers, especially the women, were different than any I had known before entering school. They wore lipstick, and they spoke and dressed differently than the rest of the women in our community. One of the male teachers even had a television. Occasionally, we walked to his house to watch it. Most days, the teachers had a big pot of beans on for lunch. Oftentimes, the families from the area would have pie suppers and auctions at the schoolhouse to raise money for Christmas or other events.

I didn't know the difference between being poor and having money until one day at school. A little girl whose family had more than most of us saw my flour-sack underwear while we were in the outhouse. She ran and told some other girls, and they all teased me about it. That was really the first time I had any inkling that we were different.

The warmth and love in our home made up for the lack of material things. My parents had a strong relationship and always seemed to be very much in love. They were visibly affectionate with one another, hugging and holding hands. One time when we were all going for a ride in our old car, Mom raced to beat us children so she could sit in the front seat right beside Dad.

It was a really old car, a black 1949 Ford. We used it to go to town or to visit families and relatives. Although it was a tight squeeze to get all of us in the car, it was always such an adventure to go for a ride. Dad would tell us scary stories when we drove the back roads. Once when we were driving home on a dirt road late one night, some tree branches hanging down brushed the windshield. Dad told us it reminded him of the time he was driving home one particularly spooky night when his windshield was brushed by low branches. He said the branches slapped hard against the windshield and startled him. The windshield was left streaked with blood. He was terrified, and drove home as quickly as he could so he could wash off the offending blood. He told us it was probably the blood of an owl that had been shot and was sitting on the branches.

We were terrified by the story. Owls are ominous birds to some Cherokees. It is believed that certain persons can change themselves into owls and travel through the night doing evil to others. One time, Dad told us, someone in our area shot an owl with a silver bullet. The next day, mysteriously, the person learned that his most bitter enemy had been found shot to death.

My father's stories were important to all of us. Our main forms of entertainment were storytelling and visiting. Either we went to see other families, or folks visited us. Mostly we saw other Cherokee people.

When I was a little girl, I usually ran off and hid if I spied any white folks coming to our house. I felt shy and embarrassed when I was around non-Indians. I would run to the woods or hide in the attic.

My wariness of white people developed when I was a little girl walking to school with my sister. Some well-dressed white ladies occasionally would drive up in their big cars. They came to bring us clothes and offer us rides to school. I suppose they felt it was their Christian duty to pick us up and take us to school. One time when we got inside their car, those ladies looked at us with sad expressions and said, "Bless your little hearts." It was not the words that got to me, but the way they said them, along with the looks on their faces. Were they being sympathetic because we had to walk? Was it because of our social situation? Was it the way we were dressed? After that, we called those women the "Bless Your Heart" ladies. Even as a child, I could tell if someone was being condescending or patronizing to me because I was Indian.

> *One of the major problems of the Indian people is the missionary. It has been said of missionaries that when they arrived they had only the Book and we had the land; now we have the Book and they have the land.*
>
> *Vine Victor Deloria, Jr.*
> Custer Died for Your Sins

Sometimes on weekends we drove to the town of Stilwell, the seat of Adair County, to spend time with my mother's Uncle Tom Sitton and his wife, Maud. It was not a very long drive, and Stilwell was a lot larger than Rocky Mountain. Those were good trips because we usually ended up getting a dime to go to the movies or buy candy. Every year in May, there was a big strawberry festival in Stilwell, and many visitors showed up to eat the berries and celebrate the harvest. The festival is still held.

Other times our great-aunt, Wilma Mankiller, came to see us. She brought us clothes and other gifts. She was a white woman who had married my father's Uncle George. They lived in a grand brick residence in Tahlequah near the old Cherokee Female Seminary. When the Mankiller allotments had been parceled out at the turn of the century, Uncle George's ancestors received land near Bartlesville, the headquarters of Phillips Petroleum Company. Oil was later discovered on my uncle and aunt's land. That is why every year Uncle George got a brand-new Cadillac. My big sister Frances was Aunt Wilma's favorite, I suppose because Frances was always nice and polite and did all her chores. I was the opposite. I would hide in the woods when Aunt Wilma came to our place.

I felt much more comfortable with my Cherokee relatives. I suppose it was because we saw them more often and we shared some of the same interests. One woman I particularly liked was my father's half sister, Jensie Hummingbird. She was small, and had hair so black it looked blue in the sunlight. She wore cotton housedresses that she had made herself. She didn't have a car, so we visited her more often than she visited us. Jensie did not speak English at all and we were not fluent in Cherokee, but we managed to communicate. It was clear to all of us kids that she was fond of us. Jensie, like many members of my father's family, had severe health problems. Most of her life, she suffered from diabetes and arthritis.

Maude Wolf was another woman we saw quite a bit. She grew up with my father, and although they were cousins, we always called her Aunt Maude. She was a tall, thin, handsome woman with prominent cheekbones and excellent posture. She particularly loved working outside, playing the traditional Cherokee game of stickball, or helping her husband, Jim Wolfe, maintain the ceremonial grounds. She also loved to walk in the woods to gather gifts of nature to prepare for a meal. Aunt Maude received no formal education, but she was wise. Her husband was a strict Cherokee traditionalist. He was an Indian doctor and a ceremonial dance leader. Maude and Jim had nine children, but because they lived away from Rocky Mountain, we didn't go to school with them. Jim never spoke English, but I remember him as a thoughtful and powerful presence with a crazy sense of humor.

We visited other folks during that time, including my father's sister, Aunt Sally Leach, her husband, Nelson, and their family. Sally was petite, even dainty, and was always meticulously dressed. Nelson, a bilingual Cherokee, always reminded me of a country squire. He was careful about his dress and had a courtly manner. He managed to look elegant even when hauling hay. Sally and Nelson lived on another portion of the Mankiller family allotment. Their house was a little better than ours, and they were more prosperous in some ways than we were. My siblings and I always enjoyed visiting so we could play with our cousins. The firstborn, Bob, inherited his mother's gentle ways and strong nature and his father's willingness to work hard. Alice and Elsie, the two girls, were quiet and strong. Larry, the youngest, was ill quite a bit in his early childhood, but eventually recovered completely. All of the Leach family spoke Cherokee.

When visiting friends, particularly the Henry Leach family, one pastime for the adults was playing cards. While the adults played, all the children would go outside for a game of hide-and-seek or just run in the woods together. Sometimes our games involved capturing bugs for hours of play. We tied long strings around June bugs and let them fly like little airplanes while we chased them. We captured lightning bugs, put them in a mason jar, and watched them flash on and off. In the end, we always released the bugs and watched them hurriedly fly out of our childish reach. Dad would warn us about staying out too late. He told us to be on the watch for mountain lions or bobcats. We knew what bobcats looked like. Once we returned from a late-night visit to friends and our headlights caught a bobcat on the roof of our storage house. Everyone was scared and excited at seeing the bobcat, because bobcats in the area were rare, even in those days. While we played and kept a wary eye out for those animals, which were more afraid of us than we were of them, Dad and the other adults sometimes played cards all night. When they did that, they would make quilt pallets on the floor for the children. We usually slept soundly, exhausted from a day and evening spent outside among the trees, plants, and animals. We loved these visitations to relatives and friends.

The one relative who impressed me most was my father's Aunt Maggie Gourd. Dad stayed with her for a while when he was growing up. She lived only about a mile and a half from our house. We often visited her, and she spoke English well. She had a striking, intelligent face and wore her very dark hair pulled back. Aunt Maggie had a nice wood-frame house—three big rooms and a porch. She also had good furniture, probably purchased when she had a much bigger ranch. Family legend has it that she married a much younger man, Looney Gourd, who sold a lot of her assets little by little until she owned very few cattle or goods. We traded farm goods and produce with Aunt Maggie. My brother Johnny and I walked to her house with eggs to swap for fresh milk. If we were lucky, Aunt Maggie had a story to tell us. I didn't know it at the time, but Aunt Maggie told stories in the old Cherokee tradition. Some of those tales were frightening and others were not, but all of her stories taught us a lesson of some kind.

My brother Johnny is only two years older than I am, but we were quite different. While my hair is brown and my eyes are hazel, Johnny has brown eyes and almost black hair. He is also built like my father—sturdy with wide shoulders. During our childhood, Johnny almost always wore overalls.

Since Johnny and I were frequently asked to watch over our younger brothers and sisters while the older ones worked, Aunt Maggie tried to impress on our young minds the importance of taking that task seriously. That is why one afternoon she told us the tale of the young Cherokee man and woman who took their baby into the woods. They stopped to make camp. They spread a blanket on the ground and put the baby on it to nap. While the child dozed, the parents moved some distance away so they would not disturb the child's dreams. They built a fire, and when it was going well and their campsite was prepared, they returned to the blanket for the baby. The infant was gone. Only the blanket remained. They searched and searched, but never found their child.

Aunt Maggie told us that the Little People, *Yunwi Tsunsdi*, who live in the woods wherever Cherokees live, had come across the baby. Believing it had been abandoned, they took it to raise as one of their own. Aunt Maggie's story had an impact. Johnny and I made a solemn vow to always keep a very close watch on our brothers and sisters and not allow them to be taken away by the Little People.

Stories of Little People have always been among the favorites of Cherokee children. The Little People look like Cherokees but are small, only about three feet tall. They speak our language. Cherokees always describe them "secondhand." It is said that if one sees the Little People and tells about it, that person will surely die. If anything is found in the forest, Cherokees assume that it belongs to the Little People. If a Cherokee woman goes out to gather hickory nuts in the fall and happens on a woven basket left by another gatherer, she can pick it up and say out loud, "Little People, I am taking this basket." Then it is hers to keep. That is her right.

Others say that the Little People assist the Cherokee "Indian doctors," those who are sometimes called medicine men. It is also said that the Little People watch out for small children in the woods, like the baby in Aunt Maggie's story. But mostly, Little People are known to be mischievous.

I grew up loving Aunt Maggie's stories. They were a rich feast. She also told us tales of the old days during territorial times. She spoke of outlaws and gunmen and posses and hidden treasure. She said famous bank robbers, such as Cherokee Bill and Ned Christie, had hidden stolen gold all around the Rocky Mountain community. To protect their loot, the bandits went to Indian doctors and asked them to make medicine. That is why when other people tried to find the treasure, terrible things always happened to them. Mysterious accidents stopped some of them. Others were bitten by rattlesnakes.

Aunt Maggie's stories were colorful and exciting. So were our visits to her house, even on those occasions when she didn't have a story to share. Just getting to her place often proved to be an adventure.

One time Johnny and I were walking to Aunt Maggie's when a coachwhip snake dropped from a tree on the path in front of us. The snake was four or five feet long with a brown tail. Such snakes are called coachwhips because they look as if they are made of braided leather like the small whips coachmen used to drive horses. It must have stirred our imaginations, because even now when recalling that incident, it seems to me that the snake deliberately jumped down at us. The snake was so infuriated at missing its mark that it chased us. Afraid to look back, we ran as fast as we could. When we finally stopped, out of breath, we were still afraid that the snake would catch up to us and whip us to death. That was what we had heard could happen. We kept going straight to our house and never turned our heads once.

Another time on our way to Aunt Maggie's house, Johnny was carrying eggs. We decided to take a shortcut across a pasture when out of nowhere came a bull charging after us. Johnny fell down and broke every single egg. He scrambled to his feet, and we made it to the safety of a fence just in time. We never could decide which was more frightening—the charging bull or the fury of our parents over those smashed eggs.

In spite of the presence of coachwhip snakes and the threat of contrary bulls, I have always loved being outside with trees, rocks, plants, and animals. I especially loved the springtime. Our place had a lot of dogwood and redbud trees. There were also dozens of different kinds of flowers. I guess my whole family loved the outdoors. My mother could name every tree, bush, flower, and edible plant we encountered in the woods. My father must have known somehow that I would love flowers because the Cherokee name he gave me is *a-ji-luhsgi*, which means "flower." I have always loved the small purple and yellow flowers that grow unattended in the woods near my house. I would sometimes examine every detail of the tiny petals.

We Indians think of the earth and the whole universe as a never-ending circle, and in this circle man is just another animal. The buffalo and the coyote are our

> *brothers; the birds, our cousins. Even the tiniest ant, even a louse, even the smallest flower you can find—they are all relatives.*
>
> Jenny Leading Cloud, White River Sioux

I much preferred playing in the woods to doing my chores. One of my jobs, along with my sister Linda, was to go to the spring to get what seemed like a constant supply of water. Linda was a stocky girl, a few of years younger than I was. She had blondish-brown hair and green eyes. She was good-natured and tended to dream a lot. I resented having to haul water from the spring, so I generally teased, prodded, and harassed Linda on our frequent trips. Our sister Frances, who was quiet and serious, did all her chores willingly and with meticulous care, while I lingered and dawdled. I spent much more time trying to figure out how to avoid chores than it would have taken to do them.

> *The Indian . . . stands free and unconstrained in Nature, is her inhabitant and not her guest, and wears her easily and gracefully. But the* civilized *[italics added] man has the habits of the house. His house is a prison.*
>
> Henry David Thoreau
> Journal, April 26, 1841

All my brothers and sisters had chores to do around the farm, and we were treated pretty fairly by our parents. At Christmas, we were given gifts of relatively equal value. Christmas usually meant I got jacks or a jump rope. My brothers got marbles or similar gifts. There were also fruit and candy, but not much more than that. Still, it was always an exciting time for us. With only a few toys, you learn to be more creative with what you have. That was the case with my brothers and sisters and me. In those days, we didn't always decorate a Christmas tree, but we had a family dinner. During some Christmas celebrations, we went outside and shot guns. In the Cherokee language, Christmas is described literally as "the day they shoot." This refers to the old Cherokee practice of shooting guns to signal the day of Christ's birth.

In addition to playing with toys such as the Chinese checkers my dad made from plywood, I recall spending a good deal of time as a little girl just reading. As far back as I can remember, there were always books around our house—a lot of books. Even today, most of my brothers and sisters prefer reading to watching television. Although none of the kids in my family was particularly crazy about going to school after we moved to California, we managed to acquire an interest in literature at an early age. This love of reading came from the traditional Cherokee passion for telling and listening to stories. But it also came from both my parents, particularly my father. Charley Mankiller loved to read. He was extremely well-read, especially in the context of his life and times. A love for books and reading was one of the best gifts he ever gave his children.

Because of that gift from my father, as well as the stories I heard from the old ones, I managed to learn the history of the Cherokee people. It is a bittersweet story, a tale of a people with extraordinary tenacity trying to survive as a culturally distinct group. At different times throughout our history, we have been described as "vanishing Americans" or have been considered relics of an ancient past. Despite all that, we not only survived—not intact, certainly—but we kept enough culture and tradition to sustain us through all the battles of the past and those yet to come.

CHAPTER 4

GENESIS OF REMOVAL

*L*ong ago, before the Cherokees were driven from their homes in 1838, the people on *Valley River* and *Hiwassee* heard voices of invisible spirits in the air. The spirits warned the Cherokees of wars and misfortunes which the future held in store, and invited them to come and live with the Nuñnehi, the Immortals, in their homes under the mountains and under the waters. For days, the voices hung in the air, and the people listened until they heard the spirits say, "If you would live with us, gather everyone in your town houses and fast there for seven days, and no one must raise a shout or a war whoop in all that time. Do this and we shall come and you will see us and we shall take you to live with us."

The people were afraid of the evils to come, and they knew that the Immortals of the mountains and the waters were happy forever, so they gathered in their town houses and decided to go with them. Those of Anisgayayi town came all together into their town houses and prayed and fasted for six days. On the seventh day, there was a sound from the distant mountains. It came nearer and grew louder until a roar of thunder was all about the town houses, and the people felt the ground shake under them. They were frightened, and despite the warning, some of them screamed out. The Nuñnehi, who had already lifted up the town house with its mound to carry it away, were startled by the cry and let a part of it fall to the earth, where we now see the mound of Setsi. They steadied themselves again and bore the rest of the town house, with all the people in it, to the top of Tsudayelunyi (Lone Peak), near the head of Cheowa.

We can still see it, changed long ago to solid rock, but the people are invisible and immortal.

The people of another town, or Hiwassee, at the place which we now call Dustayalunyi, where Shooting Creek comes in, also prayed and fasted. At the end of seven days, the Nuñnehi came and took them away down under the water. They are there now, and on a warm summer day, when the wind ripples the surface, those who listen well can hear them talking below. When the Cherokees drag the river for fish, the fish-drag always stops and catches there, although the water is deep. The people know it is being held by their lost kinsmen, who do not want to be forgotten.

When the Cherokees were forcibly removed to the West, one of the greatest regrets of those along the Hiwassee and Valley rivers was that they were compelled to leave behind forever their relatives who had gone to the Nuñnehi.

In the Tennessee River near Kingston, eighteen miles below Loudon, Tennessee, is a place which the Cherokee call Gusti, where there once was a settlement long ago. One night while the people were gathered in the town house for a dance, the bank caved in and carried them all down into the river. Boatmen passing the spot in their canoes see the round dome of the town house—now turned to stone—in the water below them, and sometimes they hear the sound of the drum and dance. They never fail to throw food into the water in return for being allowed to cross in safety.

During the winter of 1838–1839, thousands of my people died on a forced removal from our Cherokee homes in the southeastern United States to present northeastern Oklahoma, where I now live. Some of my own kinspeople came to this land during that time. The routes the federal soldiers forced our tribe to take were known as *Nunna daul Tsunyi*, which in Cherokee means literally, "the trail where we cried." In English, the removal became known as the Trail of Tears.

It was in March of 1839 when the last of the groups of Cherokees arrived in this area. One hundred fifty years later, in 1989, our tribe observed the sesquicentennial of that journey. Before it was decided that we should recognize the historic date, we had considerable discussion and hesitation because of sensitivity about the entire removal process that lingers to this day. We ultimately settled on a commemoration only after some wagon-train hobbyists, who were not affiliated with the tribe, re-traced the Trail of Tears. We needed to set the record straight. Many of our people did not make the trip in wagon trains. Far from it. They had neither that option nor that luxury. Old ones and small children were placed in wagons, but many of the Cherokees made that trek by foot or were herded onto boats. Some were in shackles. Thousands perished or were forever scarred in body, mind, and soul.

It was not a friendly removal. It was ugly and unwarranted. For too many Cherokees, it was deadly. The worst part of our holocaust was that it also meant the continued loss of tribal knowledge and traditions. So when we marked that infamous date 150 years later, there could be no celebration. There were no festivities. Nobody smiled. There was absolutely nothing to be happy about. It was a solemn observance, a very emotional time. We regarded the removal as something that happened to our family—something very bad that happened to our family. It was a tragedy. It brought us pain that never seemed to leave. Still, for me, the removal commemoration at Tahlequah did not have the historical impact on our people that an event five years earlier had.

It was in 1984 at Red Clay, Tennessee. It was a reunion of the Cherokee Nation of Oklahoma and the Eastern Band of Cherokees. During the removal in the late 1830s, several hundred Cherokees evaded the soldiers. They escaped to the mountains and remained in hiding. Those people formed the nucleus of the Eastern Band of Cherokees, now living on the Qualla Reservation in North Carolina. The meeting at Red Clay in 1984 was the first gathering of the two Cherokee groups since the removal. The reunion was very emotional. I stepped into the circle where Cherokee meetings had been held such a long time ago. I felt the anger and passion of my ancestors as they had gathered to discuss whether to fight to the death for the right to remain in our ancestral homeland, or to cooperate with the federal removal.

Besides the formal joint council meetings at Red Clay, which I co-chaired, there were wonderful ceremonial events. One of the most interesting was a stickball game. It is said that in the old days, stickball was sometimes played to settle disputes instead of going to war with another tribe. There are several variations of the game, but all of them are played in an open field. In one version, each player enters the field with a pair of ball sticks, one in each hand. The sticks are about two feet long and curved at one end, then laced with rawhide to form a kind of a racket. The ball is small and hard and covered with rawhide. Sometimes a pole, with a fish or another symbol from nature placed on top of it, serves as the goal. The object of the game is to score by capturing the ball in a ball stick, then throwing it toward the goal, striking the symbol on top of the pole.

No matter what version is played, it is a rough game with few rules. It can become extremely dangerous when the players begin to swing their ball sticks. I remember that at the stickball game at Red Clay, an ambulance was standing by in case one of the players was injured.

Today, when stickball is played in Oklahoma at the ceremonial grounds, both women and men compete. Stickball is an exciting game, and one of the few physical games I have ever really enjoyed. Teams are divided into male and female. Some women play stickball well into their seventies. The men carry ball sticks and the women use their hands. Some people say women are not allowed to use ball sticks because they have so many grievances against men, they might use the sticks as weapons of punishment.

Another important symbolic event at Red Clay was the lighting of an eternal flame by the two Cherokee groups. The flame was ignited by torches that had been lighted a few days earlier at Cherokee, North Carolina. The torches were carried by Eastern Cherokee runners along 150 miles of mountainous road. I will never forget the sight of the young Cherokee runners holding the torches high above their heads as they ran into Red Clay for our bittersweet reunion. Thousands of people were there to welcome them and to wish the Cherokees well.

The reunion at Red Clay was the beginning of regular meetings between the two Cherokee councils to discuss and act on matters of concern for all Cherokees. It also gave us an opportunity to provide public education about our history, for there is little accurate information about what modern native people are really like. There is a vacuum. Until recent times, most white Americans knew about native people only from what they saw in John Wayne–type movies.

Even in Oklahoma—in this land where so many Native Americans reside—plenty of people imagine that the state's history begins with the land run of 1889. That is because they think only in terms of white history. Our people had already been in Oklahoma for a couple of generations, and other native people had been living here long before that. We were the first ones to make this place hospitable. We had already settled this land for many years before the whites even arrived. Although it is so crucial for us to focus on the good things—our tenacity, our language and culture, the revitalization of tribal communities—it is also important that we never forget what happened to our people on the Trail of Tears. It was indeed our holocaust.

> *What began as agreements between equal nations deteriorated over time to land seizures, land allotments, assimilation, tribal reorganization, tribal termination, and, some would say, deliberate attempts to do to Native Americans what Hitler once tried to do to the Jews.*
>
> Robert Henry, former Oklahoma attorney general
> Oklahoma Today, *May–June 1992*

To truly understand how the Trail of Tears was allowed to come to pass and to comprehend the whole notion of Indian removal as practiced by the federal government, it is necessary to go back even earlier in time—much earlier. The evil seeds had been planted many years before the government soldiers arrived to push and prod our people from their homes.

The seeds of tribal removal were sown centuries before, at the very instant Christopher Columbus set foot on the beaches of San Salvador. Later, with the arrival of ironclad conquistadores, those seeds—fertilized by wholesale betrayals and broken promises—sprouted and took root. Hatred and injustice prevailed throughout the colonial period and past the 1700s.

The year 1754 marked a pivotal point in our history, with the outbreak of the so-called French and Indian War, the last of four colonial wars fought between France and England for control of North America. Our tribe reluctantly sided with the British, even though we also had some dealings with France. Our people seemed to have preferred the French to the English as human beings, yet our trading relationship with England was better. After all, some English traders had married into our tribe.

With the signing of the Treaty of Paris in 1763, ending the war, France was no longer a major problem for Great Britain. The English turned their efforts toward establishing more treaties with the Cherokees and other native tribes. Most of those treaties involved land cessions, such as the compact drawn up in 1775 in which the English secured almost all of present Kentucky from the Cherokees.

Nonetheless, our tribe's decision to side with Britain during the American Revolution was understandable. Our leaders could see that the colonies wanted to expand, and England wanted to contain the colonists. On that very important issue, British interests coincided with Cherokee interests. In addition, the majority of the licensed British traders living among our people and raising mixed-blood families were Loyalists, or Tories.

Cherokees participated in the Revolutionary War, joining the British in an attack on Charleston, South Carolina, in June of 1776. The Charlestonians managed to repulse the attack, and from then, the American Revolution—at least from the Cherokee perspective—was a furious struggle between the Americans and our tribe. The only English assistance seemed to come from the white traders living among our people. In less than a year, more than fifty Cherokee towns had been attacked and devastated. Crops and supplies were destroyed. Hundreds of our warriors died in battle. On May 20, 1777, our Cherokee leaders signed their first treaty with white Americans. With that treaty, we gave up all remaining territory in South Carolina. Only two months later, another treaty was drafted that ceded even more land.

But not all of our people went along with those early treaties. Several hundred warriors and their families, including many British Tories and mixed-bloods, under the leadership of Tsiyu-gunsi-ni, or He is Dragging Canoe (commonly called Dragging Canoe and sometimes erroneously referred to as Otter Lifter), moved to the extreme western frontier and established five new towns. They were joined there by some Creek and Shawnee people. Those defiant Cherokees were known as Chickamaugans because they had settled along Chickamauga Creek. They refused to acknowledge the treaties, and continued to honor their alliance with Great Britain. Although the American Revolution officially came to an end with the signing of the Treaty of Paris in 1782, the Chickamaugans fought against the American rebels until 1794.

Soon after the United States of America was created, it became clear that the time had arrived for the cruel harvest of those seeds of hatred planted so many years before. In 1785, just a few years after some of the Cherokees had made peace with the rebel Americans, the first Cherokee treaty with the newly established government of the United States was signed at Hopewell, in South Carolina. Known as a treaty of "peace and friendship," this benchmark agreement called for trade regulations and provided that the Cherokees were under the protection of the United States and "no other sovereign." Unfortunately, but not surprisingly, the terms of the covenant were abrogated quickly. The treaty failed to absorb some Cherokee land claimed by whites in North Carolina and Georgia. The result was the beginning of a conflict, with the Cherokees caught in the middle of a squabble between the states. It would not be resolved until the Trail of Tears. Gradually, our people learned that the only constants in the welter of treaties executed between the United States and the Cherokees were the continual loss of land and the fact that the treaties were honored by the United States only when it proved convenient.

The fledgling United States government's method of dealing with native people—a process which then included systematic genocide, property theft, and total subjugation—reached its nadir in 1830 under the federal policy of President Andrew Jackson. More than any other president, he used forcible removal to expel the eastern tribes from their land. From the very birth of the nation, the United States government truly had carried out a vigorous campaign of extermination and removal. Decades before Jackson took office, during the administration of Thomas Jefferson, it was already cruelly apparent to many Native American leaders that any hope for tribal autonomy was cursed. So were any thoughts of peaceful coexistence with white citizens.

Although some native leaders, including Cherokees, may have tried to talk themselves into believing this situation did not exist, they were only denying the inevitable. The proverbial die had been cast. What was already in motion would prove inexorable. Resistance would have been the same as going against the wind. Most native leaders were not naive enough to believe that anything could stop imminent removal.

It may seem ironic that Jefferson—an authentic genius and inspired leader who is often recalled as a high-minded man of serious conviction with a broad intellectual range—was also the principal architect of the Indian removal program. It certainly does not seem ironic to me or to any other Native American leader. Some people may find it curious that this intellectual—who was committed to liberalism and who helped to invent American democracy when, in 1776, he authored the Declaration of Independence—could also conceive a plan for moving all Native Americans who lived east of the Mississippi River to lands in the West. Again, I do not find this curious. High-minded liberals who believed in Manifest

Destiny and questioned whether Indians were human or had souls were plentiful in the days of Jefferson, and unfortunately, are still plentiful today. Contrary to today's stereotypes, racists do not always chew tobacco and drive pickup trucks with gun racks. They wear silk shirts, treat women as possessions, and talk about human rights at cocktail parties far from communities of people of color. The men in pickup trucks are just as likely to be as warm and caring as the high-minded liberals are to be racists.

When I was a little girl, we were taught at school that Jefferson was considered to be one of the nation's most eloquent champions of equality and human rights. But remember, in public schools in the 1950s and 1960s, we were still not being told that Native Americans, African-Americans, Hispanics, and Asian-Americans were victims of an insidious intellectual tyranny that had characterized the American and European cultures for centuries.

Later, as an adult, I learned that Jefferson was also one of the staunchest advocates of Western expansion. I also discovered that although he opposed the extension of slavery into the distant frontier territories, this statesman who wrote that "all men are created equal" also owned a large number of slaves. He even fathered several children by a slave with whom he carried on a liaison for many years.

Historians today use the term "presentism" when one applies contemporary standards to the past. There are critics who claim it is not appropriate to point out the flaws of historical leaders such as Thomas Jefferson or Andrew Jackson without making allowances for the prevailing historical conditions of their day. But when considering the great impact those white men have had on my heritage, I cannot be so objective. The stories of Jackson's ruthless treatment of native people are not only well known but are well documented. As for Jefferson, the ambiguity of his legacy becomes even more evident in his attitudes toward Native Americans. His actions and words seem to typify the disparity of Indian policy in the United States.

In 1776, Jefferson jotted down some thoughts about warring Indians. "I am sorry to hear that the Indians have commenced war," he wrote. "Nothing will reduce those wretches so soon as pushing war into the heart of their country. But I would not stop there. I would never cease pursuing them while one of them remained on this side of the Mississippi.... [The Indians] are a useless, expensive, ungovernable ally." A decade later, Jefferson offered a seemingly opposite point of view when he wrote "that not a foot of land will ever be taken from the Indians, without their consent."

The public shift in his attitudes remains baffling to many people. This American icon, who emerged as a central intellectual and political catalyst during the period from the Revolutionary War until the 1820s, personified vision, grace, scholarship, and character. He was the essence of what came to be known as the southern gentleman. There is no need to add any adjective; it was understood that meant *white* southern gentleman.

Most northern and southern men in the early nineteenth century applied the concept of "equality" exclusively to white males. The definition did not extend to white women or to any person of color. It certainly did not extend to Native Americans. So-called modernists of their age, such as Thomas Jefferson, thought of nature as something to be conquered, and lumped all Indians together as a group to be "civilized." The gentlemen of the white ruling class were paternalistic in their attitudes toward blacks, women, commoners and, in particular, Indians. Jean-Jacques Rousseau, the eighteenth-century French moralist and political theorist who never met a native of North America, condescendingly referred to the American Indian as "the noble savage." Although many Americans thought the European intellectuals romanticized the Indian, undoubtedly Jefferson and the more learned southern gentlemen from his circle shared Rousseau's opinion.

During the administration of President Jefferson from 1801 to 1809, the Indian policy designed in the late 1700s acquired its most rational and cogent advocate, revealing at the same time its most innate and devastating flaws. Jefferson's thoughts reflected both the high expectations and the failings of American Indian policy in the early nineteenth century. He looked at the Indian much as the eighteenth-century philosophers did. For example, as early as 1785, Jefferson stated that "the proofs of genius given by the Indians of North America, place them on a level with whites in the same uncultivated state. . . . I believe the Indian to be in body and mind equal to the white man."

Still, Jefferson believed that it was in the best interest of native people for them to take on the characteristics and qualities of the whites. He said so on several occasions. As chief executive, Jefferson was a strong proponent of bringing "civilization" to Indians. He wrote that "humanity enjoins us [whites] to teach them [Native Americans] agriculture and the domestic arts; to encourage them to that industry which alone can enable them to maintain their place in existence and to prepare them in time for that state of society which to bodily comforts adds the improvement of the mind and morals."

To realize those goals, Jefferson urged all Indian men to learn farming and Indian women to become proficient in weaving and spinning. He even went so far as to encourage intermarriage as a final solution to the "Indian problem." Jefferson argued that assimilation was the only moral path to follow.

> *If adopting or imitating the manners and the customs of the white man is to be termed civilization, perhaps the Cherokee have made the greatest advance.*
>
> William Bartram, 1789

In 1809, Jefferson offered a bold prediction to a delegation of Native Americans who came calling. "You will unite yourselves with us," he told his guests, "and join us in our great councils and form one people with us and we shall all be Americans. You will mix with us by marriage. Your blood will run in our veins and will spread with us over this great land." In those days, such words no doubt marked Jefferson as a great liberal; today, it is apparent they reflect a degree of paternalism that encouraged cultural genocide for native peoples.

> *You say, for example, "Why do not the Indians till the ground and live as we do?" May we not ask with equal propriety, "Why do not the white people hunt and live as we do?"*
>
> Old Tassel, a Cherokee

There were indeed fundamental problems with Jefferson's theory of intermarriage and assimilation. For instance, he and his supporters did not understand that it was simply impossible, if not ludicrous, for native people to suddenly adopt a completely different way of life. Another problem with Jefferson's Indian policy was that the federal government and the majority of white Americans thought the rapid acquisition of land was far more important than bringing so-called civilization to their "red brothers and sisters."

To the common man in early nineteenth-century America, the native people were not the noble beings whom Rousseau and other patronizing philosophers on the European continent had championed—far from it. To the frontiersmen, Indians were a dangerous and fierce presence. They were also expendable. Hordes of white settlers grew eager to "conquer the wilderness" and "civilize" the land. They were anxious to grab up all the salt licks, deposits of gold, stands of old-growth timber, rivers and streams, seas of lush prairie grass, beaver pelts, and buffalo hides. They wished to *own* the land. They wanted to possess everything the land had to offer. Nothing and no one—especially "heathen savages"—would stand in their way. It was, they reasoned, the white man's right. It was the will of the white man's God. It was the white man's destiny.

In their relentless march across the North American continent, those settlers did not have the slightest interest in marrying Indians or befriending them. Instead, they wanted the government to protect them from any Indians who stood in their way as they swept inexorably into the Mississippi Valley and beyond, always eager to acquire more land. Jefferson recognized that his political life relied on the support of frontier whites, especially voting white males. They were his true constituents, not our Cherokee ancestors or any of the other native people, who could not vote.

Although he continued to speak and write of Indians and whites uniting, Jefferson essentially abandoned any hope of a utopian solution to the "Indian problem" as early as 1802. Concerned by the French acquisition of the vast Louisiana Territory in 1800, Jefferson reportedly feared that Napoleonic France would regain control of the Mississippi River and all the land beyond it—land which he and other patriotic white Americans had earmarked for the expansionist needs of United States citizens. Undoubtedly, that is why Jefferson urged Governor William Henry Harrison of Indiana Territory, a future United States president, to push for all Indian people to surrender their lands as rapidly as possible. Jefferson even recommended that the more powerful Indian chiefs be encouraged to put their tribes in debt at government trading houses so they would have to pay off financial obligations by relinquishing tribal lands.

In a letter to Harrison in 1803, Jefferson wrote, "Our system is to live in perpetual peace with the Indians, to cultivate an affectionate attachment for them, by everything just and liberal which we can do for them within the bounds of reason...." That same year, in a letter to Andrew Jackson, Jefferson wrote, "I am myself alive to the obtaining of lands from the Indians by all honest and peaceable means.... I trust and believe we are acting for their greatest good."

Jefferson's fears about the French presence in North America diminished in 1803 when the United States paid $15 million to complete what became known as the Louisiana Purchase. Burdened by the extent of his campaigns in Europe, Napoleon was more willing to sell this vast parcel than in previous years. This single transaction, which included nearly the entire Great Plains between the Rocky Mountains and the Mississippi River, virtually doubled the size of the United States at a bargain cost of three cents an acre. Besides providing enough land for fifteen future states, the purchase effectively removed the threat of foreign enemies on American soil. It also made possible further expansion into new regions, and guaranteed the opportunity for the internal migration of white settlers for generations to come. It was an act with far-reaching significance, especially for Native Americans, including the Cherokees.

Any chance that native people might remain autonomous and unmolested diminished further when Jefferson determined that it was important to find out the extent of the newly acquired territory. He dispatched his neighbor Meriwether Lewis and an "Indian fighter" named William Clark to explore the vast domain and report to him. Lewis and Clark's overland journey to the Pacific required twenty-eight months.

Prior to their departure, Jefferson sent a letter to St. Louis, where Lewis was busily outfitting the expedition. Jefferson's letter included instructions on how to interact with any Indians encountered so that "henceforward we become their fathers and friend... we shall endeavor to become acquainted with them as soon as possible, and [hope] that they will find us faithful friends and protectors." Jefferson recommended that Native Americans, such as the Cherokees and other tribes living in the Southeast, might be better off if they were relocated to the new territory. The lands they surrendered could then be occupied by white settlers.

> *When the Indian passed in dignity, disturbing nothing and leaving Nature as he found her; with nothing to record his passage, except a footprint or a broken twig, the white man plundered and wasted and shouted; frightening the silences with his great, braying laughter and his cursing.*
>
> John Joseph Matthews
> Wah' Kon-Tah, 1932

Some Cherokees had already left their homeland in the Southeast long before Jefferson disclosed his theory of Indian removal. It is difficult to say precisely when the first of our people crossed the Mississippi, but according to the history that has been passed down, there was never a time in the experience of the tribe when our warriors and hunters were not accustomed to venturing beyond the wide river.

As early as the late eighteenth century, some Cherokees had already moved west of the Mississippi River. They were people who did not wish to adopt the white ways, or to live as white farmers. Most of them were steadfast Chickamaugans who had fought as allies with the British throughout the Revolutionary War. They received permission from the Spanish governor at New Orleans to settle in what was then Spanish territory in the unspoiled hunting grounds in the Arkansas country.

Before too long, others from our tribe followed those who had headed west. In 1794, a band of Cherokees in present Alabama moved from their home on the Tennessee River to west of the Mississippi after a dispute that became known as the Muscle Shoals Massacre. Depending on whose version of the story you choose to believe, the altercation between the Cherokees and a party of white boatmen over a deal gone sour resulted in injuries and loss of life on both sides.

This band of Cherokees was under the leadership of a Cherokee called "the Bowl" after the translation of his native name, Diwa-li. He was born in 1756. Our tribal chiefs at first formally repudiated the action of this group of warriors, but ultimately the Bowl and his followers were exonerated. It did not matter. They were long gone and did not wish to return. The Bowl led his band to desirable land in the valley of the St. Francis River in southeastern Missouri. Other Cherokee people joined them from time to time, and they remained there until December of 1811, when the largest known earthquakes in American history began to occur in the area. So tremendous were the quakes that for several hours the Mississippi River flowed northward, and tremors were felt over three hundred thousand square miles. Fearful of further disturbances and believing that their land was "under the ban of the Great Spirit," as anthropologist James Mooney later expressed it, those Cherokees moved farther westward.

They finally settled in present Arkansas, between the White and Arkansas rivers, where they became known as the Cherokee Nation West. Between 1819 and 1820, the Bowl took sixty families to territory promised to them by the Spanish authorities, on the Sabine and Neches rivers in the Mexican province of Texas, but most of the Cherokees stayed in Arkansas. Those people of the West, the ones who settled in Arkansas many years before the Trail of Tears, came to be called Old Settlers.

Some of the Cherokees who moved west before the Trail of Tears were promised by the United States that in exchange for land in the eastern part of the country, they would be left alone forever. Believing this promise, they settled the area, built farms and communities, and began their lives over again, far from the political, social, and economic system they had always known. They left behind not only their kinspeople, but essentially everything they were familiar with to come to the new land in the West. Soon they realized that the United States would break its promise to the Cherokees again and intrude on their new homeland as well. Betrayal by the United States government was by then a familiar story to the Cherokees.

> *The sacredness of their [the Indians'] rights is felt by all thinking persons in America as much as in Europe.*
>
> Thomas Jefferson, 1786

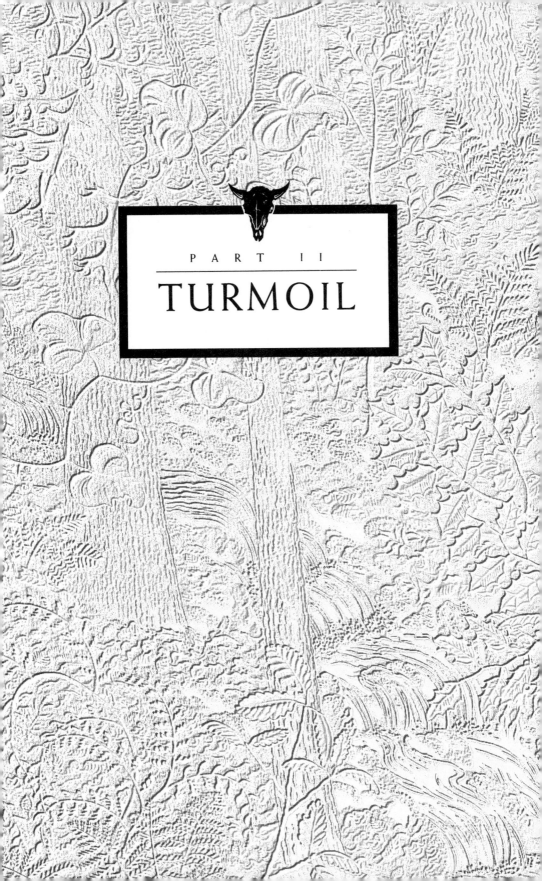

PART II

TURMOIL

CHAPTER 5

HARD TIMES

*W*hen the first lands were sold by the Cherokees, in 1721, part of the tribe
bitterly opposed the sale. They said if the Indians once consented to give up any of
their territory, the whites would never be satisfied, but would soon want a little more
and a little again, until there would be none left for the Indians. Finding that all they
could say was not enough to prevent the treaty, they determined to leave their old homes
forever and go far into the West, beyond the great river, where the white men could
never follow them. They gave no heed to the entreaties of their friends, but began
preparations for the long march, until the others, finding that they could not prevent
their going, set to work and did their best to fit them with packhorses loaded with bread,
dried venison, and other supplies.

When all was ready, they started, under the direction of their chief. A company
of chosen men was sent to help them in crossing the great river. Every night until they
reached it, runners were sent back to the tribe and out from the tribe to the marching
band to carry messages and keep each party posted as to how the other was getting
along. At last they came to the Mississippi, and crossed it by the help of those warriors
who had been sent with them. These then returned to the tribe, while the others kept on
to the west. All communication was now at an end. No more was heard of the wanderers,
and in time, the story of the lost Cherokees was forgotten, or remembered only as an
old tale.

Still the white man pressed on the Cherokees, and one piece of land after another
was sold. As years went on, the dispossessed people began to turn their faces toward

the west as their final resting place, and small bands of hunters crossed the Mississippi to learn what might be beyond. One of those parties pushed on across the plains, and there at the foot of the great mountains—the Rockies—they found a tribe speaking the old Cherokee language and living as the Cherokees had lived before they had ever known the white man or his ways.

I experienced my own Trail of Tears when I was a young girl. No one pointed a gun at me or at members of my family. No show of force was used. It was not necessary. Nevertheless, the United States government, through the Bureau of Indian Affairs, was again trying to settle the "Indian problem" by removal. I learned through this ordeal about the fear and anguish that occur when you give up your home, your community, and everything you have ever known to move far away to a strange place. I cried for days, not unlike the children who had stumbled down the Trail of Tears so many years before. I wept tears that came from deep within the Cherokee part of me. They were tears from my history, from my tribe's past. They were Cherokee tears.

People who refuse to put any stock in the adage that history repeats itself undoubtedly do not know any Cherokees. Although most Native Americans have learned hard lessons from the experiences of the bygone years, it seems that as often as not, we are still doomed to revisit some of the bleakest episodes from our tribe's past. Much of the repetition of our history concerns ownership of land and property rights.

A people without history is like the wind on the buffalo grass.

Sioux saying

From the very start of our relationship with whites, we spent much of the time moving large numbers of our population to appease others. The relocation of the Cherokees certainly did not stop with the punitive terms imposed on us by Andrew Jackson or with the ghastly Trail of Tears. In some ways, that unhappy passage was just the beginning. In more recent times, there are significant examples of how the government meddled with our people and moved them as it had in the past.

Another Cherokee removal occurred three years before I was born. The relocation of 1942 was not nearly as devastating or on the same scale as the tragedy of 1838–1839, but for the native people who were displaced, it was every bit as upsetting and catastrophic. This removal came about in the early days of World War II when the U.S. Army decided to enlarge Camp Gruber, a military installation with an extensive reservation not far from Muskogee, Oklahoma. To accomplish its plan, the government saw to it that eighty tracts of restricted Cherokee property were condemned. The land grab included the homes on allotments of forty-five Cherokee families. Sixteen of those families raised livestock or were self-sufficient farmers. All of them were given only forty-five days to pack up their belongings and abandon their homes.

The Cherokee families affected by the condemnation had no recourse, no means of appeal. So far, the federal government has declined to entertain any legal remedy, despite the clear injustice to those Cherokee families. A tribal attorney is pursuing the matter. Compensation for the appropriated property was grossly inadequate, with the displaced families receiving no financial consideration for improvements that had been made on their property. None of the Cherokees was given any relocation assistance. Altogether, more than thirty-two thousand acres were lost. During the war, many captured enemy troops were transported to Camp Gruber, one of eight POW compounds in Oklahoma. Ironically, the military prisoners, some of whom were German soldiers from the *Afrika Korps*, were treated far better than the native people who had lost their homes and farms. It was evident that Indian affairs still remained among the lowest priorities of the federal government.

Regarding my family, we willingly became part of yet another government scheme for dealing with what was still being referred to in the 1950s as the "Indian problem." It was part of an insidious plan hatched by the Bureau of Indian Affairs. In reality, it was nothing more than another direct assault on Native American rights and tribal identities. This policy was given a name mostly associated with death camps, slaughterhouses, or penitentiaries. It was known as "termination."

The government's primary objectives in launching a policy of termination in the 1950s were to break up the system of Indian reservations across the country and to lure native people from their homeland through a program of "relocation." Although we did not live on a reservation, our family was a primary target for the resettlement plan.

The architect of this brainstorm was Dillon S. Myer. In the early 1950s, he served as commissioner of the Bureau of Indian Affairs. I am quite sure most Native Americans today would get shivers up and down their spines after only a quick glance at Myer's rather dubious record of government service. But Native Americans had little to say about his appointment.

Many Indians are still primitive.

Dillon S. Myer, unpublished autobiography, 1970

A classic example of a lifelong bureaucrat who had little regard for nonwhites, Myer was named head of the BIA as a reward for having served as director of the Japanese War Relocation Authority during World War II. For three years, Myer and his WRA staff had acted as diligent keepers of more than 120,000 men, women, and children of Japanese descent. At least two-thirds of the "evacuees," as the government called them, were American born. They were innocent United States citizens who had been rounded up and removed from their homes along the West Coast to be confined in tar-paper barracks at WRA camps scattered about the West.

The eleven Japanese-American internment camps hastily constructed on remote federal land, including two on Indian reservations in Arizona, were surrounded by barbed wire. Directors of some of the camps had been recruited from the ranks of Bureau of Indian Affairs reservation superintendents. Behind machine guns in the guard towers were military policemen with orders to shoot any inmates who tried to escape. In fact, the War Relocation Centers, as they were called, were nothing more than concentration camps.

I sincerely believe, gentleman, that if we don't handle this problem [the presence of Japanese-Americans] in a way to get these people absorbed as best we can while the war is going on, we may have something akin to Indian reservations after the war . . .

Dillon S. Myer, Congressional testimony
January 20, 1943

None of those incarcerated had been accused of any crimes, and there was no firm evidence of a single case of Japanese-American espionage throughout the war. But in the months shortly after Japan's attack on Pearl Harbor, the ancestry of all Japanese-Americans was enough to call their allegiance to the United States into question. Japanese-Americans became victims of wartime hysteria, racism, and greed. Many historians now believe that the repeated violations of these people's rights were some of the greatest infringements of the United States Constitution.

The Japanese-American camps were finally disbanded in 1945, after the bombings of Hiroshima and Nagasaki ended the war. Disillusioned and humiliated, many former detainees returned to find their farms and property lost to land speculators. Some people freshly released from the camps went home to find hateful inscriptions such as "No Japs Wanted" painted on their residences.

In 1982, a federal commission concluded that the internment had been wrong and had had no basis in national security. It took until 1988 for Congress to apologize for the relocation camps. It also passed legislation to ensure that individuals who had been interned should be paid damages. By 1992, an additional law was created to increase the amount of monetary compensation for the surviving claimants.

The Cherokees and other native tribes should have recognized that the assorted Trails of Tears of our ancestors served in large part as models for the removal of the Japanese immigrants and Japanese-Americans in the 1940s. In the case of the Japanese, however, the removal was from west to east, and the government used buses and trucks, so there was no need for a forced march. It was a most efficient operation. Dillon Myer would have made Andrew Jackson and Indian fighters Kit Carson and Phil Sheridan very proud.

Myer was even cited for his heinous wartime services. To honor Myer's efficient administration of the War Relocation Authority, President Harry S. Truman presented him with the nation's prestigious Medal of Merit in 1946. For good measure, Truman offered to appoint Myer as governor of Puerto Rico, but he turned it down. Instead, Myer stayed on in Washington. He held governmental posts until May of 1950 when, after declining the offer twice, he finally accepted Truman's proposition to head the Bureau of Indian Affairs. I suppose the reasoning behind the appointment was simple—any person who could handle "the Japanese problem" should certainly be able to take care of the Indians, even if there were, by most counts, almost four times as many of us to oversee.

Given a free hand by Truman and Interior Secretary Oscar L. Chapman on hiring and firing, Myer summarily issued walking papers to many seasoned BIA officials. Many of them had cared about Native Americans and were proven champions of our land rights and tribal self-determination. The reform-minded BIA administrators did not wait for their discharges, but willingly tendered their resignations. As replacements, Myer brought aboard some of his WRA cronies, mostly career government bureaucrats—all of them white—who knew nothing about Indian affairs or law but were proven "yes men."

Shortly after taking office, Myer unveiled several important changes in BIA administrative policy. He pointed out that encouragement of subsistence farming, which had been the policy standard of Franklin Roosevelt's New Deal years, was less viable in the postwar period. That policy had originated when the BIA was headed by John Collier, a committed protector of Indian cultural heritage. According to Myer, the serious unemployment situation on Indian reservations resulted from the return of 113,000 Native Americans who had left their land during the war. To resolve those issues, Myer said, the time had come to stop developing resources on the reservations. Instead, he and his cohorts encouraged tens of thousands of young Indians and their families to relocate in urban and industrial areas.

To Myer, the various Indian reservations and communities were little more than prison camps like those he had maintained for Japanese-American detainees during the war. He treated reservation Indians, whom he labeled as "wily," much as he had treated the inmates of his wartime camps. But even though he felt that some of the native people living on reservations were cunning, Myer was not particularly worried that any Indians were planning acts of sabotage. Instead, he contended that the Native American population had to be released from the confines of tribal communities, where their holdings were assured of government protection from white predators. Myer felt that the government's health service, schools, and other privileges did not permit Indians to behave as individuals. Therefore, he believed we would be much better off if only we could be "mainstreamed" and resettled throughout the general United States population.

A mark of progress, Myer contended, would be for us to move off our tribal and ancestral lands to big cities, where we could work "like white people." To enlighten native people in the ways of the white business world, Myer restricted Indians' access to the already limited credit funds supervised by the BIA, while encouraging them to turn to private banks and lenders for loans. By 1951, Myer had focused on what he labeled "withdrawal programming." When various native people complained about some of his decisions, Myer told his staff to proceed with plans even though they might not have Indian cooperation.

Dwight Eisenhower, the nation's thirty-fourth president, succeeded Truman in 1953. This meant there was also a change of command at the BIA—Myer would be gone. Yet this did not seem to make any difference. Political parties proved to be irrelevant. The new procedures for ending the federal trust responsibility to Native Americans became bipartisan. Termination and relocation policies planned during the Truman years were implemented throughout the Eisenhower administration.

Glenn L. Emmons, a banker and rancher from Gallup, New Mexico, followed Myer at the helm of the BIA. Emmons, as the new commissioner of Indian affairs, acted as his predecessor had. He also shared the belief that the best cures to Indian problems such as unemployment lay in the termination of federal responsibilities for all Indians, and the relocation of substantial numbers of rural Native Americans to large industrial cities. Emmons said this would bring relief for the problem of reservation overpopulation, and it would facilitate rapid assimilation for those of us who did not live on reservations.

On August 1, 1953, the Eighty-third Congress adopted House Concurrent Resolution 108. This legislation, which withdrew the federal commitment for Indian people, stated in part, "It is the policy of Congress, as rapidly as possible to make Indians within the United States subject to the same laws and entitled to the same privileges and responsibilities as are applicable to other citizens of the United States, to end their status as wards of the United States, and to grant them all of the rights and prerogatives pertaining to American citizenship."

> . . . I have no hesitancy whatever in calling it one of the most valuable and salutary Congressional measures we have had in Indian Affairs in many years.
>
> Commissioner Glenn L. Emmons
> In praise of House Concurrent Resolution No. 108

Almost immediately, Utah Senator Arthur V. Watkins, who headed the Senate subcommittee on Indian affairs and was a vigorous proponent of the termination movement, secured the passage of additional legislation to use the policy with specific tribes. Watkins labeled termination as "the Indian freedom program." He and his congressional cronies considered the policy a cure-all for the "Indian problem." Immediately, Congress passed bills seeking termination of various tribes. From 1954 until 1962, Congress imposed the policy on sixty-one tribes and native communities, effectively cutting them off from federal services and protections. It was not until 1970 that Congress censured this detestable policy, too late for most tribes that had been terminated. However, some of the tribes, including the Menominees of Wisconsin, were successful in regaining federal recognition in the 1970s.

The passage and implementation of termination bills during the 1950s shocked many Indian leaders who immediately understood that the United States government again intended to destroy tribal governments. Many of them also realized that the government intended to break up native communities and put tribal land on the market by abolishing its status as nontaxable trust land. Native Americans would soon lose control of their land. Termination also meant the imposition of state civil and criminal authority and the loss of state tax exemptions and special tribal programs. Tribes would find it increasingly difficult to remain sovereign.

The United States policy of Indian relocation did not, in fact, get under way until the mid-1950s. Large numbers of Native Americans began to move en masse from reservations and ancestral lands to targeted metropolitan areas in anticipation of receiving job training, education, and a new place to live. By 1955, about three thousand reservation Indians, mostly from the Southwest, were living in housing developments in Chicago. Many other native people had also made the move to low-rent apartments and public housing in other big cities, including Los Angeles, Detroit, St. Louis, and Seattle.

The following year, my own family experienced the pain of United States government relocation. The year was 1956. It was one month before my eleventh birthday. That was when the time came for our Trail of Tears.

We were not forced to do anything, but that did not matter—not to me. Not when the time came for our family to leave Mankiller Flats. Not when we had to say farewell to the land that had been our family's home for generations, and move far away to a strange place. It was then that I came to know in some small way what it was like for our ancestors when the government troops made them give up their houses and property. It was a time for me to be sad.

Our poverty had prompted the move. In 1955, my father first started talking to Bureau of Indian Affairs officials about the various forms of assistance for Cherokees. Relocation was a possibility. I recall hearing at that time that the relocation program was being offered as a wonderful opportunity for Indian families to get great jobs, obtain good educations for their kids and, once and for all, leave poverty behind. In truth, the program gave the government the perfect chance to take Indian people away from their culture and their land. The government methods had softened since the nineteenth century, but the end result was the same for native people. Instead of guns and bayonets, the BIA used promotional brochures showing staged photographs of smiling Indians in "happy homes" in the big cities.

Some of the BIA people came to our house. They talked to my father, explaining the particulars of the program. They said the government wanted to "get out of the Indian business," and one of the ways to do that was by helping individuals and families relocate in larger cities. Dad listened to their pitch. The BIA people came out to our place a couple of times. I think Dad initially was opposed to our leaving Oklahoma and our land. As a boy, he had been taken from his home against his will to attend Sequoyah Boarding School. He did not want to leave his community and people again. But he talked it over with some Cherokee friends, and eventually he decided it would be a good idea to move. He must have honestly believed that in a distant city he could provide a better life for his children, with all the modern amenities.

I never liked the idea of our moving away. I can still remember hiding in a bedroom in our house of rough-hewn lumber, listening while my father, mother, and oldest brother talked in the adjoining room about the benefits and drawbacks of relocating our family. We younger children tried to listen through the door. We were terrified. They were talking about possible destinations. They spoke of places we had barely heard of—Chicago, New York, Detroit, Oakland, and San Francisco. California seemed to be their favorite. Finally my parents chose San Francisco because Grandma Sitton, my mother's mom, had moved to California in 1943. A widow when she left Oklahoma, she had remarried and settled in Riverbank, a community in the farm belt about ninety miles east of San Francisco.

None of us little kids could visualize California. We had been as far as Muskogee to go to the fair on a school field trip. We had been to Stilwell and Tahlequah, but that was about it. My world lay within a ten-mile radius of our family house at Mankiller Flats. Dad and my oldest brother had traveled to Colorado to cut broomcorn. My mother had been to Arkansas to see her sister, but no farther than that. My mother was scared about leaving, and hated the idea of moving to California. She really opposed it at first, more than anyone else. But finally, knowing she would be living close to her mother, she was convinced to go along with my father, believing that life might be better for us all.

Despite my mother's decision, I still was not ready to leave. Neither was my sister Frances. We asked about the possibility of staying behind with friends, but my folks said we had to go with the others. So then we talked about running away to avoid the move, but we never did that. We kept hoping right up until the day our family left that something would happen—some kind of miracle—and we would stay put and not have to go to San Francisco. We did not have very much materially, but we really did not need much either. We had always managed to get by. From my point of view as a child, I could see no value in leaving our home. If life was not idyllic, at least it was familiar.

Finally, the day arrived in October of 1956 for us to depart for California. That day is branded into my memory. There were nine of us kids then. It was before the last two were born. My oldest sister, Frieda, was attending Sequoyah High School and did not move with us. My folks had sold off everything, including the old car. We all piled in a neighbor's car, and he drove us to Stilwell so we could catch the train headed west to California. As we drove away, I looked at our house, the store, my school. I took last looks. I wanted to remember it all. I tried to memorize the shapes of the trees, the calls of animals and birds from the forest. All of us looked out the windows. We did not want to forget anything.

When we got to Stilwell, Dad took us to a restaurant, and we had bowls of chili. We were not a very happy crew—two adults and eight children leaving everything behind for an unknown place. Just getting aboard the train was terrifying for the smaller children. It was a new experience. We settled in all over the place. Some of the children were more comfortable sleeping on the floor, others stayed on the seats or beneath them. My youngest baby sister was marking the back of a seat with a crayon. We were a wild bunch. We must have looked like a darker version of the Joad family from John Steinbeck's novel, *The Grapes of Wrath*.

My mother was still scared about the move. Dad was also worried, but he was excited about the chance for a better life for all of us. As we got settled on the train, he turned to my mother and said, "I don't think I will ever be back until I come home in a coffin." As it turned out, Dad was right. The next time he came home was more than fourteen years later when he was buried in his native land.

As soon as we were all on the train, my sister Frances started to cry. It seemed as if she cried without stopping all the way from Oklahoma to California, although I am sure she did not. The conductor came along and asked her why she was crying. She could not answer him. I cried, too. All of us did. The train headed north. Then we had to change to another train in Kansas City. The trip took two days and two nights. We finally reached California, passing through Riverbank, where my grandmother lived. We kept on going until we stopped in San Francisco.

My folks had vouchers the BIA officials had given them for groceries and rent. But when we arrived, we found that an apartment was not available, so we were put up for two weeks in an old hotel in a notorious district of San Francisco called the Tenderloin. During the night, the neighborhood sparkled with lots of neon lights, flashily dressed prostitutes, and laughter in the streets. But in the morning, we saw broken glass on the streets, people sleeping in doorways, and hard-faced men wandering around. The hotel was not much better than the streets.

The noises of the city, especially at night, were bewildering. We had left behind the sounds of roosters, dogs, coyotes, bobcats, owls, crickets, and other animals moving through the woods. We knew the sounds of nature. Now we heard traffic and other noises that were foreign. The police and ambulance sirens were the worst. That very first night in the big city, we were all huddled under the covers, and we heard sirens outside in the streets. We had never heard sirens before. I thought it was some sort of wild creature screaming. The sirens reminded me of wolves.

My mother seemed sad and confused. When we went to get breakfast for the first time, we were not acquainted with the kinds of food on the menu. Back in Oklahoma, we usually had biscuits and gravy every morning. My mother scanned the menu, and the only item she could find with gravy was a hot roast beef sandwich. So that is what we all ate for breakfast—beef sandwiches with gravy. My dad left the hotel early every morning to see about obtaining a job and a house—all the things the BIA had promised us. While he was gone, we explored around the hotel. Everything was new to us. For instance, we had never seen neon lights before. No one had bothered to even try to prepare us for city living.

NO DOGS, NO INDIANS.

Popular sign in restaurants, 1950s

One day, my brother Richard and I were standing by the stairway when we saw some people come down the hall and stop. All of a sudden, a box in the wall opened up. People got inside. Then the box closed and the people disappeared! After a minute or two the box suddenly opened again and a new bunch of people came out. Of course, we had never seen an elevator before. All we knew was that we were not about to get inside that box. We used the stairs.

After a couple of weeks, the BIA was finally able to find us a permanent place to live in San Francisco. We left the hotel and moved into a flat in a working-class neighborhood in the old Potrero Hill District. The apartment was quite small and crowded, but it seemed to be the best location for us. The rope factory where my father was able to get a job was not too far away. He was paid the grand sum of forty-eight dollars a week. There was no way, even then, that a man could support a big family in San Francisco on that salary. That is why my big brother Don also worked in the factory making ropes. He and my father walked to the factory every day and worked long, hard hours. Even with both of them bringing home paychecks, we had a tough time, and our family was growing. My brother James Ray was born while we lived in the Potrero Hill District.

Many Hispanics lived in our neighborhood, and we became good friends with a Mexican family next door named Roybal. They took us under their wing, and made our adjustment a pet project. For example, we had never had a telephone before, so the Roybals showed us how one worked. None of us had ever ridden bicycles, so they taught us how to bike and roller-skate.

Still, I did not like living in the city. I especially hated school. The other kids seemed to be way ahead of us in academic and social abilities. We could hold our own in reading because of what our folks had taught us, but the other students were much more advanced at mathematics and language skills. I spent most of the time trying my best to make myself as inconspicuous as possible.

I was placed in the fifth grade, and I immediately noticed that everyone in my class considered me different. When the teacher came to my name during roll call each morning, every single person laughed. Mankiller had not been a strange name back in Adair County, Oklahoma, but it was a very odd name in San Francisco. The other kids also teased me about the way I talked and dressed. It was not that I was so much poorer than the others, but I was definitely from another culture.

My sister Linda and I sat up late every night reading aloud to each other to get rid of our accents. We tried to talk like the other kids at school. We also thought about our old home in Oklahoma. My big sister Frances and I talked about our life back at Mankiller Flats. We tried to remember where a specific tree was located and how everything looked. That helped a little, but I still had many problems trying to make such a major adjustment. We simply were not prepared for the move. As a result, I was never truly comfortable in the schools of California. I had to find comfort and solace elsewhere.

I was not alone in my feelings. I have met many native people from different tribes who were relocated from remote tribal communities. They discovered, as we did, that the "better life" the BIA had promised all of us was, in reality, life in a tough, urban ghetto. Many people were unable to find jobs, and those who did were often offered only marginal employment. I later learned that many native people endured a great deal of poverty, emotional suffering, substance abuse, and poor health because of leaving their homelands, families, and communities. Children seemed to be especially vulnerable without the traditional support of the extended family at home. Urban Indian families banded together, built Indian centers, held picnics and powwows, and tried to form communities in the midst of large urban populations. Yet there was always and forever a persistent longing to go home. "I was as distant from myself as the moon from the earth," is how James Welch, a native writer, described the sense of alienation he experienced in an urban setting.

The termination and relocation policies of the 1950s clearly failed to solve the "Indian problem." Most of the relocatees eventually returned to their communities to live and work, some of them trying even harder to strengthen tribal communities and governments. In the end, we survived.

CHAPTER 6

THE TRAIL WHERE
THEY CRIED

Some Wolves once caught the Rabbit and were going to eat him when he asked to show them a new dance he was practicing. They knew that the Rabbit was a strong song leader, and they wanted to learn the latest dance, so they agreed and made a ring about him while he got ready. He patted his feet and began to dance in a circle, singing:

> Tlage situn gali sgi sida ha
> Ha nia lil! lil! Ha nia lil! lil!

> On the edge of the field I
> dance about
> Ha nia lil! lil! Ha nia lil!

"Now," said the Rabbit, "when I sing 'on the edge of the field,' I dance that way." And he danced in that direction. "And when I sing 'lil! lil!' you must all stamp your feet hard."

The Wolves thought it was fine. The Rabbit began another round, singing the same song, and danced a little nearer to the field, while the Wolves all stamped their feet. He sang louder and louder and danced nearer and nearer to the field until the fourth song. The Wolves were stamping as hard as they could and thinking only of the song, and he made one jump and was off through the long grass.

They were after him at once, but he ran for a hollow stump and climbed up on the inside. When the Wolves got there, one of them put his head inside to look up, but the Rabbit spit into his eye so that the Wolf had to pull his head out again. The others were afraid to try, and they went away with the Rabbit still in the stump.

After my family relocated in San Francisco, where the screams of sirens echoed off warehouse walls, I was very much like Rabbit, who found himself surrounded by Wolves. But unlike the clever Rabbit of the Cherokee myth, I had no song or dance to distract the Wolves in my life. Nor was there a hollow stump for me to crawl inside. There were not even a few blades of long grass for cover.

Wolves surrounded me. But my pursuers were not four-legged or fanged or covered with fur. They were of a species all their own. I was nagged by anxiety, doubt, and fear that silently crept from the city's shadows with the thick bay fog to sit on window sills and hover at doors. The hushed voices were more terrible than any beast's howls. I could not spit in my demons' eyes to make them leave. It was impossible to escape them.

I was not accustomed to being with so many different people—people who generally did not accept my strange clothing and even stranger accent. There was literally no place for me to run and hide—at least, not at first. In those early days, when we were all trying to figure out how to get along, there was no real sanctuary for me. We were so far from Mankiller Flats and the wooded land I knew and loved. We might as well have been on the far side of the moon.

I was sad and lonesome most of the time. Having to grapple with the worries and pressures of big-city life and contend with the ordeals of adolescence were not pleasant experiences for a Cherokee girl from the Oklahoma outland. I knew only the country and country ways. I suffered from incurable homesickness aggravated by what felt like a permanent case of the blues. I thought my despair would never go away. Everything seemed hopeless.

> *I'd rather wake up in the middle of nowhere than in any city on earth.*
>
> Steve McQueen

My parents and the rest of the family helped me to survive. We all tried our best to help one another. Somehow, we managed to get through even the worst times. There also were other comforts. When the going got especially difficult, I allowed my mind to slip away to the past. Going back in time and space can sometimes help remedy a person's troubles.

This is a technique that I developed more fully when I was older and had learned more about my tribe's history. Today, I often consider the old days of the Cherokees. I allow myself to think about "the trail where they cried," and the federal government's forced removal of our people and the other southeastern tribes. I compare their upheaval in the late 1830s to my own family's relocation in the 1950s. Remembering those Cherokees and others who were forced to move to Indian Territory and how they persisted brings me at least some relief whenever I feel distressed or afraid. Through the years, I have learned to use my memory and the historical memory of my people to help me endure the most difficult and trying periods of my life.

> *We are now about to take our leave and kind farewell to our native land, the country that the great spirit gave our Fathers; we are on the eve of leaving that country that gave us birth . . . it is with sorrow that we are forced by the authority of the white man to quit the scenes of our childhood . . . we bid a final farewell to it and all we hold dear.*
>
> *George Hicks, Cherokee leader on the Trail of Tears*
> *November 4, 1838*

That is why I continue to think about the past and to circle back to my tribal history for doses of comfort. I still contemplate the lives of my ancestors—some of those early transplants who became part of the Cherokee Nation West. That all took place long before the conclusion of the Treaty of New Echota of 1835—the controversial document that provided for the Cherokees' shameful eviction from our ancestral lands, and the tribe's inevitable removal to an alien region. The experiences of those who made that journey to Indian Territory remain an unrivaled lesson in courage and hope.

I also reflect on those times before the white men and the United States government took control of our lives, when the Cherokees thrived in the ancient homeland of what became Georgia, Alabama, Tennessee,

North Carolina, South Carolina, and Virginia. I see in my mind's eye the steady European intrusion, and how the old Cherokee people gradually blended their timeless customs with the concoctions and innovations of the whites. I visualize the events that marked those years when my people were pressured to move from the Southeast to the unknown lands west of Arkansas. Remembrances can be powerful teachers. When we return to our history, those strong images assist us in learning how not to make identical mistakes. Perhaps we will not always be doomed to repeat all of our history, especially the bad episodes.

From the annals of time, from those bittersweet years of the 1800s, the spirits of long-dead Cherokees and other native men and women from other tribes remain unsettled. Their spirits still cry out, warning us about the dangers that lie ahead. They speak of the need to read small print on documents and to search between the lines on treaties. They caution us to be aware of the droves of government bureaucrats who tend to approach native people just as those well-meaning "Bless Your Heart" ladies did in Oklahoma, the ones who tried to coax me into their big shiny cars when I was a child walking down a dirt road to school.

The spirits admonish us to be careful. They draw from their own knowledge and experience, no doubt recalling the snares and pitfalls uncovered along the way when they became "civilized" and struggled to retain some dignity and appease the white ruling class. Through the spirits' chiding, we become aware that the "civilizing" of the Cherokees did us much more harm than good in many ways. We look back on those times and, if we allow ourselves, we can learn so much.

Although many Cherokees tried to stay with the old ways, especially regarding clan dances and medicine, some adopted at least what seemed the most ideal elements of the white man's world. That is why, among our people, some became farmers, merchants, and traders. They dressed like whites. They lived in log cabins, sent their children to schools, attended Christian churches, and adopted written laws. For the most part, they abandoned many of the old traditions and customs that the whites frowned on and considered pagan and offensive.

Some Cherokees, mostly the prosperous mixed-bloods, began to treat women as second-class citizens, kept black slaves, and even owned large plantations. Some Cherokee leaders believed that if our people would only adopt the beliefs and lifestyle of the white Americans, we would be allowed to survive as a tribe in our own homeland. Perhaps the whites would leave us alone. Just maybe the song and dance would work, and the Wolves would let Rabbit be. That proved to be a costly mistake in judgment.

As early as the 1820s, the Cherokees, Chickasaws, Choctaws, and Creeks were becoming known by some whites as the "Civilized Tribes." Eventually, the Seminoles would be added to those ranks. By the late 1850s, long after all the tribes had been removed on their individual trails of tears to Indian Territory, they put aside most of their old antagonisms toward one another. They would be referred to as the "Five Civilized Tribes." Those three words—"Five Civilized Tribes"—continue to be a pejorative term still in use to this day, even by some Native Americans.

The Cherokees were able to live effectively in the Cherokee world as well as in the white world. To white society, that meant our people were the most acculturated, although we still were not—and never would be—placed on the same level as the whites. Still, the Cherokee mixed-bloods were accepted in many white circles, and their influence in the tribal communities increased. Mixed-blood surnames such as Adair, Ward, Rogers, Vann, Lowery, and Ross became well established in our tribe.

By the 1820s, the mixed-bloods, some of them with blue eyes and light hair, had acquired most of the tribal wealth. Even though they still had to share their power with the full-bloods, they held at least 40 percent of the Cherokee government posts. Although the majority of the white blood in members of the tribe came from the male side, an 1824 Cherokee Nation census noted seventy-three white women as the spouses of Cherokee men, and 147 white men as husbands of Cherokee women.

The impact of the mixed-bloods and the influence of Christian missionaries became increasingly evident. Charles Hicks, one of our tribe's mixed-blood leaders and author some of the first written Cherokee laws, adopted by the tribal council in 1808, was the chief who gave his approval to the establishment of churches and schools in Cherokee communities. "Our very existence depends upon it," Hicks reportedly told a missionary.

Early on in the nineteenth century, some of our people's spiritual needs were ministered to by various white missionaries, starting with a small group of Moravians who established a mission in Georgia in 1801. Other white Christian missionaries—Presbyterian, Baptist, Methodist, and

Quaker—all anxious to "save the savages," soon moved into our homeland. They built churches and mission schools where, in most instances, academic lessons were supplemented with an abundance of hymn singing, public prayers, and Scripture readings.

> *How can we trust you? When Jesus Christ came on earth, you killed him and nailed him to a cross.*
>
> Shawnee Chief Tecumseh, 1810

In 1819, as part of the government's commitment to "civilize" all native people, Congress authorized an annual sum of $10,000 to the War Department to support and promote the civilization of Indians by employing "capable persons of good moral character, to instruct them in the mode of agriculture suited to their situation; and for teaching their children in reading, writing, and arithmetic." Without fail, our tribe received the largest proportion of this fund each year. The five schools in the Cherokee Nation in 1809 had increased to eighteen by 1825, with the enrollment climbing from ninety-four to 314 students. There also were many mission schools, where besides the "three Rs," the standard curriculum included Bible and catechism study. Graduates of the mission schools, mostly those with more white than Cherokee blood, often were sent to colleges or academies in New England.

Typical of the religious literature of that era was a tract entitled *A Discourse or Lecture on the subject of Civilizing the Indians, in which is exhibited a New Plan to Effect their Civilization and to Meliorate their Condition.* Published in 1826 in Washington, D.C., by the Reverend J. Darneille, former rector of Amherst Parish, Virginia, the thirty-six-page pamphlet sold for a dollar per copy, a tidy sum in those days. The author, mindful of marketing strategy, explained up front that "if the intrinsic value of the work be overrated, yet you will have the pleasure of making this small donation to civilize and instruct the Indians; to remunerate and return to them, in this way, some indemnity for the fair and fertile country which you now possess and enjoy on the shores of the Atlantic, their rightful inheritance, from which their ancestors were driven by ours, and for which, in justice to them, your sympathy for their sufferings, and your bounty for their relief, can never be misapplied."

Darneille's primary intent in publishing the slim volume was to suggest the establishment of a missionary school and farm among the Old Settler Cherokees living in Arkansas. He also proposed taking his own family to the Cherokee Nation West so he could oversee the Indian school and preach the gospel to the "heathens." If Darneille would have had access to a time machine to make a forward journey to 130 years later in Oklahoma, he unquestionably would have fit right in with those "Bless Your Heart" ladies in Adair County. And no doubt those ladies—dressed to the nines for all to see—would have been in the first-row pew of his church every Sunday morning. Like those opinionated Oklahoma ladies, the pious Reverend Darneille had nothing but sympathy for the Cherokees, a sympathy that reflected his patronizing concern for what he perceived to be our "plight."

Darneille and the other sanctimonious do-gooders of that period did not have the slightest clue about the workings of the Native American culture and belief system. "The scourge of their lives pursue and seem to afflict them even after death," Darneille wrote in his treatise. "Nature prompts the survivors to bury their dead, but of this they are deprived for want of instruments to open the earth. They, therefore, enclose the body with bark, and suspend it as high as they can on a tree."

The Reverend Darneille's pamphlet was not published in Cherokee, although by 1826, the Cherokee syllabary, publicly demonstrated a few years earlier, had been printed for the first time.

Most historians credit Sequoyah, the most famous Cherokee, with the invention of the syllabary. However, some oral historians contend that the written Cherokee language is much, much older. But even if there was an ancient written Cherokee language, it was lost to the Cherokees until Sequoyah developed the syllabary. The development of the syllabary was one of the events which was destined to have a profound influence on our tribe's future history. This extraordinary achievement marks the only known instance of an individual creating a totally new system of writing.

Born in the 1770s in the Cherokee village of Tuskegee on the Tennessee River, Sequoyah was a mixed-blood whose mother, Wureth, belonged to the Paint Clan. Sometimes the young man was known by his English name, George Gist or Guess, a legacy from his white father. Sequoyah, reared in the old tribal ways and customs, became a hunter and fur trader. He was also a skilled silver craftsman who never learned to speak, write, or read English. However, he was always fascinated with the white people's ability to communicate with one another by making distinctive marks on paper—what some native people referred to as "talking leaves."

Handicapped from a hunting accident and therefore having more time for contemplation and study, Sequoyah supposedly set about to devise his own system of communication in 1809. He devoted the next dozen years to his task, taking time out to serve as a soldier in the War of 1812 and the Creek War. Despite constant ridicule, criticism from friends and even family members, and accusations that he was insane or practicing witchcraft, Sequoyah became obsessed with his work on the Cherokee language.

> It is said that in ancient times, when writing first began, a man named Moses made marks upon a stone. I, too, can make marks upon a stone. I can agree with you by what name to call those marks and that will be writing and can be understood.
>
> Attributed to Sequoyah

Some historians say that ultimately Sequoyah determined the Cherokee language was made up of particular clusters of sounds and combinations of vowels and consonants. The eighty-five characters in the syllabary represent all the combination of vowel and consonant sounds that form our language. In 1821, Sequoyah's demonstration of the system before a gathering of astonished tribal leaders was so dramatically convincing that it promptly led to the official approval of the syllabary.

Within several months of Sequoyah's unveiling of his invention, a substantial number of people in the Cherokee Nation reportedly were able to read and write in their own language. Many mixed-bloods were already literate in English, but the syllabary made it possible for virtually everyone in the Cherokee Nation, young and old, to master our language in a relatively short period of time.

The Christian missionaries opposed the new syllabary at first, but later saw how it could be used to further their conversion work. Soon, they made sure that laboriously copied Cherokee translations of the Bible and other religious works were being distributed among our people. Our tribal council was resolved to put the syllabary to good use in other ways also. Stimulated by this achievement, our entire tribe advanced rapidly, much to the chagrin of those whites who still regarded all native people, even those with "book learning," as pests who stood in the way of the whites' progress.

In 1827, the Cherokee council appropriated funding for the establishment of a national newspaper. Early the following year, the hand press and syllabary characters in type were shipped by water from Boston and transported overland the last two hundred miles by wagon to our capital of New Echota, established two years before in Georgia. Elias Boudinot, whose true name was Buck Watie, or Galagina, "the Buck," was selected as the first editor. Formally educated in Connecticut, Watie took the name Elias Boudinot after becoming friends with a Revolutionary War hero of the same name, who had written a book claiming that the Cherokees were one of the ten lost tribes of Israel.

The inaugural issue of the newspaper, *Tsa la gi Tsu lehisanunhi* or the *Cherokee Phoenix*, printed in parallel columns in Cherokee and English, appeared on February 21, 1828. It was the first Indian newspaper published in the United States.

The name given to the newspaper was a fitting choice. The power of that mythical bird—which was swallowed by flames but rose from its ashes—reminds us of the Cherokees' eternal flame. It has come through broken treaties, neglected promises, wars, land grabs, epidemics, and tribal splits. According to our legend, as long as that fire burns, our people will survive.

> *We would now commit our feeble efforts to the good will and indulgence of the public... hoping for that happy period when all the Indian tribes of America shall arise, Phoenix-like, from the ashes, and when the terms "Indian depredation," "war whoop," "scalping knife," and the like, shall become obsolete.*
>
> Elias Boudinot's *first editorial*
> Cherokee Phoenix, *February 21, 1828*

A written Cherokee Constitution, adopted on July 26, 1827, by a convention of elected delegates from the eight districts whose representatives had gathered at New Echota, was produced in both languages on the new national printing press. Modeled after the United States Constitution, the document provided for three branches of government, two legislative houses, a legal system that included a supreme court and jury system for trials, and a national police force to enforce our written laws. It boldly proclaimed the existence of an independent Cherokee Nation with complete dominion over our tribal lands in Georgia, Tennessee, North Carolina, and Alabama.

Some of our people frequently single out the many positive events of the late 1820s as the high point of the Cherokee Renaissance, from the conclusion of our war with the Creek people in 1814 to the mid-1830s. In terms of lifestyle and culture, the Cherokees had a highly developed society, as opposed to the largely ignorant frontier riffraff in the South, made up of many whites who envied Indian achievements, coveted their land and, generally, treated them as savages. The great majority of white political leaders and citizens from Georgia—the nerve center of the Cherokee Nation—had no respect for native people. They found the concept of "civilized" Indians and the notion of Cherokees forming their own republic most offensive; such radical ideas only served to undercut the proposed federal removal policy.

More important to the white Georgians, gold was discovered in July of 1828 on Ward's Creek near the present town of Dahlonega, not far from New Echota in the heart of Cherokee country. De Soto's dream seemed to be coming true. The discovery of gold caused even more of a stampede of white settlers into the region. More than ever, the whites clamored for the removal of the Indians. Georgia's political vanguard immediately began to draft restrictive legislation. Our tribal leaders did not dare to admit it, but the fate of the Cherokee Nation was sealed. The old myth about Rabbit and his Wolf enemies suddenly applied. But this time, Wolves were all around, and Rabbit's song and dance did not divert the enemies' attention. Even trying to act like Wolves and mimicking their way of life did not work. Wolves pressed in, and Rabbit had no place to run.

Besides the discovery of gold, Georgians remained alarmed because of the adoption of the written Cherokee Constitution asserting that our people were independent and had complete jurisdiction over our own territory. A further complication for our people loomed on the horizon—the election of Andrew Jackson as president of the United States in 1828. An intensely ambitious Tennessean and proud son of the southern frontier, the cunning Jackson was a seasoned "Indian fighter," an outspoken advocate of Indian removal, and a well-known antagonist of the Cherokees.

Just a month before "Old Hickory" won the presidential election in

November of 1828, John Ross—the primary author of our constitution and a tireless guardian of Cherokee rights—was elected as principal chief of the Cherokee Nation, an office he would be reelected to until his death in 1866. Although only one-eighth Cherokee, Ross always will be remembered as one of our most remarkable chiefs, a dedicated and beloved leader who became the hope of the Cherokees as the whites swept our people forever from our rightful land.

Ross was born in 1790 at Turkeytown in what is now northern Alabama. His mother was Molly McDonald, a quarter-blood Cherokee and the daughter of the Tory agent among the Chickamaugas. Ross's father was Daniel Ross, a Scottish immigrant who was traveling through Cherokee country on a trading mission before the American Revolution when he encountered a war party of Dragging Canoe, the fearless Chickamauga warrior. The warriors spared Daniel Ross's life and made him a member of the Cherokee Nation. Two years later, he married Molly. John was their oldest son, the third of nine children.

Even though John Ross was seven-eighths Scottish, it is important to note that the influence of the United States government in the area of identifying Indians by degrees of native blood had not yet had its effect on our tribe. To the Cherokee mind at that time, one's identity as Cherokee depended solely on clan affiliation. Ross's mixed-blood mother was a Cherokee by definition because she and her sisters were members of the Bird Clan. Cherokee children belong to their mother's clan and retain membership for life, so Ross, too, was a Cherokee of the Bird Clan.

Ross's Cherokee name was Guwi Sguwi, usually spelled Cooweescoowee, referring to a legendary white bird. Although Ross and his siblings were raised by their father "like white aristocrats," as one writer put it, they were ardently Cherokee at heart. After his mother's death, the family moved to Georgia, where the diminutive Ross—with fair skin, reddish hair, and blue eyes—was well educated by tutors and at schools. He became a polished gentleman and eloquent speaker. He married a Cherokee named Quatie, whose English name was Elizabeth Brown Henley. Ross established a trading post, operated a ferry, and became a successful merchant and planter. He also served as an aide and confidant to tribal leaders.

During the War of 1812, Ross and hundreds of other Cherokees sided with the Americans and fought against the British and their Creek allies. Ross, along with adopted Cherokee Sam Houston and Tennessee frontier scout Davy Crockett, served under Andrew Jackson in 1814 at the Battle of Horseshoe Bend, when a Cherokee warrior saved Jackson's life. Houston and Crockett remained on friendly terms with our people, and later vehemently opposed our tribe's removal westward. Jackson, however, proved to have little appreciation for the help he had received from the Cherokees.

> *I have long viewed treaties with the Indians an absurdity not to be reconciled to the principles of our government.*
>
> Andrew Jackson
> Letter to President James Monroe, 1817

By 1817, Ross, already actively involved in tribal politics as a member of the Cherokee National Council, advocated tribal unity and opposed the ceding of any more Cherokee land to the whites. Later, he chaired the Cherokee National Committee, and in 1827, he helped to draft our Cherokee Constitution while serving as president of the constitutional convention. Beloved by the majority of Cherokees, or "the people" as he preferred to call his kinsmen, Ross favored taking "the white man's road" in the hope that an acceleration in "acculturation" would fortify the Cherokee Nation, bolstering its position in the eyes of white Americans.

Sadly, this strategy of adopting white culture backfired. The policy of appeasement failed to satisfy anyone. As a result, the strength of our people diminished, especially given the increased influence of the mixed-blood population, which also greatly changed the status of Cherokee women. The clan system and the time-honored practice of descent through maternal lines began to erode. The Cherokee Constitution further limited women's rights by excluding them from all government offices and prohibiting them from voting. Cherokee women were expected to become subservient and domesticated like white women, who were home oriented.

When Ross became principal chief of the Cherokee Nation in 1828, he at once set about to demonstrate to the whites that our nation was, as the *Cherokee Phoenix* claimed, "a land of civil and religious means." But Ross faced the dilemma of having to deal with angry white Georgians who were plainly outraged by what they considered to be the impudence of the Cherokee claims outlined in our constitution. Those whites found a vigorous champion in Washington, D.C., in the person of President Jackson, who took office in March of 1829.

In his first message to Congress, Jackson candidly informed the Cherokees that they could not expect any support for their constitutional position. He contended that Indians had no right to occupy land within the United States, and that it was only because of the government's generosity that native people had any land at all. He and his supporters urged the rapid passage of legislation to enable the southeastern tribes to be removed as soon as possible to lands in the West.

After bitter debate, Jackson's backers in Congress pushed through, by a narrow margin, the Indian Removal Act of 1830, authorizing the president to establish districts west of the Mississippi to exchange for Indian-held lands in the Southeast. Jackson immediately signed the bill into law. The seeds of removal sowed by Thomas Jefferson years before had taken root. The Cherokee Nation—Jackson's former ally—and other native people of the Five Tribes were about to reap the bitter harvest.

The removal bill became the law of the land despite pleas from Davy Crockett. His opposition to Jackson's Indian policy supposedly cost him reelection to Congress as a Democrat later that year. Although he returned as a Whig two years later and served another term, Crockett eventually left in search of further adventure in Texas, where his legend was burned into eternity when he perished at the siege of the Alamo in 1836. Besides the much mythologized Crockett, others also opposed Indian removal, including noteworthy political leaders of conscience such as Henry Clay and Daniel Webster.

After the passage of the removal act, Jackson arranged for a meeting of the southern tribes in hopes that he would be able to convince them to obey the new law. The Cherokees refused to attend, but the Creeks, Choctaws, and Chickasaws sent delegations. In the next two years, those three tribes signed individual treaties of removal. They soon found themselves severed from their homes in Mississippi and Alabama, headed west on their own paths of tears and misery to Indian Territory. Many died on the journey.

The Seminoles fought removal by taking up arms and ensconcing themselves in the Florida Everglades, where they engaged in a guerrilla war against the United States Army for almost eight years. Some Seminoles were finally removed to the West. Those who remained in their Everglades refuge refused to make peace with the government officially.

They became known as "the tribe which never surrendered." Although the Cherokees also refused to give in to the whites, they did not wish to go to war. Our leaders were convinced that it was imperative to maintain independence through peaceful methods.

Even before the removal legislation was enacted, the Georgia legislature had passed a series of anti-Cherokee measures. The worst of those statutes nullified all our people's laws, confiscated Cherokee property and gold, and prohibited native people from testifying in court. It also forbade whites to live among the Cherokees without first swearing an oath of allegiance to Georgia, made it illegal for an Indian to speak out against immigration to the West, and provided for a survey of Cherokee land and a lottery to distribute that land to white Georgians.

Most of our leaders, especially Chief John Ross, were determined to resist. They traveled to Washington and appealed to President Jackson, but to no avail. They did not give up. They tried again. They were committed to mend the wounds and restore our people's balance.

Among our old notables at that time was Gulkalaski, a great warrior acquainted with Jackson from years before at the bloody clash against the Creeks at Horseshoe Bend. He was the Cherokee known for supposedly having saved Jackson's life by slaying a Creek warrior who had Jackson at his mercy. Aware of those circumstances, Chief Ross sent Gulkalaski to Washington to appeal to Jackson. But the ploy did not help. After he heard Gulkalaski's petition, Jackson reportedly snapped at him., "Sir, your audience is ended, there is nothing I can do for you." One version of the tale is that after being refused help, Gulkalaski uttered, "Detsinulahungu," which means "I tried, but could not." After that, he was always known as Tsunu lahunski, or "One who tries, but fails."

> If I had known that Jackson would drive us from our homes, I would have killed him at the Horseshoe.
>
> > Attributed to Tsunu Iahunski,
> > on the Trail of Tears

Editorials in the *Cherokee Phoenix* attacking the removal policy were reprinted in newspapers across the United States and Europe. Ministers in Boston, New York, and other large cities preached fiery sermons based on the editorials. Some of our tribe's most eloquent speakers brought the

Cherokee case to the public by lecturing throughout the northern states. Proficient in political and legal matters, Chief Ross made frequent trips to Washington to confer with the nation's leading statesmen and power brokers, including Jackson, John Quincy Adams, James Monroe, and John Calhoun. Nothing changed, however. Jackson would not be swayed. Finally, our tribal leaders had no recourse but to turn to the United States Supreme Court. Ross and his followers were confident that the Court would intercede on behalf of the Cherokee Nation and foil the plans of Jackson and other foes of the Indians.

In 1831, the case of the *Cherokee Nation v. Georgia* was finally heard by the Supreme Court. Lawyers hired by the tribe urged the learned justices to uphold our rights. They argued that Georgia could not legally enforce its laws in Cherokee country, and that Jackson and the government had no authority to forcibly evict our people from their own land. Cherokee counsel, maintaining that the tribe was a sovereign nation, sought an injunction against Georgia's encroachment on Indian property in violation of treaty guarantees.

On March 18, 1831, Chief Justice John Marshall, in handing down the Court's decision, effectively sidestepped the issue. He broadly hinted that he and his fellow justices considered the Cherokee Nation as "a distinct political society separated from others, capable of managing its own affairs and governing itself." But even though he was sympathetic to the Cherokee cause, Marshall was also aware that a ruling in behalf of the tribe would have the authority of the Supreme Court. That meant if the Court could not enforce its own decree in behalf of the Cherokees, its authority would be compromised. In writing for the majority, Marshall held that the Cherokee Nation was a "domestic dependent nation," or a ward of the federal government, and therefore could not bring suit in federal courts. Georgia state law still applied to our people.

Disappointed, but far from ready to admit total defeat, our leaders continued to believe that the Supreme Court was the Cherokees' best protector of tribal rights. They did not have long to wait before another test of those rights came before the Court. When the Reverend Samuel Austin Worcester and Elizur Butler, white missionaries living among the Cherokees in Georgia, refused to take the oath of allegiance to the state, they were arrested and charged as felons. Tried and convicted, the two men were sentenced to four years of hard labor. Worcester appealed to the United States Supreme Court.

In 1832, the Supreme Court suddenly reversed itself in the celebrated *Worcester v. State of Georgia*. This time, the Court found that Indian nations were capable of making treaties, and that under the United States Constitution, such treaties were the supreme law of the land. They ruled that the federal government had exclusive jurisdiction within the borders of the Cherokee Nation, and that state law had no power within those boundaries. The Georgia statute was declared unconstitutional.

Georgia officials were furious. They responded by denying the Court's jurisdiction and refusing to obey the judgment. A Supreme Court special mandate that ordered Worcester's release from prison was also ignored. A devoted clergyman who later moved to Indian Territory before the Cherokees were finally forced to leave the Southeast, Worcester languished in a Georgia prison for almost another year before he was released.

The federal government, beset by technicalities concerning enforcement, was stymied from further action. Jackson, of course, refused to help. He simply disregarded the judgment, declaring that "the decision of the Supreme Court has fell still born, and they find that they cannot coerce Georgia to yield to its mandate." Jackson also supposedly made the sarcastic pronouncement, "John Marshall has made his law; now let him enforce it."

Cherokees and other native people remained at the mercy of the whites, who continued to seize Indian property, then being divided into lots of 160 acres and gold lots of forty acres and parceled out in the lottery to white Georgia citizens. In the spring of 1834, during one of John Ross's many treks to Washington on behalf of his people, his fine estate was confiscated. He and his ailing wife moved their children and possessions into a small cabin across the border in Tennessee.

The situation, exacerbated by the dismal outcome of the tribe's two major Supreme Court cases and by Andrew Jackson's reelection in 1832, was enough to convince some Cherokees that they could do nothing more to halt the removal process. Some Cherokees, on their own volition, moved west to join the Old Settlers. As morale continued to deteriorate, a minority faction of our tribe began to support the official surrender of Cherokee land to Georgia while a deal could still be struck with the whites.

Surprisingly, the majority of the dissident faction once had been violently opposed to removal. They rather abruptly changed their minds after they became convinced that the tribe's only choice was to pull an about-face and move elsewhere or risk annihilation. The group was led by Major Ridge, a powerful Cherokee orator, his ambitious son, John, and Ridge's nephew, Elias Boudinot, or Buck Watie. In 1832, Boudinot had resigned as editor of the *Cherokee Phoenix* under pressure from Ross when Boudinot had begun to write editorials that seemed to support immigration. To Ross, the public discussion of the removal question was contradictory to the traditional Cherokee approach to resolving political disputes. The two Ridges and Boudinot were joined by Boudinot's younger brother Stand Watie, who later became a brigadier general in the Confederate Army and a political rival of John Ross. Those who were proponents of signing a removal treaty with the whites became known as the Ridge Party or, eventually, the Treaty Party. Considered traitors by Ross and most of our tribe, they thought of themselves as true patriots.

Some historians have inferred that the pro-removal mavericks in the Ridge Party were inspired as much by their own ambitions as by true concern for the tribe. Grace Steele Woodward, in her book, *The Cherokees*, suggests that there was a conspiracy of sorts between the Ridge Party and the authorities in Georgia. According to Woodward, the Ridge followers felt that they knew what was best for the Cherokee Nation and were willing to bypass the tribal process for their own benefit. Whatever their motivations, members of the Ridge Party had little support within the Cherokee Nation. Although the tribe was becoming more divided on the issue, the majority of Cherokees adamantly opposed removal. They remained loyal to Chief John Ross and the Ross Party.

The Ross majority and the rival Ridge faction continued to send independent delegations to Washington to hammer out an agreement. Early in 1835, with the Ridge Party completely in favor of removal, Jackson appointed the Reverend John F. Schermerhorn, a retired Dutch minister whom most Cherokees called "Devil's Horn," as treaty commissioner to our tribe. It was Jackson's hope and Schermerhorn's intent to arrange for an acceptable removal treaty as expeditiously as possible. The treaty that resulted was rejected in October of 1835 by the Cherokee Nation, meeting in full council. The Ridge followers went off to lick their wounds and to scheme. Later that year, Ross again prepared to go to the nation's capital to negotiate on behalf of the tribe for more favorable terms.

In a blinding rainstorm on the evening of December 5, twenty-five members of the Georgia Guard—a band of whites on horseback who had recently confiscated the *Cherokee Phoenix* press—crossed into Tennessee and swept down on the Ross family's cabin. They arrested Ross and his houseguest, John Howard Payne, a playwright and the composer of "Home, Sweet Home," who was gathering material for a book about the Cherokees. The guard seized Payne's manuscript and Ross's personal documents, and carted the two men off to a squalid log cabin in Georgia that served as a jail. Shackled near them was the son of the speaker of the Cherokee tribal council. Ross and Payne remained in chains for almost two weeks before they were released, without any charges having been lodged against them. The undaunted Ross finally reached Washington, but while he was there, Schermerhorn organized a parley of the pro-removal council members at New Echota to sign the rejected Ridge treaty.

On December 29, 1835, fewer than five hundred Cherokees of a tribal population of at least seventeen thousand answered the summons to appear at New Echota. Despite the overwhelming opposition, twenty-one proponents of Cherokee removal, including most notably Major Ridge, John Ridge, Elias Boudinot, and Stand Waite, scrawled their names or left X marks on the document. Not a single elected tribal officer signed the contentious covenant. However, as a result of the fraudulently obtained Treaty of New Echota, the Cherokee Nation relinquished to the United States all of its remaining land east of the Mississippi River for $5 million. The Treaty Party also agreed to leave the Southeast within two years of the treaty's ratification and move west to Indian Territory, the land that was guaranteed to be ours forever.

Ross protested the treaty "in the name of God and the Cherokee Nation." The Cherokee National Council denounced it as fraudulent. Ross again journeyed to Washington, bearing a petition of protest signed by many thousands of Cherokees. Jackson—granitelike—would not be moved. In spite of the evidence that the tribe's constituted authorities and most Cherokee people were firmly opposed, Congress ratified the removal treaty on May 23, 1836, with a one-vote majority. Bands of our people, including the Treaty Party leaders and some of the Christian missionaries, eventually left for the West. Chief Ross and his followers—the greater part of the Cherokee tribe—remained in the Southeast. They continued to resist removal and to speak out against the treaty, which they branded as a sham.

When the federal government's designated deadline for the Cherokees to leave the Southeast arrived in the spring of 1838, very few of our people—only about two thousand—had "voluntarily" vacated their homeland. Anxious for the removal to begin, the War Department dispatched army units with orders to help supervise the forcible expulsion of all remaining Cherokees. Martin Van Buren, Jackson's successor as president, was no different than those who had come before him. "No state can achieve proper culture, civilization, and progress in safety as long as Indians are permitted to remain," Van Buren stated. He sent General Winfield Scott to the Cherokee Nation to carry out the terms of the treaty and to direct the removal operations.

Although Scott, who considered his assignment distasteful, gave strict orders for the troops to conduct the removal process in a considerate and humane manner, there were many reports of soldiers dragging Cherokees from their cabins and fields at bayonet point. Homes were looted and crops burned; women and girls were raped. Mixed-blood girls, whom the white soldiers found more desirable, were passed from man to man like bottles of whiskey. Just as the other southern tribes had lost thousands of victims to cholera, pneumonia, and exposure during their confinement and forced removal to the West, the Cherokees also experienced wholesale hardship and brutality.

> *I fought through the Civil War and have seen men shot to pieces and slaughtered by the thousands, but the Cherokee removal was the cruelest work I ever saw.*
>
> *Georgia volunteer Z. A. Zele, later a*
> *Confederate colonel, reflecting on the 1838 removal*

Without sufficient clothing or food and water, our people were rounded up like cattle and placed in stockades where they awaited departure for Indian Territory. Some groups made the journey by riverboat, but most were forced to go overland on foot or horseback. Ill and elderly people were permitted to ride in crowded wagons. Several hundred Cherokees managed to evade the soldiers. They escaped to the mountains and remained in hiding.

After witnessing the heavy loss of life among the captive tribal members, Ross urged General Scott to allow him to supervise the removal of approximately seventeen thousand Cherokees, a few whites, free black people, and slaves. It should be remembered that hundreds of people of African ancestry also walked the Trail of Tears with the Cherokees during the forced removal of 1838–1839. Although we know about the terrible human suffering of our native people and the members of the other tribes during the removal, we rarely hear of those black people who also suffered.

> *Being acquainted with many of the Indians and able to fluently speak their language, I was sent as interpreter into the Smoky Mountains country in May 1838, and witnessed the execution of the most brutal order in the history of American warfare.*
>
> *I saw the helpless Cherokees arrested and dragged from their homes, and driven at the bayonet point into the stockades. And in the chill of a drizzling rain on an October morning I saw them loaded like cattle or sheep into ... wagons and start toward the west.*
>
> *One can never forget the sadness and solemnity that morning. Chief John Ross led in prayer and when the bugle sounded and the wagons started rolling many of the children rose to their feet and waved their little hands good-bye to their mountain homes, knowing they were leaving them forever.*
>
> *John G. Burnett, former army private*
> *Eightieth birthday story, December 11, 1890*

Although Jackson had warned Van Buren not to yield to Chief Ross, Van Buren followed Scott's advice and agreed to Ross's request to supervise the removal himself. In October of 1838, the first organized contingent of one thousand Cherokees began the twelve-hundred-mile westward trek. By March of 1839, twelve more groups had followed.

Altogether, at least four thousand Cherokees died in the detention camps or along the way. Among those who perished was Quatie Ross, the wife of Chief Ross. A witness of the Trail of Tears later said that Quatie gave her only blanket to a sick child, soon developed pneumonia, and died on a bitterly cold night. She was buried far from her mountain home.

> *... murder is murder whether committed by the villain in the dark or by uniformed men stepping to the strains of martial music. Murder is murder and somebody must answer, somebody must explain the streams of blood that flowed in the Indian country*

in the summer of 1838. Somebody must explain the four thousand silent graves that mark the trail of the Cherokees to their exile. I wish I could forget it all, but the picture of . . . wagons lumbering over the frozen ground with their cargo of suffering humanity still lingers in my memory.

John G. Burnett, December 11, 1890

CHAPTER 7

CHILD OF THE
SIXTIES

A hunter was in the woods one day in winter when suddenly he saw a panther coming toward him and at once prepared to defend himself. The panther continued to approach, and the hunter was just about to shoot when the animal spoke. Suddenly it seemed to the man as if there were no difference between them, that they were both of the same nature. The panther asked the man where he was going, and the man said he was looking for a deer. "Well," said the panther, "we are getting ready for a green-corn dance, and there are seven of us out after a buck, so we may as well hunt together."

The hunter agreed, and they went on together. They started up one deer and another, but the panther made no sign, and said only, "Those are too small; we want something better." So the hunter did not shoot, and they went on. They started up another deer, a larger one, and the panther sprang on it and tore its throat, and finally killed it after a hard struggle. The hunter got out his knife to skin it, but the panther said the skin was too much torn to be used, and they must try again. They started up another large deer, and this the panther killed without trouble. Then, wrapping his tail around it, he threw it across his back. "Now, come to our town house," he said to the hunter.

The panther led the way, carrying the captured deer on his back, up a little stream branch until they came to the head spring. It seemed as if a door opened in the side of the hill, and they went in. The hunter found himself in front of a large town house, with the finest detsanunli (ceremonial ground) he had ever seen. The trees around were green, and the air was warm, as in summer. There was a great company there *getting ready for the dance, and they were all panthers, but somehow it all seemed natural to the hunter. After a while, the others who had been out came in with the deer they had taken, and the dance began. The hunter danced several rounds, and then said it was growing late and he must be getting home. So the panthers opened the door and the hunter went out, and at once found himself alone in the woods again. It was winter and very cold, with snow on the ground and on all the trees. When he reached the settlement, he found a party just starting out to search for him. They asked him where he had been so long, and he told them the story. Then he found that he had been in the panther town house for several days instead of only a very short time as he had thought.*

He died within seven days after his return, because he had already begun to take on the nature of the panther, and so could not live again with men. If he had stayed with the panthers, he would have lived.

My family's relocation experience in San Francisco was disturbing in many ways. But in retrospect, our ordeal was not nearly as harsh or painful as the problems encountered by the Cherokee people who had been forced to take the Trail of Tears in the late 1830s. At least we did not have to walk hundreds of miles through snow and sleet. We did not worry about getting bayoneted or shot by some soldier or bushwhacker. Our relocation was voluntary and not by federal mandate. There were some parallels, however. For instance, even after we had settled down in our two-family flat in the Potrero District, we still felt as alienated as our ancestors must have felt when they finally arrived in those unfamiliar surroundings that became their new home. Despite the decades that separated us, we shared a feeling of detachment with the Cherokees who had come before us.

I know that many native people who turned up in San Francisco as part of the BIA's removal program in the 1950s considered California to be the land of new beginnings. At least that was their hope. They wanted to believe the promotional literature that spoke of good jobs and happy homes waiting for those who had relocated. I was only a youngster, but I did not accept the government propaganda. Instead, I was convinced that my parents had made the wrong decision when they bought the BIA's bill of goods.

At first, nothing about the city was very appealing. The overt discrimination we encountered is what got to me the most. It became obvious that ethnic intolerance was a fact of life in California, even in the urbane and sophisticated world of San Francisco. Not only did African and Hispanic Americans feel the sting of racism, so did Native Americans.

I recall an incident that drove home for me the concept of racial bias. Soon after we moved to California, a woman came up to my mother and told her straight out that we were all "nigger children." Then she called my mother a "nigger lover." The woman said those things because of my father's dark complexion. Mother was outraged by that repulsive word of contempt. Prompted by blind hatred and ignorance, it was intended to inflict pain. It must have stung like a hard slap on the face. My soft-spoken mother was so distraught by such a blatant display of malice that she jumped the woman!

Most of the time, however, people who had a problem with our being different did not say what they thought about us to our faces. They made snide remarks behind our backs. It was then that we found out the place where we lived was hardly exempt from racial prejudice.

All ethnic minorities in California have suffered from various kinds of unjust treatment and bigotry over the years. The abuse of Native Americans began with the white settlement of California and was the worst kind of oppression that any minority group has experienced there. Except for the cessation of violent acts in recent years, the shoddy treatment of California's original inhabitants still continues.

At one time, the state sustained a much larger number of Native Americans than any other region of comparable size on the continent north of Mexico. Native people hunted, fished, gathered food, and generally learned to get along without killing one another. By the time the first Spanish settlement was founded in the mid-1700s, there were at least 275,000 Indians living in present California. That changed very quickly. By 1900, less than sixteen thousand native people remained.

Throughout history, beginning with the Spanish conquerors and continuing with the white settlers, the Indians of California endured genocide, disease, starvation, and overt oppression. In many instances, widespread violence became wholesale murder. While the Cherokees and the other Five Tribes adjusted to their new homes in Indian Territory, in California the white settlers, miners, and armed posses had a field day indiscriminately slaughtering native people. The law of the white man was, in fact, no law at all.

In many ways, California in the middle to late 1800s was much like violence-plagued Bosnia, where "ethnic cleansing" in the 1990s has become the norm. Wholesale genocide and rape became standard in California. According to a study conducted by the University of California, at least one thousand Indian women in the 1850s alone were raped so brutally that most of them died. Thousands of other native women were forced to become white men's concubines. During that same period, almost four thousand Indian children were kidnapped and sold into slavery. Considered to be obstacles to white men's progress, Native Americans were hunted like wild game. As late as 1870, there were communities in California actually paying bounties for Indian scalps or severed heads.

> The only good Indians I ever saw were dead.
>
> General Philip Henry Sheridan, January 1869

Some whites tried to halt the carnage. In the early 1880s, New England author Helen Hunt Jackson, noted for her espousal of the Native American cause, distributed to every member of Congress a copy of *A Century of Dishonor*, her book about governmental mistreatment of Indians. It set the standard for muckraking books that followed two decades later, and it became one of the most influential books of the late nineteenth century. Jackson was made a member of a special commission to study the problems of native people in California. The report that resulted had little impact on Congress, but by serving on the commission, Jackson came up with enough material to write *Ramona*. Some critics labeled this 1884 novel about the criminal abuse of the Mission Indians as the "*Uncle Tom's Cabin* of California."

Other whites also made attempts to help Native Americans. In 1901, a group in Los Angeles led by Charles F. Lummis founded the Sequoya League, named for our noted Cherokee linguist. Incorporated to "make better Indians"—whatever that meant—the organization had as its main objective giving aid to native people in obtaining food and clothing, or financial and legal assistance.

California Indians faced difficulties that most tribes elsewhere in the United States did not always encounter, because only a small number of the California Indians were ever placed on reservations. Treaties proposed in the nineteenth century that provided for reservations were never ratified, so the majority of California Indians were left without any land. They were forced to get along to the best of their abilities and wits. A great number of native people did not survive. Of those who did pull through, many of them became agricultural workers in the vast California growing fields. Others ended up destitute and homeless. They were shoved aside and written off as burdens to society.

> *I know what the misfortune of the tribes is. Their misfortune is not that they are red men; not that they are semi-civilized, not that they are a dwindling race. Their misfortune is that they hold great bodies of rich lands, which have aroused the cupidity of powerful corporations and of powerful individuals. . . . I greatly fear that the adoption of this provision to discontinue treaty-making is the beginning of the end in respect to Indian Lands. It is the first step in a great scheme of spoliation, in which the Indians will be plundered, corporations and individuals enriched, and the American name dishonored in history.*
>
> *California Senator Eugene Casserly,* 1871

Some of the questions I am asked most frequently today include what happened to native people, such as those in California? Why do native people have so many problems? How is it that they ended up facing high unemployment, low educational attainment, low self-esteem, and problems with alcohol abuse? I answer that all one needs to do is look at our history. History clearly shows all the external factors that have played a part in our people being where we are today.

Regardless of all the problems Native Americans faced, they became the fastest-growing minority group in California in the twentieth century. This took place without their reaping much of California's extraordinary affluence. From fewer than sixteen thousand in 1900, at least forty thousand native people lived in the state by 1960, just a few years after my family arrived. Some sources claim that the 1960 population count could have been as high as seventy-five thousand, because census takers did not identify as Indians all native persons who were using Anglo or Hispanic surnames. Only a small percentage of those native people lived on reservations or *rancherias;* most had homes in the Los Angeles or San Francisco areas.

Several factors account for the dramatic rise in the Indian population in California, especially since World War II. First of all, native people were starting to be treated a little better. Numerous social and economic troubles remained, but an awakening of consciousness began among some whites in the late 1920s and continued to gain momentum. About the time our family moved west, California was attempting to abolish barriers separating Indians from non-Indians in terms of education, welfare assistance, and other public services. The substantial Indian immigration from Oklahoma, the Dakotas, and the Southwest throughout the postwar years helped to boost the Native American population in California. The BIA's removal program accounted for a great many Native American individuals and families moving to California, including the Charley Mankiller brood, direct from Mankiller Flats in Oklahoma.

Nonetheless, our troubles did not disappear, even though the old days of exterminating Indians had ceased and California's Native American population was increasing. There were still problems to solve and predicaments to face. Besides the poverty and prejudice we encountered, I was continually struggling with the adjustment to a big city that seemed so foreign and cold to me.

The San Francisco I experienced as a young girl in the late 1950s and early 1960s was not the sophisticated city of palatial Nob Hill mansions, picturesque cable cars, fancy restaurants, and elegant hotels. My family did not lunch amid the tourists at Fisherman's Wharf or dine at Trader Vic's. We did not meet friends to watch from the Crown Room high atop the Fairmont Hotel as the mists rolled in on the bay. Folks who did those things were on a much higher rung of the economic and social ladder than we were. Our family was more familiar—and comfortable—with the crowd that shopped for bargains at Goodwill or St. Vincent de Paul. We ate simple meals at home, wore hand-me-down clothes, and got by from paycheck to paycheck. Our family's meager budget could not handle any nonessentials or luxuries.

After we had lived in San Francisco for a little more than a year, my father, with help from my older brother Don's salary contributions, was able to scrape together enough money for a down payment on a small house. So we left the crowded flat in the Potrero Hill District and moved into a new home in Daly City, just south of San Francisco on the southern peninsula in San Mateo County. Daly City had come into being as a result of the earthquake and fire of 1906, when many San Franciscans fled to John Daly's dairy ranch. It grew into a residential area that mushroomed during the boom years after World War II, when it became one of California's fifty most populous communities.

Our new residence looked as if it had come straight out of a cookie-cutter mold. There were three small bedrooms, a full basement, and not many frills. My sisters and I shared bunk beds. I would describe it as modest, just like the hundreds of other ticky-tacky houses in endless rows that climbed up and down the landlocked hills flanked by the Pacific Ocean and San Francisco Bay.

For our family as a whole, the move to Daly City was a good one. It represented a marked improvement over our first dwelling. We were moving up in the world. At about that same time, my father started to become active at the San Francisco Indian Center, where we met and spent time with other native people living in the area. That had a positive impact on the family. But for me, nothing had changed. I still loathed being in California, and I particularly despised school.

I was uncomfortable. I felt stigmatized. I continually found myself alienated from the other students, who mostly treated me as though I had come from outer space. I was insecure, and the least little remark or glance would leave me mortified. That was especially true whenever people had to teach me something basic or elementary, such as how to use a telephone. I was convinced that they must think it odd to be teaching an eleven- or twelve-year-old how to pick up a phone, listen for a tone, and then dial a number.

In Daly City, I was getting ready to enter the seventh grade. The thought of that depressed me a great deal. That meant having to meet more new kids. Not only did I speak differently than they did, but I had an unfamiliar name that the others ridiculed. We were teased unmercifully about our Oklahoma accents. My sister Linda and I still read out loud to each other every night to lose our accents. Like most young people everywhere, we wanted to belong.

Also, there were changes going on inside me that I could not account for, and that troubled me very much. I was experiencing all the problems girls face when approaching the beginning of womanhood. I was afraid and did not know what to do. Besides having to deal with the internal changes, I was also growing like a weed and had almost reached my full adult height. People thought I was much older than twelve. I hated what was happening. I hated my body. I hated school. I hated the teachers. I hated the other students. Most of all, I hated the city.

I did not hate my parents or the rest of the family. I always loved them very much. But it was a time of great confusion for me. I was silently crying out for attention, but nobody heard me. My dad was constantly busy trying to make a living and, at the same time, deal with his own frustrations and confusion about city life in California. My mother was doing her best to help all of us with our problems while she kept us fed and clothed. Then on top of everything, my oldest brother, Don, announced that he was going to get married. He had met a nice young Choctaw woman named LaVena at the Indian Center. They had fallen in love. Everyone was very happy about the news, but there were long discussions about Don leaving home with his bride and how that loss of income would affect the rest of the family.

With so much going on, I felt like nobody had any time for me. I felt there was not one single person I could confide in or turn to who truly understood me. My self-esteem was at rock bottom. That is when I decided to escape from all of it. I would run away from home. At the time, that seemed my best and only option.

I ran off to Grandma Sitton, who lived at Riverbank. She was an independent woman. I had gotten to know her better since our move to the West Coast, and I liked her very much. I thought perhaps my grandmother would understand and comfort me and help with my problems. Also, I liked Riverbank because Oklahoma families who had come out during the Dust Bowl period were living in the area. I felt more comfortable around them.

My younger sister Linda and I had stashed away a little bit of money saved from baby-sitting jobs we had gotten through meeting other families at the Indian Center. We did not have much, but it was enough to buy a bus ticket. Of course, as soon as I got to her house, my grandma called my folks and said, "Pearl's here, you better come get her." My parents were upset—very upset—and my dad drove out and took me back. But that did not end it. That first time was just the start of a pattern of behavior that lasted until I became a teenager.

I waited a little while, and then I ran away a second time and went straight to my grandmother's house. My parents and I went through the same routine. But I did not stop. I did it again. Once more, my dad drove to Riverbank and took me back to Daly City. One time my sister Linda ran away, too. She took off for somewhere on her own. I am not sure where she went. My folks found her and brought her home. But I kept running away. Every single time, I went to Grandma Sitton's. Over a year or so, I guess I ran away from home at least five times, maybe more.

My parents could not control me. Eventually, they decided that I

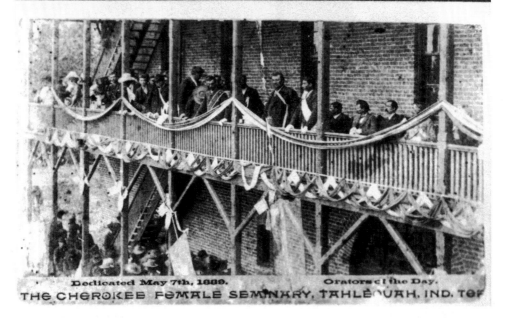

ABOVE: Dedication ceremony of the rebuilt Cherokee Female Seminary, May 7, 1889. *(Courtesy John Vaughan Library, Northeastern State University, Tahlequah, Oklahoma.)*

BELOW: Cherokee Senate, 1889. *(Courtesy John Vaughan Library, Northeastern State University, Tahlequah, Oklahoma.)*

Teacher Janana Ballard at Cherokee Female Seminary, circa 1887. *(Courtesy R. Lee Fleming.)*

BOTTOM LEFT: Cherokee Keetoowah Society Meeting, September 12, 1917. Standing left to right: Steve Sand, Tim Alex, Charley Scott, Bluford Sixkiller, Redbird Smith, William Rogers, Jim Hogshooter, Sam Lacy, Steve Cary. Seated: Peter Nix, Osie Hogshooter, and Tom Horn. *(Courtesy Oklahoma Historical Society.)*

Redbird Smith with the Nighthawk Keetoowahs. *(Courtesy Oklahoma Historical Society.)*

Principal Chief John Ross and his wife Mary Stapler Ross. *(Courtesy Cherokee National Historical Society.)*

BELOW: Cherokee National Council, Tahlequah, 1889. *(Courtesy John Vaughan Library, Northeastern State University, Tahlequah, Oklahoma.)*

OPPOSITE TOP: A late-nineteenth-century Cherokee woman named Walini, probably one of the traditionalists, Cherokee, North Carolina. *(Courtesy of the Smithsonian Institution.)*

ABOVE: Two unidentified Cherokee women making pottery at Cherokee, North Carolina, in 1888. *(Courtesy of the Smithsonian Institution.)*

RIGHT: A serious young Cherokee girl, born in 1887, dressed in a very formal style. *(Courtesy of the Smithsonian Institution.)*

LEFT: Cherokee chicken-and-bean dinner, early twentieth century, Elm Springs, Oklahoma. *(Courtesy Western History collections, University of Oklahoma Library.)*

Rosa Hildebrand, taken in the late nineteenth century. She was a member of an important Cherokee family. *(Courtesy of the Smithsonian Institution.)*

Portrait of Susan Sanders, a Cherokee woman whose dress is evidence of a complete rejection of traditional Cherokee dress or is simply the way she dressed for this pose. *(Courtesy of the Smithsonian Institution.)*

Very early-twentieth-century paternal family photo. Back row: Dad's Aunt Maggie Mankiller on left and my grandfather John Mankiller on right; two unidentified women in the middle. Front row, left to right: second from left, my great-grandfather, Jack Mankiller; fourth from left, Colson; fifth from left, Mary Mankiller. The others cannot be identified.

BELOW LEFT: My maternal grandparents, Robert Bailey Sitton and Ethel Pearl Sitton, Stilwell, Indian Territory, 1902.

OPPOSITE BOTTOM: Early-twentieth-century paternal family photo. Back row, left to right: Jenny Mankiller Christie, Colson (George) Mankiller, and Mary Mankiller Hughes. Front row, left to right: my paternal Aunt Sally, Grandfather John, holding my father, Charley, and my grandmother, Betty Bolin Canoe Mankiller.

OPPOSITE TOP: My maternal aunt Sadie Sitton and my mother, Irene, Stilwell, Oklahoma, 1922.

BELOW: My siblings on the porch of our rented house near Stilwell, Oklahoma, 1945. Left to right: John, Frances, Robert, Frieda, and Don.

My siblings and I at Mankiller Flats near Rocky Mountain, Oklahoma, in 1949. Back row, left to right: Robert (partially obscured), Louis (Don) Frieda. Middle row, left to right: John, Frances, Wilma. Front row: Linda.

Wilma Pearl Mankiller, junior high school, San Francisco, 1959.

MIDDLE: My brother, Robert Charles Mankiller, getting ready for a date, San Francisco, 1959.

BOTTOM: A family outing with my parents and brothers and sisters at Golden Gate Park in San Francisco, 1961. Back row, left to right: Richard, Wilma, Linda, John, Mom and Dad. Front row, left to right: James and Vanessa.

OPPOSITE BOTTOM: My father, Charley Mankiller, at a family outing, California, mid-1960s.

OPPOSITE RIGHT: My maternal grandmother, Pearl Sitton, and I at Riverbank, California, 1961.

OPPOSITE LEFT: I am attending a powwow with a friend in the San Francisco Bay Area, dressed in a borrowed buckskin dress, 1962.

My parents, Irene Sitton Mankiller and Charley
Mankiller, in their youth, Stilwell, Oklahoma.

had become incorrigible. They saw that I truly did not want to live in the city. I wanted no part of it. So they gave in and let me stay with my grandmother. By then, she had outlived another husband. She sold her home and gave the money to her son and his wife—my Uncle Floyd Sitton and Aunt Frauline. They had moved to California after Uncle Floyd's return from World War II and his discharge from the service. He used the money my grandmother gave them to buy a dairy ranch north of Riverbank, near the town of Escalon. In exchange for helping them buy their "dream place," Grandma Sitton moved in with my uncle and aunt and their four children, Tommy, Mary Louise, and twins about my age, Eddie and Teddie.

I was preparing to begin the eighth grade when I joined my grandmother and the other Sitton relatives at their ranch. The agreement was for me to stay with them for one year. Ultimately, it turned out to be a very positive experience, but at first there were difficulties. There was a fair amount of conflict between my cousins and me, but they finally got used to my living there. Our problems sprang not from my Native American blood, but from a rivalry between the four of them and me. In a nutshell, we were all competitive kids. We were pure country, too, and that meant we would not run from a fight. When I arrived, it took only the slightest agitation to provoke me. I was highly sensitive and self-conscious.

One time in particular, I recall, several of us were walking back from the fields following Uncle Floyd. My cousin Teddie kept taunting and teasing me until I could not take any more. When he pulled my hair again, I whirled around and punched him in the jaw so hard that he dropped to the ground. I got into trouble over that incident, and there was some talk about shipping me back home to the city. That finally passed. I settled down, and the teasing stopped. The conflict faded. My life seemed to improve.

I began to gain some confidence. As I felt better about myself, I felt better about others. My grandmother deserves much of the credit. Even though she was strict, she was never judgmental. At a very critical point in my life, she helped me learn to accept myself and to confront my problems.

School even seemed more palatable. When I moved to the farm, I did not have one single friend my age at school. I relied on my tough demeanor to protect myself, and I found that this really turned off people.

My cousins had told all the other kids at the small community school we attended that my parents had sent me to live with them because they could not handle me. That was not a good way for me to begin. During lunch and recess, I was usually by myself. Although I got off to a bumpy start, I had made some friends and had developed a routine by the close of the school year. I got along better with my cousins and enjoyed the work on the farm.

All in all, the year I spent on the dairy farm was just what I needed. I slept in the same bed with my grandmother, and we all got up every day at 5:00 A.M. to milk the cows and take care of chores. My main job was to help keep the barn clean. Besides the dairy cows, my uncle and aunt had some pigs and a horse. There was a big vegetable garden. I even helped my Aunt Frauline deliver a calf during a difficult birth. The hard work and fresh air at the farm were so good. We also found time to explore the fields and swim in the creeks.

During our year together, my grandmother helped shape much of my adolescent thinking. I spent much of my time with her, and never considered a single moment wasted. Although she was small, only about four feet ten inches tall, she was solidly built. She also was opinionated, outspoken, tough, and very independent. She was deeply religious and sang from her hymnbook every day. Her favorite song was "Rock of Ages." My grandmother also loved to garden, raise chickens, and pick peaches. Grandmother Sitton and my father—two of the people I most admired as a young woman—valued hard work. I believe it was their examples more than anything else that contributed to my own work ethic.

I continued to visit the farm every summer during my high school years. Some of my brothers and sisters usually came too, and we would help tend the crops or pick fruit to earn money for new school clothes. We worked alongside some white people in the fields, and my mistrust of whites certainly did not apply to them. The people whom some Californians derisively called Okies or Arkies were great friends—hardworking people, close to the land, and quick to share what little they had with others who had even less. The farm work was demanding, but those were summers of freedom. We swam in the canals, went to drive-in movies, and sipped cherry Cokes or limeades at the local Dairy Queen. Sometimes we headed to the nearby town of Modesto to cruise the streets. Later,

Modesto was the setting for *American Graffiti*, the film about teenage life in small-town America directed by George Lucas, a native son.

I looked forward to those visits with my grandmother. After I was married, I still went to see her. I would sit on her lap, and we teased each other and laughed. Full of spirit and energy, my grandmother married her third and last husband when she was in her eighties. During their courtship, she had me dye her hair black because she believed it would make her look her best. I obliged. Later, I helped her get all prettied up before they went to Reno, Nevada, for a quick wedding. Pearl Halady Sitton never stopped enjoying life. She canned vegetables and fruit, kept chickens, worked in the garden, and sang those hymns until shortly before she died. I am inspired whenever I think about her and all those good times we had.

> *Guided by my heritage of a love of beauty and a respect for strength—in search of my mother's garden, I found my own.*
>
> Alice Walker
> In Search of Our Mothers' Gardens, 1974

At the end of the year I spent with my mother's family, I returned to the Bay area, but not to our house in Daly City. My family no longer lived there. While I was gone, my brother Don and his girlfriend, LaVena, had married. LaVena got a job with the telephone company, and Don went to work for Pacific Gas and Electric. They set up housekeeping at their own place not far from Candlestick Park. As was expected, the loss of Don's income meant my parents were forced to make budgetary adjustments. That meant giving up the house in Daly City. I came home to a more affordable residence my father had found for us, in southeastern San Francisco on a spit of land projecting into the bay. It was a place known as Hunter's Point.

Named for Robert E. Hunter, a forty-niner from the last century who had planned to create a city on the site, Hunter's Point eventually had become the home of a huge U.S. Navy shipyard and dry docks. It flourished during World War II and continued to thrive for some years afterward when a severe housing shortage occurred. Ironically, Japanese-Americans returned to the Bay area after their long confinement in Dillon

Myer's camps only to find that black workers, attracted by plenty of jobs at the shipyards and defense plants, had moved into the "Little Tokyos" of the city. But thousands of black families also occupied the housing built on tidelands adjoining the shipyard at Hunter's Point. Many of those black families had migrated from Oklahoma, Texas, and other states that whites also had fled during the Dust Bowl years.

Hunter's Point may sound like the name of an affluent residential development where polo players and stockbrokers lived, but it was far from that. The only thing fancy about it was the name. Shipyard employees and hourly wage earners made their homes there. Although the shipyard did not close until 1974, jobs started to become more and more scarce in the 1960s. The workers who resided at Hunter's Point fell into financial difficulties, and the housing area became little more than a ghetto.

We found a few Native Americans living at Hunter's Point, including another Cherokee family. They had come to California from Locust Grove, an old Cherokee Nation town in eastern Oklahoma and the home of the late Willard Stone, the wood sculptor whose claim of Cherokee ancestry recently created a great deal of controversy. That other Cherokee family at Hunter's Point was also part of the relocation program masterminded by the BIA.

At Hunter's Point, my perceptions of the world around me began to take shape. Most police, teachers, political leaders, and others in positions of power and authority were whites. There were a few white people living at Hunter's Point, perhaps a few Asians, and several Samoan families. Regardless of the ethnic sprinkling, Hunter's Point was primarily a community of black families. Black culture had a profound impact on my development. When the rest of America was listening to Pat Boone, the Beach Boys, or Elvis, my friends and I listened to Etta James, Dinah Washington, Sarah Vaughan, B. B. King, and others. I talked endlessly with my best friends, Johnnie Lee and LaVada, about things which girls our age were obsessed with—music, boys, parents, and growing up. We sometimes put on makeup, fixed our hair, played records, and danced, pretending we were at a party far away from Hunter's Point. Even today, more than thirty years later, the sisterly company of black women is especially enjoyable to me.

My mother also became good friends with people from different backgrounds. She developed a close relationship with a Filipina woman who lived next door. This neighborhood of diverse cultures was where we remained for several years. Those outside our community called our new home "Harlem West."

We lived in one of the typical little houses, but to everyone's amazement, it had a surprisingly pleasant interior. The rooms were small, but the house had two stories and was not as tiny as some of the other places we had lived. More important, there was not a rat in sight. The kitchen and bathroom were satisfactory, and the wooden floors were in fairly decent shape.

Outside was another story. There was a great deal of animosity between the black youths and Samoan youths of Hunter's Point. Sometimes it seemed like a war zone when rival gangs clashed on the streets. Now and then there were enormous battles. Upstairs, in the bedroom I shared with my sister Linda, we could gaze out the window at the beauty of the sky and water, or we could lower our eyes to the streets where the gangs fought furiously.

I was taught invaluable lessons on those mean streets. They were part of our continuing education in the world of urban poverty and violence.

In many ways, Hunter's Point appeared to be like everywhere else we had been, yet it was also a very different world. Most of the differences, I found, were a matter of perception. I learned that in the "hood," there is a constant fight against racial prejudice. There is a struggle to keep the children off the streets and away from drugs. This takes place in an environment of overwhelming frustration among many diverse people who are alienated from the rest of America in many ways other than by simple geography. Living there was really like one long, hot, boring, lazy afternoon—nothing to do, no place to go, and no promise of anything better in the future.

I will not forget the time I was choking on something, and I became so distraught that my father called an ambulance. It was late at night, and when my father gave our address to the person on the telephone, he was told that no ambulance would come to Hunter's Point after sundown. My father finally cleared my throat and I was fine. We never discussed what would have happened to me if he had not been successful. Another time, I recall a police car driving around our neighborhood. When the officers stopped to make a call and left their car unattended, every window was shattered. That was standard procedure. All of the police, across the board, were considered to be "the enemy." They were never looked upon as concerned individuals who could help. Hunter's Point was like a "no man's land" that was constantly under siege.

Still, Hunter's Point was my home. I would not trade my experiences there for any amount of money. We were living there when my brother Bob died in Washington, when I decided to get married, and when my father made the decision to leave San Francisco for Castroville in Monterey Bay. Many important moments in my life took place there.

Living in Hunter's Point also gave me an insight into cultures I otherwise might not have ever known. In 1991, when I saw the film *Boyz N the Hood*, I was struck by how familiar the families in the film seemed to me, even though more than thirty years had passed since I had lived in a similar place.

Whenever I hear or read about inner-city crime, drugs, and gangs, I filter it through my own experiences at Hunter's Point. Although communities such as Hunter's Point have tremendous problems, they also have strengths that few outsiders ever recognize or acknowledge. The women are especially strong. Each day, they face daunting problems as they struggle just to survive. They are mothers not only of their own children but of the entire community. Poverty is not just a word to describe a social condition, it is the hard reality of everyday life. It takes a certain tenacity, a toughness, to continue on when there is an ever-present worry about whether the old car will work, and if it does, whether there will be gas money; digging through piles of old clothes at St. Vincent de Paul's to find clothing for the children to wear to school without being ridiculed; wondering if there will be enough to eat. But always, there is hope that the children will receive a good education and have a better life.

> *There are tens of millions of Americans who are beyond the welfare state. Taken as a whole there is a culture of poverty . . . bad health, poor housing, low levels of aspiration and high levels of mental distress.*
>
> Michael Harrington
> The Culture of Poverty, 1962

By the time we moved to Hunter's Point, in 1960, my father had left the rope factory and was working as a longshoreman on the docks. He began to augment his income by playing poker. People used to come to our house for big poker games that lasted well into the night. Before they left, my dad usually had picked up a little money. He had a lot of confidence. That was important. Some of those who played cards with him were men he worked with, but many were other native people he had met at the San Francisco Indian Center.

Located upstairs in an old frame building on Sixteenth Street on the edge of the very rough and tough Mission District, the Indian Center became a sanctuary for me. It was my safe place for many years. At last, the mythical Rabbit had finally found a hollow stump the Wolves were not able to penetrate.

In many ways, the Indian Center became even more important to me than the junior high and various high schools I attended. During my teen years, I transferred from an inner-city school dominated by violence to another public high school with a predominantly Asian student body, because it offered a calmer atmosphere. However, changing schools did not help me very much. I had made some headway in gaining self-esteem, but like many teens, I remained unsettled as far as goals, with no sense of direction. I was not sure what I wanted to do once I finished school and had to make my own way in the world. But a moody and self-absorbed teenager could count on one thing—at the end of the day, everything seemed brighter at the Indian Center. For me, it became an oasis where I could share my feelings and frustrations with kids from similar backgrounds.

There was something at the center for everyone. It was a safe place to go, even if we only wanted to hang out or watch television. For the younger children, the center provided socialization with other native people through organized events such as picnics and supervised outings. Older kids went there for dances, sports programs, and an occasional chance to work behind the snack bar to earn a little money. Adults played bingo, took part in intertribal powwows and, most important, discussed pertinent issues and concerns with other BIA relocatees from all across the country. We would jump on a city bus and head for the Indian Center the way some kids today flock to shopping malls.

The Indian Center was important to everyone in my family, including my father. Always a determined person who stuck to his principles, even if they turned out to be lost causes, Dad ultimately quit working as a longshoreman to become a shop steward and union organizer with a spice company based in San Francisco. Besides his union activities, he also became more involved with projects at the Indian Center. For instance, when the question arose about the need for a free health clinic for Indians living in the Bay area, he rallied the forces at the Indian Center to get behind the issue. In an effort to heighten public awareness, he appeared on a television panel discussion about the urban clinic. Perhaps at that time, he influenced my life in ways I could not imagine then.

When he believed in something, he worked around the clock to get the job done. He was always dragging home somebody he had met, someone who was down on his luck and needed a meal and a place to stay. It was a tight fit, but we made room. My dad never gave up on people. I think my father's tenacity is a characteristic I inherited. Once I set my mind to do something, I never give up. I was raised in a household where no one ever said to me, "You can't do this because you're a woman, Indian, or poor." No one told me there were limitations. Of course, I would not have listened to them if they had tried.

The exception would have been my father. I always listened to him, even if I did not agree with what he had to say. From the time I was a little girl, we discussed all the topics of the day. Our very best debates concerned politics. Sometimes those conversations would get a bit heated. After my political awakening as a teenager, I became aligned with the party of Franklin Roosevelt, Harry Truman, and a rising young star of the sixties—John F. Kennedy. My father, on the other hand, was a registered Republican, which was not unusual among older members of the Five Tribes, especially the Cherokees. Folks who know our people's past can usually figure out why so many of the older Cherokees belonged to the Republican party. The story goes that a historian once asked an Oklahoma Cherokee why so few of the old-timers became Democrats. The Cherokee supposedly replied, "Do you think we would help the party that damned ol' Andy Jackson belonged to?" For the elders, the choice was obvious—Republicans were the lesser of two evils.

Despite our political differences, my father and I enjoyed our discussions, and especially our time spent at the Indian Center. Throughout the sixties, my entire family considered the Indian Center to be a stronghold. At the center, we could talk to other native people about shared problems and frustrations. Many families we met there were like us. They had come to the realization that the BIA's promises were empty. We all seemed to have reached that same terrible conclusion—the government's relocation program was a disaster that robbed us of our vitality and sense of place. That is why the Indian Center was so immensely important. It was always there for us. It was a constant. During the turmoil and anguish of the 1960s, it was where we turned.

In 1960, when my brother Robert was killed, we went to the Indian Center for solace. Bob was only twenty years old when he died. He had joined the National Guard, boxed a little bit, and worked at various odd jobs. He did not seem to have any real plans. My dad wanted him to settle down and find steady employment. But Bob was restless. He and his pal, Louie Cole, a quarter Choctaw, decided to leave the city. Louie was nineteen, and I thought of him as my first real boyfriend. He and my brother took off one morning, intent on making money for a grubstake. Then they planned to go off on their great adventure and discover the rest of the country.

Bob and Louie had been gone for two or three weeks and were up the coast in Washington state when they found work as apple pickers. The boys lived in sharecroppers' cabins near the orchards. When they got up early in the morning, it was still cold and dark outside, so they would start a fire in a wood stove using a little kerosene to get the flames going. One morning, my brother was still groggy with sleep when he lit the fire. Instead of the kerosene, he mistakenly picked up a can of gasoline. The cabin exploded in flames. The door was locked with a dead bolt, so by the time the boys got outside, they were severely burned. Louie was burned over much of his body, but Bob was in far worse condition.

My parents, my brother Don and my oldest sister, Frieda, who still lived in Oklahoma, went to Washington to be with Bob. The doctor told them that if Bob lived for seven days, he would probably survive. Among Cherokees, the number seven is considered sacred. We have seven clans, our sacred fire is kindled from seven types of wood, and there are seven directions—north, south, east, west, up, down, and "where one is at." We thought maybe the seven days would bring luck to Bob.

Attractive and charming, Bob always had been the best looking of all of us. He was tall and athletic, a happy-go-lucky type. I looked up to my big brother Don, but for my carefree role model, I had Bob. I think all of us wondered what his life would be like if he survived. It was clear that he would never be the same.

When it seemed that there was a slim chance Bob might pull through, my father, who had to return to his job, left my mother in Washington to stay with Bob through his long recovery. But as it turned out, Bob could not be saved. He lived for seven days and no more. On the seventh day, he died. I am not so sure the number failed him.

When they brought him home to California, he was buried at Oakdale, a community on the Stanislaus River not far from my grandmother's place. Bob's death stunned all of us. It left me in a state of shock. I cannot remember who told me that Bob had died. Probably it was one of my older sisters. All I know is, I just stood there and screamed. I screamed as loud as I could, hoping that my screams would drown out those awful words I did not want to hear. I was fifteen years old, and the loss of Bob was the closest I had ever been to death up to that point.

My parents, of course, were devastated. The loss of a child is the worst kind of death experience. You never expect to outlive your offspring. But after that tragic event, something very good happened to our family. My mother, who was forty years old, became pregnant the same month my brother Bob died. Everyone was quite surprised. Nine months later, my brother William was born. No one can take someone else's place, but after losing Bob as we had, all of us were happy when Bill arrived.

Louie Cole remained hospitalized in Washington for several months before he was allowed to return to California. He lived near Riverbank, where I had first met him when I stayed with my grandmother. We stayed in touch after he came home to recover, but we were never girlfriend and boyfriend again. Every so often, we wrote to each other, and then finally that stopped.

Many years later, long after I had come home to Oklahoma and had became involved in tribal politics, Louie came to visit me. He had been married several times, and he still collected disability because of the injuries he had received in that fire so many years before. I was not totally comfortable seeing Louie again. There was something brooding about him, and he wanted only to focus on the past, especially the bad times. About a year after his visit, I received a letter from Louie's mother informing me that he had been shot and killed by one of his former wives during a quarrel.

Louie was my first boyfriend, but it was not as if I had a whole string of them. In fact, I was basically shy with boys. However, I did meet several young men at the Indian Center who interested me. One of them was Ray Billy. I was about sixteen when I started to date him. He was Pomo, a California tribe, and was a little older than I was. He had his own apartment. I dated him for about a year. My dad liked him, and that counted for something. Occasionally, Ray got the use of a car, and he would come to our house at Hunter's Point and ask my dad if he could take me for a ride. Other times, my dad let us go for rides in our family car. Everyone liked Ray. He was a gentleman—most of the time.

He was also crafty, and I had to watch my step. One night we were down on the beach. I was getting cold, so he suggested that we go to his place to get a jacket and warm up. It was a classic trick, and I almost fell for it! When we got to his apartment, he said he was tired and we ought to rest on his bed for a while. I came to my senses. I put my foot down and would not cooperate. He thought I was stupid for reacting as I did. A short time later, he dropped me for a girl who had just been crowned Miss Indian San Francisco, or some such title. Ray and I did not see each other again. I was hurt by his treatment, but I pulled through. I learned that most first crushes—even second or third crushes—can be survived.

Friends and family helped me mend my broken heart and get over Ray Billy. Our music was also a big help. My girlfriends and I listened to rock and roll and to soul music. "Hit the Road, Jack" and "I Found my Thrill on Blueberry Hill" were popular then. We listened to two soul stations, KDIA and KSAN. We dreamed of the time we would be out of school and free.

Most of the time, I was only going through the motions of attending classes. I was never much of a scholar, and I do not have many memories from my years in high school. Those I do have are not of much consequence. My grades ranged from A to F, depending on the subject and my level of interest. Science and math were my downfalls, but I had an affinity for English and literature courses. None of my teachers left enough impact for me even to remember their names. I was not much of a joiner. I did not go in for glee club or the yearbook staff or sports or any of the organizations except Junior Achievement. I did participate in that for a while, and I liked it.

Mostly, I went to the Indian Center. That is still my best teenage memory. Much more was going on at the center besides pingpong games and dance parties. It was the early 1960s, and change was in the air. A person could almost touch it. During that time, many people, including my friends and siblings and I, were aware of the currents of restlessness.

The new decade promised to be a time of momentous social movements and open rebellion. There would be sweeping legislation and great achievements, as well as devastating war and senseless tragedies.

Even before the 1960s, the entire Bay area had become a magnet for artists and rebels who were ready and willing to act as the merchants of change. Now a new generation was getting its voice, testing its wings. I was part of that generation. San Francisco was the place to be. We were ready to proceed with the decade and with our lives.

INDIAN TERRITORY

At the time of creation, an ulunsuti, or crystal, was given to the white man, and a piece of silver to the Indian. But the white man despised the crystal and threw it away, while the Indian did the same with the silver. In going about, the white man afterward found the silver piece and put it in his pocket and has prized it ever since. The Indian, in like manner, found the crystal where the white man had thrown it. He picked it up and has kept it since as his talisman, just as money is the talismanic power of the white man.

In the 1960s, a multitude of people—ranging from intellectual dissidents and civil-rights advocates to antiestablishment ideologists and rebel youths—decided it was time for the United States to amend its ways. The kind of stormy societal dislocation and cultural transition that occurred during that period was not at all new to Native Americans. We had been looking for the balance to return for a very long time. Some of us had just about given up hope.

Tribal people were not novices when it came to the difficult process of modifying our lives. Whether the situation called for compliance or, more rarely, aggressive behavior, we were accustomed to making adjustments and concessions. Our ability to adapt had become an effective survival technique ever since the whites first forced themselves on native tribes. That adaptability continued as the federal government instigated an endless string of treaties and promises that were never honored.

> As long as the moon shall rise,
> As long as the rivers shall flow,
> As long as the sun shall shine,
> As long as the grass shall grow.
>
> Common expression for terms of
> treaties with Native Americans

The troubles of the Cherokee Nation did not end when our people arrived in Indian Territory in the late 1830s. In many ways, the real ordeal was just beginning. There were Cherokees who survived the hardships of the journey only to be stricken with disease. Some reports from those times speak of thousands of Trail of Tears survivors dying from illness, or complications related to the removal, before the end of the first year in their new homeland. But perhaps one of the worst problems of all was internal strife.

Jealousies and bitterness surfaced among three distinct Cherokee groups then residing in Indian Territory. There were the Arkansas Cherokees, or Old Settlers, made up of people who, prior to the Treaty of 1835, had voluntarily moved to the lands west of the Mississippi, and who later moved to Indian Territory under a regularly established form of government all their own. Next was the Treaty or Ridge Party, that portion of the Cherokee Nation led by Major Ridge, John Ridge, Elias Boudinot, Stand Watie, and others who had encouraged and approved the Treaty of New Echota of 1835. Finally came the Ross Party, composed of the majority of Cherokees who followed John Ross, who had been such a vehement opponent of the 1835 treaty. Given the disparity of these three groups, a confrontation was unavoidable.

After the last of the Cherokee immigrants arrived in Indian Territory, the Ross Party insisted that all tribal members adopt a new system of government and code of laws to regulate the entire nation. But the Old Settlers and the Treaty Party joined forces in disagreement, claiming that they had already established a suitable government. Although this faction was outnumbered almost three to one by the Ross Party, the new alliance insisted that the Old Settlers continue to rule, at least until the autumn of 1839, when a general election to select a new tribal legislature would be held. About six thousand Cherokees representing all sides met beginning on June 10, 1839, at Ta-ka-to-ka. After almost twelve days of heated debate, none of the parties budged. No agreement was reached.

On June 22, immediately after adjournment of the tribal meeting, the three most prominent leaders of the Treaty Party—Major Ridge, John Ridge, and Elias Boudinot—were killed in separate attacks. It was at once evident that they had been slain, in part, for their roles in the treaty negotiations that had led to the Trail of Tears.

The slayings sent tremors across Cherokee country. John Ridge had been seized at his residence by a swarm of armed men. They dragged him outside, where his terrified family was forced to watch as he was repeatedly stabbed and his throat slashed. A few hours later and forty miles from the scene of his son's murder, Major Ridge was shot in an ambush while riding horseback not far from the Arkansas line. Struck by at least five rifle shots, Ridge fell to the ground and was trampled by his rearing horse. The unsuspecting Boudinot was stabbed and his brains were bludgeoned by a band of killers wielding Bowie knives and tomahawks who came to his Park Hill home under the pretense of seeking medicine.

The unknown assassins reportedly were sympathetic to the Ross Party. It was said that the men who acted as executioners drew lots after agreeing that Ross was never to know anything about their mission. Friends of the principal chief, fearing reprisal, immediately rallied to his protection and posted a volunteer guard of six hundred armed tribesmen to patrol the countryside surrounding the Ross residence.

Ross, a man of peace and intellect, vehemently denied any knowledge of the murders. His supporters pointed to a Cherokee Nation law dating from preremoval days, drafted by John Ridge and passed by the National Council in 1829. The statute called for the penalty of death to be applied against any Cherokee convicted of having agreed to the exchange or sale of tribal property. To many Cherokees, the slayings of the three men were their just and proper punishments. It was blood revenge in accordance with the customs of the tribe.

Shortly after the deaths of the Ridges and Boudinot, the National Council passed decrees posthumously designating the three men and their allies as outlaws. The council also ruled that the slayers were guiltless of murder, and absolved them of any criminal acts.

Stand Watie, the younger brother of Boudinot, had also been targeted by the assassins for his support of the New Echota Treaty. But Watie was warned of the execution plot by the Reverend Samuel Worcester, and reportedly used the missionary's sleek horse, Comet, to make his escape. Others who had signed the removal treaty also fled to the safety of the garrison at Fort Gibson, near Muskogee. Watie vowed vengeance, and continued to be a thorn in Chief Ross's side for many years to come.

Meanwhile, our tribe did its best to get on with the business of recreating a way of life that some believed was almost lost forever. On July 12, 1839, a general convention of all Cherokees met in Indian Territory to pass a momentous act which stated, "We, the people comprising the Eastern and Western Cherokee Nation, in National Convention assembled, by virtue of our original and unalienable rights, do hereby solemnly and mutually agree to form ourselves into one body politic, under the style and title of the Cherokee Nation."

Less than two months later, a national convention convened at the settlement of Tahlequah in Indian Territory. The first order of business was to make Tahlequah the new Cherokee Nation capital. Next, the convention promptly adopted the new tribal constitution, which was similar to the old document. It provided for three branches of government; affirmed the Cherokee practice of holding property in common, although individuals owned improvements; and stipulated that anyone who moved out of the Cherokee Nation gave up all rights to be a Cherokee. There were more conflicts among the various factions, but by 1840, the new constitution had been accepted by many of the Old Settlers. Except for the small band of Cherokees left in the mountains of North Carolina, most of our people were reunited under our own constitution and laws, with John Ross remaining as principal chief.

Even though Ross and his followers were in power and a new constitution was in place, political strife and general unrest continued among the various factions in our tribe. Too many differences and old grudges remained. Many of those who adhered to the Treaty Party or the Old Settlers could not accept Ross as chief of the entire Cherokee Nation.

For several years, the threat of civil war hung over our people like a deadly fog. Armed bands representing all the alliances roamed the countryside. Often, the internal chaos resulted in more assassinations and other acts of violence. Among our people and others outside the Cherokee Nation, this time was known as "the reign of terror." Some Cherokees, such as Tom Starr and his kinsmen, became little more than outlaws as they menaced the nation until the gang's leaders were killed. In 1845 and 1846 alone, at least thirty-four politically related murders were committed in the Cherokee Nation. By then, there was so much bloodshed that many Cherokees, particularly those who remained loyal to Stand Watie and the Treaty Party, left Indian Territory to seek refuge in Arkansas.

From 1841 to 1846, Chief Ross spent much of his time in Washington, attempting to rectify interpretations of the various pacts between our people and the federal government, including the New Echota Treaty. Old Settler and Treaty Party delegations also went to the capital, pressing their case for a division of the tribe. They presented their views to federal commissioners representing the administration of President James K. Polk. After much debate among all the parties, articles were drafted for yet another treaty.

The Treaty of 1846 provided for a unified Cherokee Nation by healing some of the factional wounds that had plagued our tribe for so many years. The treaty was a compromise. Chief Ross agreed to recognize the New Echota Treaty, and the Old Settlers acknowledged that the Ross Party had rights to land in Indian Territory. Conflicting financial claims and reimbursements were adjusted, and a general amnesty was proclaimed for all past offenses committed within the Cherokee Nation.

> *I have entered into this treaty of amnesty in all sincerity; I intend to be peaceable, and have no doubt that others who have less to forgive will follow the example which the leaders have set.*
>
> Stand Watie, August 1846

Despite the bickering and conflict within the tribe in the 1840s, our people also took positive steps toward building a new society and advancing cultural achievements. It was a remarkable period for the Cherokees, as several of our old institutions were rejuvenated.

A national printing press was established at Tahlequah. The first issue of our revived tribal newspaper, called the *Cherokee Advocate*, appeared on September 26, 1844, making it the first newspaper published in what is now Oklahoma. Like the *Cherokee Phoenix* before it, all of the *Advocate's* columns were printed in Cherokee and English. The newspaper's first editor was William Potter Ross, a graduate of Princeton University and a nephew of Chief John Ross.

Under the editorship of W. P. Ross, the *Cherokee Advocate* published news of other native tribes as well as editorials about internal concerns within our own nation. The newspaper's motto—"Our Rights, Our Country, Our Race"—summed up the Cherokee people's spirit of pride and nationalism. But critics, including angry and defiant Stand Watie, labeled the bilingual newspaper as nothing but a propaganda tool for the editor's uncle and the views of the Ross Party.

> *The great mass of the Cherokees remained uncorrupted and incorruptible. But some were changed by glittering silver, some became drunkards, some idlers, and others were seduced from the path of virtue and innocence. From among those last enumerated, may be found some of those depraved but unfortunate beings, who, while indulging the habits and vices imbibed from the whites, commit the crimes that are occurring in our country.*
>
> Cherokee Advocate, *May 1, 1845*

Besides reestablishment of a national press, other periodicals were launched in Indian Territory, such as the *Cherokee Messenger*, printed by the Park Hill Mission Press under the guidance of the Reverend Samuel Worcester, who had moved with our people from our eastern homelands to the West. The steadfast Worcester, who died in 1859 after spending thirty-five years as a missionary among our people, used the mission press to publish and distribute such books and pamphlets as *Treatise on Marriage, Cherokee Hymns,* and *Cherokee Primer.* At the same time, he led a temperance crusade built around what he called his "Cold Water Army," made up of Cherokees whom he had convinced to sign pledges against strong drink.

Our people also made education a high priority during those years. A public school system for the tribe had been established in 1841. Within only a few years, as many as eighteen schools were functioning within the Cherokee Nation. Through the hard work of John Ross, two exceptional seminaries, or preparatory schools, for young Cherokee scholars were in operation by May of 1851—the Cherokee National Male Seminary near Tahlequah, and the Cherokee National Female Seminary at Park Hill.

The establishment of a school exclusively for Cherokee women was thought of as quite radical because most white Americans at that time regarded females as intellectually subordinate to men. Generally, nineteenth-century women were afforded few, if any, educational opportunities. Our women's seminary was modeled after Mount Holyoke Female Seminary, today's Mount Holyoke College, in South Hadley, Massachusetts. Chartered in 1835, Mount Holyoke was the oldest institution for the higher education of women in the United States. It was considered one of the most progressive schools in the nation, and it set a superb standard for our people to follow. Mary Lyon, founder of Mount Holyoke, helped to devise the curriculum at the Cherokee seminary and sent graduates of her college to Indian Territory to serve as some of our first teachers.

Built of native brick, both of the stately seminaries were supported financially by the Cherokee Nation, with students paying only a modest annual fee to cover room and board and the cost of textbooks. After completing four years of training at the seminaries, which included courses in several languages, philosophy, astronomy, and logic, young Cherokee men and women with academic promise were sent to colleges in the East for further study. Many of them returned to Indian Territory to work as teachers, lawyers, ministers, and physicians. In 1852, the *Cherokee Advocate* boasted that "the number of adults in the Cherokee Nation not able to read or write may be counted on your fingers."

In the 1850s, the Cherokee Nation enjoyed an era of revitalization throughout their domain in Indian Territory. Cherokee wealth, particularly among the mixed-blood aristocracy, also increased because of successful farms and livestock operations, which were kept running in some instances by the continued and quite despicable use of black slaves. I have tried to find some comfort in the knowledge that only a tiny fraction of Cherokee families owned slaves, but I cannot. The truth is that the practice of slavery will forever cast a shadow on the great Cherokee Nation. It is no wonder that during that same time, the role of women in the Cherokee Nation was also diminished.

That was a period of prosperity for the Cherokees. The overall economic future of the Cherokee Nation seemed even brighter. But that golden era was about to be shattered in 1861, with the outbreak of the Civil War. It was one of the darkest chapters in the history of the Cherokees.

It was not surprising that some Cherokees, like the other tribes that had been removed from the southern states, were sympathetic to the Confederate cause. But even as the clouds of war gathered, it became obvious that support for the Confederacy was not unanimous throughout the Cherokee Nation. Our loyalties most definitely were divided.

The old Treaty or Ridge Party, headed by Stand Watie and supported by secret secession organizations such as the Blue Lodge and the Knights of the Golden Circle, chose the Confederate side. In full support of slavery and ever loyal to the South, the Treaty Party forces perceived the coming war as a prime opportunity to topple the regime of John Ross. Pro-Confederacy Cherokees were opposed by a large number of full-bloods and traditionalists who favored the abolition of slavery. That did not mean that all of them were prepared to fight for the Union. Even some of the Cherokee slave owners such as John Ross, who grew wealthy by the sweat of his own slave force, leaned toward the North, yet did not wish to get involved in the coming conflict.

On the one hand, the Ross coalition could not rationalize taking up arms in support of ruthless southerners who had demanded the Cherokee removal. Many of the whites in the South who were clamoring for war were some of the same ones who had forced our tribe to give up sacred land that would forever hold our ancestors' bones. Although the federal government had not always been equitable and had treated all Native Americans harshly, the transgressions of the South were equally difficult to forgive. Instead of choosing sides, Ross and his followers opted for neutrality—at least, at first.

> *Our locality and situation ally us to the South, while to the North we are indebted for a defense of our rights in the past and that enlarged benevolence to which we owe our progress in civilization.*
>
> Chief John Ross, 1861

To counterbalance the Knights of the Golden Circle and other mixed-bloods who had assumed a pro-Confederate stance, Ross counted on the support of a very old secret society whose members were pledged to defend Cherokee autonomy. In English, this highly patriotic group was called the Keetoowah Society, from the name Kituhwa, an ancient town in the old Cherokee Nation which at one time had formed the nucleus of the most conservative element of our tribe. Shortly before the Civil War, the Keetoowah Society resurfaced in the Cherokee Nation West, possibly encouraged by Evan and John B. Jones, a Baptist missionary father and son. Keetoowah Society members hoped not only to cultivate national pride, but also to counteract the influence of the wealthier slaveholding class of the Cherokees.

Ross and his loyal followers soon found it was impossible to straddle the fence for very long. Almost fifteen years of relative peace and tranquillity for the Cherokees was about to come to a close. Confederate artillery opened fire on Fort Sumter in Charleston harbor at 4:40 A.M. on April 12, 1861, and the Union garrison surrendered the next day. The Civil War had begun. Indian Territory would become embroiled in the struggle, and in the Cherokee Nation, the old wounds of factional animosity would be torn open. The loss of a great deal of property, livestock, and possessions and, more important, thousands of lives from both sides would soon prove inevitable. As with most wars, few survivors would think the cost worth it—especially the widows and orphans.

From the start, the Confederacy was interested in Indian Territory and the native people who resided there. General Albert Pike of Arkansas, commissioner for the Confederate states, visited Indian Territory in an effort to enlist the services of several tribes. Pike conferred with the Treaty Party leaders, and urged Ross to reconsider the Cherokees' position of neutrality and join in the fray. At last, the pressure was too great for Ross to resist.

Union troops had been withdrawn from the forts in Indian Territory. Lacking the protection he requested from the federal government, Ross reluctantly decided to sign a treaty with the Confederates. On October 7, 1861, the treaty was concluded at Tahlequah, joining the Cherokees with the Confederacy. The Creeks, Choctaws, Chickasaws, Seminoles, Osages, Comanches, and several smaller tribes had already aligned with the Confederates.

Two Cherokee regiments raised as militia to guard the Cherokee Nation were placed in Confederate service under the command of Stand Watie and Colonel John Drew, a Cherokee. Cherokee soldiers, including some recalcitrant full-bloods, carried the Confederate banner at several skirmishes and engagements in Indian Territory and elsewhere. They were part of the forces gathered for the Battle of Pea Ridge, fought on March 7–8, 1862, in northwestern Arkansas, regarded as the most decisive battle in the state. The Confederate forces at Pea Ridge were soundly defeated, limiting their ability to protect neighboring Indian Territory from a Union invasion. Union forces later swept into the Cherokee capital of Tahlequah.

The Ross faction, especially the full-bloods who had joined with the Confederates only under great duress, saw Pea Ridge as a turning point. It gave them an opportunity to separate themselves from Watie and his mixed-blood rebels, as some Cherokees already had done in late 1861.

During the war, Cherokees fought Cherokees. Some of those on the Union side were members of the Keetoowah Society. They also became known as the "Pins" or "Pin Indians" because of their insignia of two crossed pins worn under the lapels of their coats and hunting shirts. Pins also had other secret signs, including the custom of touching their hats as a salutation when they encountered other society members. At night when two Pins met, one would ask the other, "Who are you?" The reply was, "Tahlequah—who are you?" The proper response was, "I am Keetoowah's son." Among our people, it was also known that Pins who had rebelled against the Confederacy and had fought for the North tied strips of split corn husk in their hair before they went into battle.

Unafraid and thoroughly convinced that slavery must end, the Pins repeatedly clashed with Watie and his Confederate Cherokees and Creeks. Pin Indians attacked and burned the homes of southern sympathizers in the Cherokee Nation, and the Watie supporters retaliated with raids on the Unionist faithful. Thousands of fugitive Cherokees and other native people fled to Kansas, where they were cared for—although poorly—by the federal government. Hundreds of Indian refugees died in Kansas during the first winter of the war.

Meanwhile, Chief Ross, whose heart had never been with the southern cause, revealed his true feelings when he welcomed the Union troops as they entered Indian Territory in 1862. He then left under protective custody. The aging chief spent the remaining war years shuttling between Philadelphia and Washington, attempting to convince the Lincoln and Johnson administrations that the Cherokees had been coerced into signing the Confederate treaty.

In February of 1863, the Cherokee National Council, meeting at Cowskin Prairie in the Cherokee Nation, passed bills to abolish slavery in the Cherokee Nation and to abrogate the Confederate treaty. Ross, in the East, forwarded the document to federal officials. The National Council's action came nearly six weeks after Lincoln's Emancipation Proclamation had gone into effect.

When Ross had departed for the East, Stand Watie saw his chance and declared himself the new principal chief of the Cherokees. But the majority of our people refused to recognize Watie or his government, even as he removed others from political office and passed a law drafting men into the service of the Confederacy. Cherokees who still wished to remain neutral were forced to go into hiding to escape fighting for something they opposed. Those households left unprotected were easy prey for raiders from all factions, including Confederate forces led by Watie, who by 1864 had been promoted to brigadier general. That made him the only Native American to achieve the rank of general in the Civil War.

Despite the promotion, Watie had become more cynical, even about the Confederacy. In describing the Confederate government's promised protection of Indian Territory, he labeled the effort as "a useless and expensive pageant." Nevertheless, Watie and his men fought on.

> *I believe it is in the power of the Indians unassisted, but united and determined, to hold their country. We cannot expect to do this without serious losses and many trials and privations; but if we possess the spirit of our fathers, and are resolved never to be enslaved by an inferior race, and trodden under the feet of an ignorant and insolent foe, we, the Creeks, Choctaws, Chickasaws, Seminoles, and Cherokees, never can be conquered by the Kansas jayhawkers, renegade Indians, and runaway Negroes.*
>
> General Stand Watie, 1864

Watie's troops harassed Union relief columns and supply trains. The Pins and their northern allies struck back. Old feuds and past troubles returned to haunt our people. Many innocent victims were caught in the cross fire. In only a few terrible years, nearly two decades of prosperity for the Cherokees were swept away by vicious guerrilla fighting.

The Civil War officially ended on April 9, 1865, when General Robert E. Lee surrendered his Confederate army to Union General Ulysses Grant at Appomattox, Virginia. Confederate President Jefferson Davis, who hoped to continue the war west of the Mississippi, fled in an effort to avoid capture. He was taken prisoner on May 10 in Georgia, and by month's end, the scattered remnants of Confederate forces had given up.

However, the Confederate Cherokees led by General Stand Watie continued to wage war until late June. Then they finally laid down their arms, making Watie the last Confederate general to surrender. Many Cherokees gave thanks that at last the nightmare was over.

The Civil War left the Cherokee Nation devastated. Losses in livestock alone were estimated at more than three hundred thousand head slaughtered or driven off. Schools, churches, and public buildings had been torched. Libraries had been destroyed and homes burned to the ground, including the residence of John Ross at Park Hill. By the close of the war, seven thousand Cherokees—at least one-quarter of the tribal population—had lost their lives. So many of our people died that one of the main priorities became the construction of an orphanage. Our frontier homeland was in ashes.

The United States, however, was apparently not satisfied that the Cherokee Nation and the other members of the Five Tribes had suffered enough. The tribes' association with the Confederacy provided a convenient excuse for whites to take more land as a penalty for secession.

This became clear in September of 1865, when the federal government summoned delegates from the Five Tribes and several other tribes to a conference in Fort Smith, Arkansas, with representatives sent by President Andrew Johnson, in office less than five months since Lincoln's tragic death. Johnson would go down in history as one the country's worst chief executives. Not many Native Americans would argue otherwise.

> If the savage resists, civilization, with the Ten Commandments in one hand and the sword in the other, demands his immediate extermination.
>
> President Andrew Johnson
> Message to Congress, 1867

At the start of the thirteen-day Fort Smith council, the federal commissioners stated that because the Five Tribes had violated their treaties by siding with the Confederates, they also had forfeited all of their rights. They were at the mercy of the federal government. All Indian delegates were given a list of stipulations, and instructions that each of the tribes must enter into a treaty for permanent peace with the United States. The drafting of those stringent Reconstruction treaties had a dramatic effect on the five Native American republics in Indian Territory.

Provisions of the treaties with the Five Tribes stipulated that the government would begin to relocate other tribes, especially Plains Indians, throughout the western half of Indian Territory. Unlike the Five Tribes, the newcomers would be placed on federal reservations, not to be considered as independent nations.

The Cherokee treaty was completed in Washington, D.C., on July 19, 1866. By terms of the pact, the Cherokee Nation was "brought back under the protection of the United States." The treaty officially abolished slavery. All former slaves, or freedman, residing in the Cherokee Nation were granted tribal citizenship.

Our people had to give up eight hundred thousand acres in Kansas, called the Neutral Lands, that were coveted by white settlers. We also had to grant rights-of-way to railway companies so they could begin construction of rail lines across the Cherokee Nation. The United States informed us that, with our permission, they could move other Indians onto our land. Within a few years, nearly a thousand Delawares from northern Kansas and more than seven hundred Shawnees, also from Kansas, were relocated in our country and became Cherokee citizens under that provision of the treaty.

On August 1, 1866—ten days before the Cherokee treaty was ratified—John Ross died in Washington, D.C. He passed away peacefully, fully aware at the very end of his life that yet another treaty had been consummated between his beloved people and the federal government.

Ross, dignified and stubborn to the end, was seventy-five years of age. Fifty-seven of those years had been given to the service of the Cherokee Nation, with nearly forty years as the officially recognized principal chief of the Cherokees. He was buried in Delaware, but in 1867, his body was brought back to Indian Territory, where he was laid to rest at Ross Cemetery near Park Hill. In his honor, one of the nine districts of the Cherokee Nation was given his Indian name, Cooweescoowee.

> *I am an old man, and have served my people and the Govt of the United States a long time, over fifty years. My people have kept me in the harness, not of my seeking, but of their own choice. I have never deceived them, and now I look back, not one act of my public life rises up to upbraid me. I have done the best I could, and today, upon this bed of sickness, my heart approves all I have done. And still I am, John Ross, the same John Ross of former years, unchanged.*
>
> Chief John Ross, April 3, 1866

Stand Watie, longtime foe of Ross, outlived him by only a few years. Watie, forever respected by some of our people for his bravery as a warrior under fire, died in 1871. By that time, younger leaders had emerged to guide the Cherokee Nation through the balance of the nineteenth century and beyond.

After Ross's death, his nephew William P. Ross, first editor of the *Cherokee Advocate*, was chosen to fill the unexpired term as principal chief. In 1867, Lewis Downing, formerly a lieutenant colonel in the Union army and the assistant principal chief, took the reins of the tribe. During his years as chief, Downing and his followers successfully realigned old political factions, and united the former Ross Party and the southern Cherokees in a new organization that focused on the increasing demands for the opening of Indian Territory to white settlement. Known as the Downing Party, this group came to dominate Cherokee politics for many years.

In 1871, during Downing's second term as principal chief, the seal of the Cherokee Nation was adopted by the National Council to commemorate the unification conference held in 1839. In the seal's center, the mystic seven-pointed star symbolizes the sacred number of our people and the seven matrilineal clans in our ancient tribal tradition. The wreath of oak leaves, surrounded by the name of the Cherokee Nation in English and Cherokee, signifies strength and everlasting life. Oak is significant because it is used for the sacred fire kept perpetually burning. For our people then and now, the seal is a symbol of great promise.

After Downing's death in 1872, W. P. Ross again assumed the role of principal chief, until 1875. Although he served in other political offices until his death in 1891, the Ross dynasty in the Cherokee Nation had come to an end. The Downing Party was reorganized in the late 1880s, and from that time until the United States greatly diminished the Cherokee government in 1907, almost all of the principal chiefs of the Cherokee Nation came from the Downing Party.

As Reconstruction came to an end, our people recovered from the catastrophic effects of war and started to prosper once again. Herds of livestock were replenished, and thousands of acres of crops were cultivated and fenced. New homes and stores appeared in many of the Cherokee communities scattered across the hills of Indian Territory. Schools were restored. Our capital of Tahlequah became a popular mecca for cultural and educational activities.

In 1870, the *Cherokee Advocate*, which had been suspended in the late 1850s, resumed publication. Our citizens did not feel cut off from the outside world. The railroad began to lay tracks across our tribal territory. The first line was the Missouri-Kansas-Texas system, better known as the

"Katy." By 1872, its rails followed the old Texas Road and ran the length of Indian Territory across the Red River into Texas. Train tracks soon crisscrossed the prairies, linking our people with the rest of the continent. Towns sprang up along the railroad lines. Although the coming of rail service meant more rapid economic growth for some Cherokees, the railroads also gobbled up much of our people's land through the right of eminent domain.

Besides losing valuable property to rail construction, our people knew the trains would bring more land-hungry homesteaders and squatters. So did the cattle trails running north and south across our land, when Texas cattlemen began to drive their herds to the railroad towns in Kansas. Tribal leaders kept a wary eye as a steady flow of rambunctious cowboys, renegades, drifters, whiskey peddlers, prostitutes, gamblers, and con artists drifted into Indian Territory. Undesirables of every type regarded Indian Territory as a paradise on earth because tribal courts had no jurisdiction over any of the whites crowding onto our lands.

> *It is sickening to the heart to contemplate the increase of crime in the Indian country . . . if crime continues to increase there so fast, a regiment of deputy marshals cannot arrest all the murderers.*
>
> Fort Smith, Arkansas,
> newspaper editorial, 1873

Finally, in 1875, the federal government named Isaac Charles Parker as the new judge on the federal bench in Fort Smith, just one hundred yards east of the Indian Territory line. A stickler for meting out justice, Parker was determined to restore peace to Indian Territory, which was under his jurisdiction. After giving them a good dose of Scripture reading, Parker sent dozens of condemned killers, robbers, and rapists to the gallows, presided over by a dour Bavarian hangman named George Maledon.

During the twenty years Parker presided at Fort Smith, his reputation spread far and wide. Outlaws and law-abiding citizens called him "the hanging judge," a moniker he detested. Parker appointed two hundred deputy marshals. The federal government would not allow Indians to exercise jurisdiction over whites, even on our own land. The tough lawmen dispatched by Parker had a thankless mission, trying to patrol an area the size of New England. They called themselves the "men who rode for Parker." Although the ground they tried to cover was mostly wooded hills and was much too large for effective law enforcement, they helped to diminish the criminal activity that raged in Indian Territory for many years.

Although felons and fugitives from justice abounded in hideouts and haunts throughout the territory, our people used their remarkable recuperative powers to make significant advances in the decades after the Civil War. Growth came at a time when the United States government not only continued, but stepped up, its policy of blatant oppression against all Native Americans. This appeared to be especially true on the Great Plains and across the mountains of the North and West, where the army worked very hard at exterminating as many native people as possible.

> *The idea that a handful of wild, half-naked, thieving, plundering, murdering savages should be dignified with the sovereign attributes of nations, enter into solemn treaties, and claim a country 500 miles wide by 1,000 miles long as theirs in fee simple, because they hunted buffalo or antelope over it, might do for beautiful reading in Cooper's novels or Longfellow's* Hiawatha, *but is unsuited to the intelligence and justice of this age, or the natural rights of mankind.*
>
> Supreme Court Decision,
> United States v. Lucero, 1869

> *My people, some of them, have run away to the hills, and have no blankets, no food; no one knows where they are—perhaps freezing to death. I want to have time to look for my children and see how many I can find. Maybe I shall find them among the dead. Hear me, my chiefs! I am tired; my heart is sick and sad. From where the sun now stands I will fight no more forever.*
>
> Chief Joseph, Nez Percé, October 7, 1877

> *We tried to run but they shot us like we were buffalo.*
>
> Louise Weasel Bear,
> survivor of Wounded Knee massacre, 1890

Despite the instability and unlawfulness in Indian Territory and beyond, the sheer number of Cherokee accomplishments in the late 1800s was staggering. Senator Henry L. Dawes, of Massachusetts, visited the Cherokee Nation in the early 1880s, and his report revealed that our people were flourishing. "The head chief told us there was not a family in that whole nation that had not a home of its own," wrote Dawes. "There was not a pauper in that nation, and the nation did not owe a dollar. It built its own capitol . . . and it built its schools and its hospitals."

Countless achievements marked the entire forty-two years between the end of the Civil War in 1865 and Oklahoma statehood in 1907. During that time, several important "firsts" took place in the Cherokee Nation. They included the establishment of our first free and compulsory public education system; the installation of the first telephone west of the Mississippi; and the graduation of more students from college than in Texas and Arkansas combined. But not everyone was impressed or understood why our people were doing so well.

> *The mental capacity of the Indian is of superior order. His perceptive faculties are remarkably developed, and his reasoning powers are not to be despised, however crude. He is thoroughly master of all branches of education necessary to the the comfort and safety of his savage life, thus giving evidence of capacity for a higher order of education. . . . And it must be conceded that the Indian behaves much better than we have any right to expect.*
>
> Colonel Richard I. Dodge, 1882

Unfortunately for the Cherokees and other native people with "reasoning powers," pejorative whites continued to look at all Indians as little more than chattel. This was especially true of inflexible military leaders and conniving politicians.

In the Cherokee Nation, our people were making great strides forward, but there were other forces at work—forces with the power and authority not only to curtail Native American progress, but also to wreck any sense of balance we might have regained. One of those forces was Senator Dawes, who had spoken in such glowing terms of the Cherokee Nation after his visit in the early 1880s. But in addition to praising our work ethic and our ability to construct homes and schools, Dawes had found flaws with the philosophy that formed the basis of our world.

"The defect of their system was apparent," noted Dawes. "They have got as far as they can go, because they own their land in common . . . and under that there is no enterprise to make your home any better than your neighbors. *There is no selfishness* [italics added], which is at the bottom of civilization. Till this people will consent to give up their lands, and divide them among their citizens so that each can own the land he cultivates, they will not make much more progress."

Dawes and his congressional allies convinced themselves that tribal ownership of land was an abysmal failure. If government officials were going to alter the native people's culture—and, more important, get to the natural wealth contained on much of the Indian lands—they had to eliminate tribal governments and tribal ownership of land. They had to abolish, eradicate at any cost, our rampant selflessness. Like many white politicians throughout history who claimed they always had native people's best interests in mind, Senator Dawes, too, had his plan. It was more like a scheme, a plot. The Dawes proposal was soon scrawled out on paper. It was destined to become federal law.

That is precisely what occurred in 1887, when President Grover Cleveland signed into law the Dawes Act, named for the senator, who had drafted the measure. Also known as the General Allotment Act, the law had as its primary aim the assimilation of all native people into white society by bringing them under federal jurisdiction and teaching them farming techniques and the values of private ownership. White proponents of the new law figured that if they could get an Indian to abandon the concept of tribal ownership, they would also be able to change his culture.

The act called for dividing the lands held in common by native people into separate parcels, with the heads of families to receive 160 acres each, or a quarter of a mile–square section. Single persons older than eighteen would be allotted eighty acres each, and all other tribal members would receive forty acres each. Any surplus land was to be opened to white settlement.

> *The purpose to fill up Oklahoma with settlers will never sleep, and ought never to sleep, until it is accomplished . . . we know that an empty house, though swept and furnished, cannot be guarded against demonic possession.*
>
> *Charles C.C. Painter*
> The Proposed Removal of Indians to Oklahoma, *1887*

Our people and the others of the Five Tribes emphatically opposed the entire concept of assimilation and allotment. Because of this vehement opposition, Congress excluded the Five Tribes, the Osages, and a few other tribes from the Dawes Act. But it would prove to be only a temporary reprieve. It was the same old story—we had won the battle, but in the long run, we were doomed to lose the war. In 1887, when the Dawes Act became law, Native American land totaled more than 138 million acres. Less than fifty years later, when the allotment policy was finally abandoned, only forty-eight million acres remained in the hands of native people. It was one of the most massive thefts in American history.

Just two years after passage of the Dawes Act, the newly organized Territory of Oklahoma emerged, the word *Oklahoma* coming from the Choctaw phrase meaning "red people." Oklahoma Territory was created from the western half of Indian Territory. It was the new home for tribes being removed from other parts of the country, where white people wished to live or raise cattle or grow crops or cut timber or drill for oil or rip minerals from the earth. Our part of the world—what everyone knew as Indian Territory—served as a place to move entire communities of Native Americans who had been displaced from their homelands as the whites marched onward in their pursuit of Manifest Destiny.

Soon the government had assigned each native person an allotment of property, leaving millions of acres which the federal government declared to be "excess" land. Under the Dawes Act, this meant the surplus land was qualified to be opened up to hordes of anxious homesteaders. The flood gates were about to burst.

Newly inaugurated President Benjamin Harrison proclaimed the nearly two million acres of "Unassigned Lands" in Oklahoma Territory—the center of the original Indian Territory—open to settlement at high noon on April 22, 1889. Existing federal land laws would be in force. Fifty thousand homesteaders, every one of them anxious to get a hunk of real estate, lined up at the borders waiting for the signal. When the bugle blasted and the soldiers' pistols cracked, they were off on horseback, in wagons, on bicycles, and some even on foot. By dusk, every homestead had been staked out, as well as the lots for several towns. This was the first of five dramatic Oklahoma "land runs." Each spelled increasing woes for the Five Tribes.

Creation! Hell! That took six days. This was done in one. It was history made in an hour—and I helped make it.

Yancey Cravat,
fictional character in Edna Ferber's Cimarron

Throughout the Cherokee Nation and all across Indian Territory, there was a tremendous sense of loss, not only with the run of 1889 but with each repeated run as well. Our people learned what to expect as western tribes were forced to accept allotments, and their surplus lands were surveyed and opened to the white settlers. Black settlers came as well, and they obtained homesteads and established several all-black towns. From the first land run, the majority of newcomers moving into Oklahoma Territory pushed for statehood. It took them eighteen years of struggle, but they finally achieved their goal in 1907.

There was disagreement about whether the "Twin Territories" should enter the Union as one or two states, but the proponents of "single statehood" won out. Oklahoma Territory and Indian Territory had to be rejoined. That required the altering of the land system in Indian Territory, where our Five Tribes still remained free of the impositions of the Dawes Act. We resolutely opposed accepting allotments, and held our lands in common, self-governed as five separate nations.

Change came in 1893. Congress established a government panel to investigate the reorganization of Indian Territory and the absorption of the Five Tribes into the United States. President Cleveland, back for a second term after Benjamin Harrison had served his four years, named Henry Dawes, recently retired from the Senate, to head a group of bureaucrats. They became known as the Dawes Commission, and their influence and shameful legacy continue to echo through the twentieth century. Members of the commission spent several years in Indian Territory, negotiating with the leaders of the Five Tribes to convince them to accept allotments and terminate our tribal governments.

To understand the significance of the Dawes Commission, one must first understand associated events. In 1893, the same congressional act that provided for the Dawes Commission ratified the sale of the 6.5 million acres which made up the Cherokee Outlet, a band of rich grasslands just below the Kansas line. Popularly known as the Cherokee Strip, the outlet had been ceded to the United States by the Cherokees at the close of the Civil War to be used as a home for other Native Americans. However, now that the federal government had purchased the outlet, it was to be opened to white settlers for homesteading.

Until 1883, when the Cherokee Strip Live Stock Association was chartered under Kansas law, our tribal government had collected grazing fees from individual cattlemen. The association's contract with our tribe, worked out in 1883, called for a yearly usage fee of $100,000. That lease expired in 1888, and later that year, a new five-year lease was worked out with the association, doubling the fee. But then the federal government stepped in and, yielding to pressure to open the outlet to settlers, declared the lease null and void. The cattlemen were ordered to remove their stock and find rangeland elsewhere.

The Cherokee people finally settled for the government's offer of only $1.29 per acre, although in 1961, after many years of tedious litigation, we were awarded an additional $14.7 million for our outlet property. The money was too little and came too late. Nothing could atone for the theft. In 1893, Congress quickly approved the original sale agreement, and it was approved by our National Council. All that was needed was for the signal for the land opening to be given.

That came on September 16, 1893. The opening of the Cherokee Outlet was the largest land run in American history. More than one hundred thousand land-crazed settlers raced for the forty thousand claims waiting to be staked.

Tired of the Five Tribes' resistance to allotment, Congress empowered the Dawes Commission to assign allotments to our people without approval from tribal leaders. In 1898, Congress delivered the final blow to the tribally held Cherokee Nation through passage of the Curtis Act. Drafted by Charles Curtis—a conservative Kansas congressman of Kaw descent who later became vice-president under Herbert Hoover—this legislation effectively ended tribal rule. The Curtis Act not only abolished tribal laws and courts, but made native people subject to federal courts. It also provided for the survey of townsites; the extension of voting rights to hundreds of thousands of nonnative people, although denying native people the right to vote; and the establishment of free public schools for the white children in Indian Territory.

Still, the great Cherokee Nation refused to cooperate. Many Cherokees, including some members of the Keetoowah Society, remained opposed to allotments and the organization of Indian Territory into a federal state. But after two agreements failed, a third was approved by the Cherokees on August 7, 1902, during a special election. Senator Dawes's allotment scheme was at last going to be imposed on the Cherokees and on the others of the Five Tribes. Under this agreement, all members of the Cherokee Nation were duly enrolled by the Dawes Commission. They were given allotments of 110 acres each of average land from the tribal domain.

The last chief of the Cherokees before statehood, William Charles Rogers, was elected in 1903. Under provisions of the agreement made between the United States and the Cherokee Nation at Muskogee in 1902, that was to be the last election held in the Cherokee Nation. Rogers, however, was retained as principal chief of the Cherokees until his death in 1917. The federal government allowed this so that Rogers, as the properly authorized representative of the Cherokee Nation, could sign the deeds transferring the title of community lands to individual allottees.

In the fleeting years before statehood, some citizens of the Five Tribes tried to form an independent state, to be named Sequoyah for the Cherokee who had developed our syllabary. In 1905, a convention was held to consider a constitution for the Indian "State of Sequoyah," but the document was rejected when the delegates sent it to Congress.

Instead, in 1906, Congress passed the Oklahoma Enabling Act, permitting the people of Oklahoma Territory and Indian Territory to come together for the purpose of drafting a constitution. A constitutional convention was convened in Guthrie, the capital of Oklahoma Territory. Members of the convention drew up a reform constitution, containing many ideas that were intended to "return democracy to the people," although few native people were involved with the convention. The document was sent to Washington for congressional approval.

Finally, on November 16, 1907, President Theodore Roosevelt issued a proclamation declaring Oklahoma the forty-sixth state of the Union. Officials in Washington telegraphed the news to Guthrie. Throughout the new state, there was much celebration—fancy parties, down-home barbecues, whiskey toasts, and prayer services.

But not everyone was caught up in the revelry. I feel sure that Cherokee families gathered in countless rural homes to talk about the illegitimate birth of Oklahoma. Perhaps they discussed the federal government's long-forgotten promise that in exchange for the loss of our ancestral homeland, we would be left alone in Indian Territory. Statehood day was a sad day for the Cherokee Nation. Some people even erroneously assumed that the Cherokee Nation had ceased to exist.

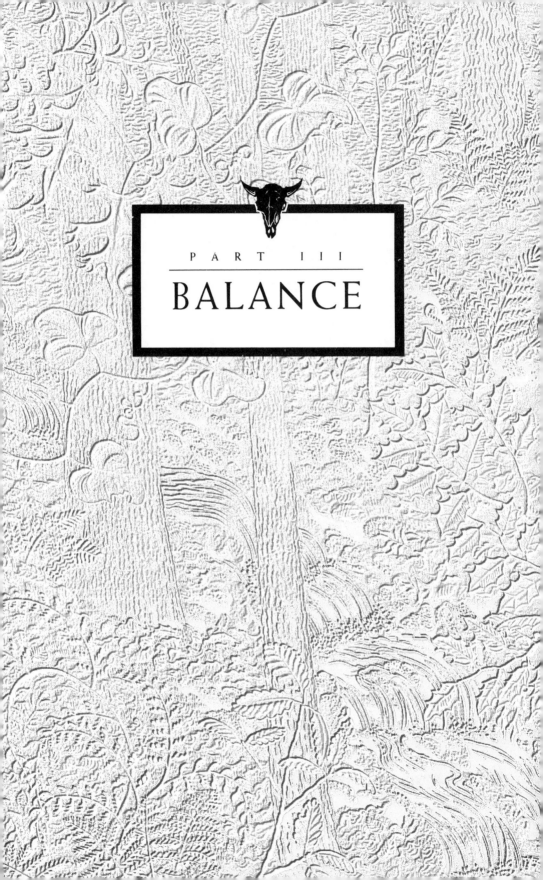

PART III
BALANCE

CHAPTER 9

REVOLUTION

Once while all the warriors of a certain Cherokee town were off on a hunt or attending a dance in another settlement, an old man who had been left behind was chopping wood on the side of a ridge.

Suddenly a party of enemy warriors from some other tribe came upon him. The old man threw his hatchet at the nearest one, and then he turned and ran for the house to get his gun and defend the village as best as he could. When he came out of the house with the gun, he was surprised to find a large body of strange warriors driving back the enemy. There was no time for questions, and taking his place with the others, the old man fought hard until the enemy was pressed back up the creek. Finally, they broke and retreated across the mountain.

When it was all over and there was time to breathe again, the old man turned to thank his new friends, but found that he was all alone. They had disappeared as though the mountain had swallowed them. Then he knew that they were the Nuñnehi, the Immortals, who had come to help their friends the Cherokees.

June 1963. It was less than fifty-six years since Oklahoma had become a state, and precisely ninety-eight years since Cherokee General Stand Watie had surrendered his Confederate force. On June 2, 1963, those few who remembered silently marked the thirty-ninth anniversary of the passage of the Snyder Act, giving citizenship to all Native Americans born in the United States.

June 1963. It had been 120 years since Chief John Ross had summoned a Native United Nations Treaty Conference. Four thousand people representing several Indian nations had responded to his invitation and camped at Tahlequah for a month of deliberations about United States–Native American relations and other issues.

June 1963. Like so many other months throughout the sixties, the weeks were filled with transition and change. During those thirty days, a Buddhist monk set himself ablaze to protest South Vietnamese government persecution, nearly two years before the United States committed itself in a major war in Vietnam. Dr. Martin Luther King, Jr., was working on his "I Have a Dream" speech for the upcoming march on Washington in August.

In the United States, June 1963 was a month of civil disorder and violence. Defiant Governor George Wallace temporarily halted his fight to stop two black students from enrolling at the University of Alabama when President John Kennedy dispatched National Guardsmen to the Birmingham campus. Only a few days later, in Jackson, Mississippi, a sniper killed black civil-rights leader Medgar Evers in front of his home, sparking riots throughout the South. The voices of Martin Luther King, Jr., Malcolm X, and James Baldwin—all active in the civil-rights movement—cried out for freedom.

During that month, the U.S. Supreme Court banned the reading of the Lord's Prayer and the Bible in public schools; a young American boxer still using the name Cassius Clay won a big fight in London; and a crowd of enthusiastic West Berliners turned out to hear JFK tell them, *"Ich bin ein Berliner."*

June 1963. In San Francisco, I was fully aware of many of the truly momentous world and national events that were transpiring, but I also had other things on my mind. Mainly, I was just happy that at long last, June of 1963 had finally arrived. For me, there was one event that month that outweighed all the others—my high school days were over. That meant no more associating with people I did not like, people who did not like me.

I was ready to get going and take my place in the world. I moved in with my sister Frances. That gave me some measure of independence. I was, at least, kind of living on my own. I had a great deal of personal freedom. I went right out and got a real day job. There were never any plans for me to go to college. That thought never even entered my head. People in my family did not go to college. They went to work. And certainly none of the other people around me—friends and neighbors and kids I knew from the Indian Center—went on to college.

So I took a job with a finance company. I did clerical chores, telephone work. It was very basic—a nine-to-five routine job. I was only seventeen years old and did not have a care in the world. Seventeen is a romantic age. Childhood may be over, but full adulthood has not yet arrived. It is a limbo time.

All I knew was that I was seventeen, and at long last, I felt as if I was making my way in. the world. I was actually earning some money, maybe not much, but certainly more than I had had before. I was poor, but I felt good. Besides, I was starting to fall in love, or at least I thought I might be in love.

His full name was Hector Hugo Olaya de Bardi. I called him by his middle name. He was always just Hugo. Hugo Olaya.

Hugo was a native of Ecuador, and he was four years older than I was. Carmen Roybal, one of our neighbors years before in the Potrero Hill District, was the one who introduced us. Carmen took me to a Latino dance in the city. It was springtime. In came Hugo with a dashing soccer wound on his head. His team had just won a big victory, and so there was much ado. That is how I met him.

I liked him immediately, but it was not love at first sight. He was charming and handsome. He was the classic Latin in every respect—very dark, very macho, with a definite touch of class. He was sophisticated, and he handled himself very well. But to say that I loved him from the start would not be true.

Hugo's father was a physician who had come to the United States to start a new life. He left his wife and children behind in Ecuador. He had a daughter and three sons, counting Hugo, who was the oldest. His father said he would send for them later, after he was established in this country. That never happened. He settled here, but he never sent for his family. As far as I could ever determine, he never applied for a medical license either. Truthfully, I never knew exactly what Hugo's father did. I thought of him as sort of a playboy type. Although he deserted Hugo's mother, he still visited his children and kept up with them.

Hugo's mother was from an old-line Italian family that had settled in Ecuador. They were very "old money"—a refined, aristocratic family. That was how Hugo was raised, in that kind of upper-class atmosphere. The family owned several businesses—a construction firm, a pharmacy, a shirt shop, and other enterprises. There are many Indians living in Ecuador, but there definitely was not a drop of Indian blood flowing in Hugo's veins. That was quite clear.

Hugo was a schoolboy when he left his family's home in the large Pacific coast city of Guayaquil, and moved to the United States to pursue his academic studies. He had other relatives besides his father living in this country, including some in the Bay area. When I met Hugo, he was attending San Francisco State College, studying business and accounting. I found him to be quite bright, but again, I was not swept off my feet. He was interesting and pleasant—the basic nice guy.

In a way, Hugo reminded me of my old boyfriend, Ray Billy, the last person I had really been interested in—the fellow who had left me for a beauty queen. Like Ray, Hugo also was someone who had been around. He was worldly and, to a real ghetto kid like me, that was very impressive. I was a teenager, dating an exotic South American who was going to college and driving his own car. He was dashing and different and good-looking.

Hugo took me to a variety of places, where we did and saw things that were all brand-new to me. After I spent the day working at the finance company, it was so much fun to go out to a restaurant or club with Hugo. He introduced me to different types of music and cultures. It was a whirlwind summer, and through it all we maintained what I can best describe as a kind of partying relationship. You might call it one continuous spree. And what better city to be in for this than San Francisco? There was so much in the Bay area I had never been able to experience before meeting Hugo. Now, with Hugo as my guide, all of that had changed.

It was pure fun—very pure. I never allowed our physical relationship to go too far. That was very important to me. We dated quite a lot during the summer of 1963. All the while, Hugo constantly pressed me for some kind of commitment. He told me he wanted to marry me. I kept putting him off, but finally, I decided I would take him up on his offer. It was a rather sudden decision. It happened one night in October. As usual, we were out on the town. At the time, I was having some sort of problem—

I cannot even recall exactly what it was—and I thought that perhaps if I married Hugo, all my problems would disappear. I accepted his proposal.

I went to my parents to tell them what Hugo and I were going to do. I wanted to get their permission. I was still only seventeen, a month from my eighteenth birthday. My father was not too pleased about the prospects of my marriage. He was never overly fond of Hugo. Dad had liked Ray Billy, and wished that he were the one I was going to marry. My mother liked Hugo a little bit more than my father did. She thought Hugo was OK. Neither of my parents said very much about my young age. After all, my mother had been only fifteen years old when she went against her family's wishes and ran off to marry my father. Hugo's family did not object to our plans to marry.

When we went to get our wedding rings, I realized I did not even know for sure what Hugo's last name was. He had such a long name, and it was all in Spanish. I thought maybe it was Bardi. So there I was with the man I was about to marry, picking out wedding bands and having to ask him to explain his name.

Hugo's father bought the rings for us, and we took off. We went to Reno to get married. That was my very first airplane experience. We were all by ourselves. No one from our families attended, not my parents, not any of my brothers or sisters. It was just Hugo and I. I wore a dressy cream-colored suit. We went to one of those wedding chapels that Nevada is so famous for, with a justice of the peace. We were wed on November 13, 1963. It was a Wednesday afternoon. I became Wilma Olaya. I was five days shy of turning eighteen.

As soon as the brief ceremony was over, we got on an airplane and returned to the Bay area. From there, we left on our honeymoon. Hugo's father had presented us with one thousand dollars to be used for a wedding trip. We decided to go to Chicago. We took the bus. All the time we traveled across country, I started to really consider what I had just "gone and done." I had behaved impulsively on many occasions in the past, but my sudden marriage to Hugo had to top the list. All I could do was plunge ahead and make the best of it.

That was my first visit to Chicago, so it was exciting when we drove into the city. We were still in Chicago on Friday, November 22, when the startling news flashed around the world that President Kennedy had been shot and killed that afternoon in Dallas. One of the most tragic events in American history occurred during my honeymoon. In a way, I was experiencing my own loss of innocence and, on a much larger scale, so was the rest of the nation.

This electrifying young man of compassionate vision and open mind, who inspired my generation and understood the human potential, was snatched away from us in an instant of madness. The promise of John Kennedy's presidency had seemed to me almost unlimited. The Dillon Myer era of Indian policy was vanishing. It was a very hopeful time. Kennedy's death marked a very personal disillusionment for me. I remember that church bells tolled throughout the city and across the countryside. Like everyone else, we sat transfixed before the television, watching in disbelief the horrifying and sad occurrences of those bleak November days. It was a somber time. It was a time to cry. It was a time to remember.

> *When we forget great contributors to our American history—when we neglect the heroic pasts of the American Indian—we thereby weaken our own heritage. We need to remember the contributions our forefathers found here and from which they borrowed liberally.*
>
> *John F. Kennedy, 1961*
>
> *America wept tonight, not alone for its dead young President, but for itself. . . . Somehow the worst prevailed over the best. . . . Some strain of madness and violence had destroyed the highest symbol of law and order.*
>
> *James Reston, 1963*

When we returned to San Francisco, I was still very bewildered by what had taken place in Dallas. The senseless death of John Kennedy would haunt me for a long time. It would stay with many of us.

Hugo and I came back from our honeymoon only to go our separate ways. It was not that we wanted to be apart, but we had no choice. Neither of us had a place big enough for both of us to live. I squeezed back in with my younger sister at my parents' home in Hunter's Point, and Hugo went to his apartment. It was only temporary. After just a few days of searching and telephone calls, we found a place. Hugo and I moved in with his cousins, Rose and Tito Bastidas. They generously made room for us in their house in the Mission District. Hugo's cousins Tito and George Bastidas, who were brothers, were very close to each other and to Hugo. Rose and Judy Bastidas, married to Tito and George, respectively, were my closest friends during that time. The men all played soccer while we cheered them on. We held large family gatherings after the games. We shared the births of our children, our twenty-first birthdays, and the transition from youth to womanhood. Our friendship has stood the test of time.

We settled right into our new roles as husband and wife. Hugo took a job working the night shift with Pan American Airlines while he finished the course work for his degree at San Francisco State. I continued with the finance company, but my job was not very challenging. Most of the time, it amounted to tracking down people who were delinquent in their loan payments. It was all rather unpleasant. I would call them, ask them to come up with some money toward paying off their bills, and then write down whatever they said to include in our files. There was not much satisfaction in doing that same old thing day in and day out.

In January of 1964, just a couple of months after Hugo and I were married, I was home alone one evening when I suddenly felt very ill. I was not sure what was wrong. I became feverish, had pains in my back, and was unable to keep any food down. It was getting worse and worse. Finally, I called my father, because Hugo was at his night job at Pan Am. Dad came right over and took me to the emergency room at San Francisco General Hospital. They put me through tests, and after several hours of anxious waiting, a doctor came out to tell us they had found the source of my problems.

He told me my back pains and fever were caused by a kidney infection, which could be treated. When I asked about the nausea, the doctor smiled. He said that was the result of yet another condition— pregnancy. I was going to have a baby.

That news was astounding. For all my street smarts, I still did not have the kind of knowledge needed to prevent pregnancy. Like other eighteen-year-olds at that time, I suppose I suffered a little bit from the "it can't happen to me" syndrome. Hugo and I had talked about taking precautions and I had planned to see a physician to discuss birth-control options, but I just had not gotten around to it.

The doctor at the hospital was correct. Some prescription medicine cleared up my kidney problems—at least at first. None of us knew it at the time, but that initial kidney infection was only the symptom of what eventually would be diagnosed as a very serious disease. But that was far from my mind. I had my first pregnancy to deal with.

I did not have an easy time. It was so difficult that I had to quit my job early on, and I stayed sick throughout the pregnancy. My problems included high blood pressure and profound edema, swelling caused by an abnormal accumulation of fluid in the cells and body cavities. The kidney infections also returned, with such fury that I was forced to spend much of the time bedridden. Sometimes, because Hugo was so busy with his job and school, I went to my parents' home so my mother could watch over me. I thought my ordeal would never end.

On August 11, 1964, the time came to deliver my baby. I was taken to St. Luke's Hospital. It was only fitting that the top tune on the charts that week was the Beatles' "A Hard Day's Night." I was in for a strenuous ordeal, and neither my husband nor my mother could comfort me. I asked for my father to come to the hospital to be with me, and he did. I knew he would have to miss work to be there, but at that point, I did not care, and of course, neither did he.

At last, after I had endured twenty-seven exhausting hours of exertion and pain, the doctors induced labor and my child was born. A little bit of simple arithmetic showed us that the baby had arrived almost exactly nine months after my marriage. I had conceived during our honeymoon in Chicago. Something positive—a new life—had come out of that November week when so much else in this country went wrong. Now I had a healthy daughter. We called her Felicia, a name that means "happiness."

Shortly after my daughter's birth, we moved from the home in the Mission District that we shared with Hugo's cousins. We rented a house all our own in a pretty San Francisco neighborhood. It was quiet and tidy, and there were shops nearby. Hugo kept up his schedule of going to school by day and working for the airline every night. I stayed home with my baby daughter. I kept house, shopped, cooked, and cleaned. I evolved into my role of young wife and mother. I felt there was some order, perhaps some of that old Cherokee balance, in my life, but I was not completely sure I was comfortable with my situation. That feeling would nag at me for a long time.

I was very busy with my baby and keeping up with my brothers and sisters and their families. Then in June of 1966, less than two years after Felicia was born, I had my second daughter. We named her Gina.

She was born by natural childbirth, and I had little difficulty with her delivery. I was delighted to have two healthy children.

Shortly after Gina's birth, one of Hugo's younger brothers from Ecuador moved to San Francisco. His name was Santiago. Unlike Hugo, he used the family's entire last name, Olaya de Bardi. At our invitation, Santiago lived with us for a short time. He was not an unpleasant house-guest. I liked having him around. He was very mellow and laid back, and I thought he made a good contrast to his big brother, who often was just the opposite.

By then, Hugo and I had been married for about three years. We had two children, a home, and security. But despite all that, I was begin-ning to think that our relationship had become somewhat damaged or fractured. No major fissures were yet evident, just the tiniest, the slightest of cracks. As is usually the case, I first noticed our problems arising from seemingly insignificant causes.

As much as I loved my family and home, I was starting to feel restricted by the routine required of the traditional wife. I had not yet celebrated my twenty-first birthday. Sometimes, I wanted to get out of the house and flex my wings a little bit. It did not take all that much to make me happy. For me, the ideal way for us to spend an evening together was to go to my folks' house to play cards. That was really all I needed to stay content.

Hugo needed more. He, too, was restless. I think he missed the old days from our whirlwind summer of courtship, before the girls were born. He longed for the times when he did not have so much to worry about. Whenever we had a chance to step out, Hugo wanted to do more than sit around with my family shuffling cards at the kitchen table. Our personal tastes and backgrounds were so dissimilar. He was interested in the more formal style of socializing, going to clubs and parties. At first, none of those differences was too troublesome. I grew more conscious of them the longer we were married.

Regardless of our disparate preferences and priorities, Hugo and I had no problem with our location, although sometimes we flirted with the idea of moving to the suburbs. San Francisco was an exciting place to be for nearly everyone, but especially those of us who were caught up in those times and everything that was going on around us. Turn-of-the-century novelist Frank Norris once described San Francisco as "a city where almost anything can happen." His words were still true throughout the 1960s. During those early years of my marriage, I became more aware of the San Francisco I had not had the opportunity to learn about while living in Daly City and at Hunter's Point. For that, I am grateful.

The entire Bay region—from Sausalito to Berkeley—has always served as a magnet and proving ground of the arts and culture. In the mid- to late 1950s, when my family was still shaking the Oklahoma dust from its clothes, an arts movement that became known as the San Francisco Renaissance was under way. A group of bohemian artists and writers emerged, calling themselves the Beat generation. The high priests of that movement included Allen Ginsberg, Gregory Corso, Jack Kerouac, Gary Snyder, and Michael McClure. They gathered at City Lights, Lawrence Ferlinghetti's North Beach bookstore, to argue, discuss, and read one another's work.

At the "hungry i" and other local nightclubs, folk singers, balladeers, and comics performed. The Kingston Trio and the Smothers Brothers were there. Ken Kesey and his busload of Merry Pranksters were preparing to go on the prowl. Dr. Timothy Leary held forth on the merits of LSD beneath a perfumed cloud of marijuana, Bob Dylan sang from the depths of his soul, and out of Carmel and the Big Sur country emerged Joan Baez with her sweet laments. Abstract painters and sculptors, drawn to the city, turned to a new realism. It was a time when prose writers, poets, and playwrights lived in "pads," experimented with pot, and practiced Zen. Each evening, they met at one of the city's many cafés or coffeehouses to sip espresso or glasses of golden Napa wine while devouring freshly composed poems.

By the time the 1960s were under way, any self-respecting radical, nonconformist, or renegade knew the place to be was San Francisco.

The Bay area was very much a place of ferment and apprehension. In cosmopolitan and compact San Francisco, bounded on three sides by water, a tremendous building boom in the 1960s altered the way of life. The skyline was transformed when a flock of skyscrapers rose like phoenix birds out of the landfills and climbed the city's steep hills. Many residents found the growth repulsive. They described the new building craze as the "Manhattanization" of their treasured city.

By that time, the Bay area, including Oakland, had become a center for relocation of native people from all over the United States. As families arrived, usually fresh from rural isolated communities, the earlier relocatees would help them adjust to the sometimes bewildering new lifestyle. The new relocatees were accustomed to living with few amenities or even basic necessities, but at least at home they had been surrounded by family, friends, and neighbors who were willing to share what little they had with one another. In the Bay area, they were exiles living far from their native lands. There were lots of other poor people who cried out for decent places to live. Minority racial forces were gaining strength across the country, and their voices were heard loud and clear in California. They were on a quest for better housing, more jobs, and an end to discrimination.

After the devastating Watts riots of August 1965 and March 1966 in Los Angeles, a smaller disturbance erupted in September 1966 at Hunter's Point, my former home. That riot, much like those in Watts, stemmed from a police incident. At Hunter's Point, a police officer shot a suspected teenage car thief. Like the outbursts in southern California, the riot occurred on a hot day when everyone was on edge. The gunplay and brutal weather were key factors in the disorder, but many residents knew it was only a matter of time until the lid blew off the pressure cooker. Hunter's Point lay there like a cauldron—a neighborhood where a riot was waiting to happen.

For too many years, the black families who came to San Francisco after World War II had been pushed into bad flats in isolated ghettos—the inadequate housing at Hunter's Point or the decaying Victorians in the Fillmore district, where slum landlords got away with charging exorbitant rents. I knew from my own experience that because of the level of poverty, widespread unemployment, and broken families, residents from those neighborhoods had very little, if anything, to look forward to in life. But some of them did retain their pride and, if they were lucky, their dreams. That is what got them through.

> *We shall overcome, we shall overcome,*
> *We shall overcome some day*
> *Oh, deep in my heart I do believe*
> *We shall overcome some day.*
>
> > *Old religious song adapted for*
> > *the 1960s civil-rights*
> > *movement*

Fortunately, no buildings were set on fire and no one was killed in the Hunter's Point disturbance. San Francisco Mayor John F. Shelley, backed by the National Guard, quickly imposed a curfew and restored calm. Mindful of California's law forbidding employment discrimination, Shelley openly condemned what he called "the medieval practice" of racial bias in some of the area labor unions. Hunter's Point began to receive substantial annual grants from the Model Cities Program. Eventually, new businesses were launched and job-training programs were introduced in the community.

Still, many black people and other racial groups remained bitterly frustrated with their plight. Militancy became a preferred tactic in some circles. In October of 1966—just one month after the Hunter's Point mêlée and one month before a conservative Republican by the name of Ronald Reagan was elected governor of California—Bobby Seale and Huey Newton founded the Black Panthers in nearby Oakland. Other fiery militant black leaders such as Angela Davis and Eldridge Cleaver came forward to repudiate the conventional white culture and to advance the war cry that for them said it all—"Black is Beautiful." But beyond that catchy axiom was a definite self-help message in the Black Panthers' rhetoric. They established free breakfast programs and alternative schools. During the group's heyday, it was not uncommon to see Huey Newton on local talk shows discussing civil rights and police harassment of young black men. The first activist group I truly identified with was the Black Panther Party. They talked about problems I was familiar with. I had never before seen any minority stand up to police, judges, and other white people.

At the same time black militants in the Bay area and around the country were attempting to gain a different lease on life, Hispanics in California were making their presence known. For too many years, they had been acquiescent, fully resigned to their place in the barrios and the growing fields. But they also knew wholesale poverty and prejudice. They felt the frustration of sending generation after generation to public schools where their language and history were shunned. The Hispanics also desired change. They did not want to wait anymore.

My spirits were buoyed in the mid-1960s whenever I heard more news from the San Joaquin Valley about the National Farm Workers Association, led by Cesar Chavez, and their successful rallies and strikes against California's major grape growers on behalf of the migrant workers, who labored under deplorable conditions. I could identify with that group of activists. I had worked on farms every summer during my teen years. I attended several of their benefits and consciousness-raising events held throughout the Mission District. I met several people who worked with Chavez, and later I became acquainted with his associate Delores Huerta.

Using the image of a black eagle as their symbol of solidarity, the farm workers fought off the rich owners and their thugs who were hired to terrorize them. It was a form of coercion not unlike the use of hired bullies to scare off Dust Bowl Okies when they came to California to rebuild their lives. In San Francisco in the mid-1960s, sympathetic longshoremen began to refuse to load grapes picked from the farms being struck. Nationwide product boycotts were launched. Chicano power had had an impact.

Of course, this restlessness stirred also in various groups of the white community. Driven by the spirit of change, civil-rights proponents came not only from the ghettos and barrios and inner cities, but also from middle-class America and college campuses.

As President Lyndon Johnson began to ship more and more combat troops to Vietnam in 1965, many young people already involved in the civil-rights struggle realized that the insanity of what some people were calling an immoral war traced its origins to the internal problems of our nation. Selma and Montgomery were important victories, but Da Nang and the Mekong Delta represented great setbacks. Our country had mixed up its priorities, and an ever-widening gap developed between those seeking peace and social progress and the false patriots and prophets of the status quo.

> *If we ever let the Communists win this war, we are in great danger of fighting for the rest of our lives and losing a million kids.*
>
> Bob Hope, 1969

> *War is not healthy for children and other living things.*
>
> Popular 1960s poster

> *What if they gave a war and nobody came....*
>
> Popular 1960s slogan

A tangible feeling of skepticism and consternation with the leadership of the nation and state poured forth from the University of California at Berkeley, site of the "Free Speech" movement and a large number of protests throughout the decade. If San Francisco was the great bastion of liberalism in the 1960s, then Berkeley, just across the bay, had to be the inner sanctum for student revolutionaries.

A broad spectrum of America's sons and daughters dared to question the prevailing Establishment. Many of those young people came together in San Francisco, a revered mecca. Most of them were about my age or a little younger. They had dropped out of school or had left upper middle-class homes to become part of the counterculture.

Adorning themselves with beads and tie-dyed T-shirts, feathers and fringed leather vests, they took on a sort of back-to-nature look with a definite Native American influence. They often lived together communally as family units or "tribes" in "crash pads" scattered throughout a neighborhood of old Victorian homes. It was not far from a strip of Golden Gate Park known as the Panhandle, near where two streets—Haight and Ashbury—intersect. Spiritual descendants of the Beats and bohemians of earlier days, these denizens of Haight-Ashbury were called *hippies*, from *hipster*, a term supposedly created by writer Norman Mailer.

By early autumn of 1966, new recruits were moving into the Haight area every day. Rock musicians also took up residence there, providing a rhythm and adding an air of celebrity. The Grateful Dead lived at 710 Ashbury, and the Jefferson Airplane could be found on nearby Fulton Street. Unfortunately, by the last years of the decade, the area had gone into decay. The peak time for Haight-Ashbury was in 1966, spilling over into the following year. Thousands of young people—literally with flowers in their hair, the scent of patchouli on their bodies, and love in their hearts and minds—descended on the city. Their favorite buzz words were *peace, spare change,* and *freedom.*

When my daughters were still quite small, I frequently took them to Haight-Ashbury. In retrospect, I think the people of the Haight had to be as curious about us as we were about them. My daughters wore their shiny patent-leather shoes and little-girl dresses, and I looked like what I was at the time, a young housewife who liked to observe what was going on around me, but was unwilling to get fully involved. Yet there was something comfortable and inviting, at least for a little while, about that uninhibited culture of psychedelic art and rock-and-roll poets.

We enjoyed strolling through the street fairs and perusing the crowded shops filled with smoky incense and other accoutrements of the "love generation." We attended concerts and listened to sidewalk musicians sing their delicious ballads of hope and tranquillity. I also was drawn to Glide Memorial Church, a rather famous counterculture sanctuary in San Francisco, where the Reverend Cecil Williams presided in a brightly colored dashiki. Sometimes I still think about him and hope that he has not changed and become a moderate like so many of the rest of us from that time.

Whenever I do pause to reflect, I find that many of my hopes and aspirations were formed during those wonderfully sad and crazy years of the 1960s in San Francisco. Everything that was happening in the world at that time—Vietnam, peace demonstrations, the civil-rights movement, and the seeds of the native-rights movement—had a lasting influence on me. I began to question so many things in my life, including, once again, my marriage. I would come home from an afternoon in the Haight or after spending time with some of my politically active brothers and sisters and wonder what I was doing, what the future really held for me.

Although I knew something was terribly wrong with my marriage, I tried to stick it out. We thought about our options, including a change of location, which we had considered earlier. Perhaps moving out of the city to the suburbs would help. We even went out to look at a couple of places, but something held me back. I could not make that commitment to move.

I distinctly recall going to visit a family at a suburban home northeast of Oakland. I had nothing against those folks, but that visit really did it for me. The whole time I was there, I felt as if I were suffocating. All around us in the city were people—interesting people—discussing politics, music, theology, world events—but there we were in the suburbs talking about lawn mowers at a house that looked exactly like all the others on the street.

I knew I did not want to live like that. I had no wish to become the kind of woman who would later be called a "Stepford wife." If we moved to the suburbs, that is surely what would happen. That was the night I realized I had to institute some serious changes. I cried all the way home.

In the late 1960s, I made an important step toward finding the independence I wanted. I started to college. It began with my taking a few courses at Skyline Junior College, south of the city in San Bruno. At first, I was very tentative because school had never been a pleasant experience for me. I had hated it so much, but I knew that if I wanted to really find a niche in life, my continuing education was important. I took a couple of courses each semester. I looked for subjects that interested me, such as literature or sociology. I even took a criminal-justice class. When I did well in those courses, I thought to myself, "Hey, this isn't that bad." Besides the college study, I also worked off and on at various jobs. Sometimes I worked in law offices as a paralegal, typing briefs and wills.

Then it was time for me to move along. A Klamath woman named Gustine Moppin, whom I had met right after we moved to California, eventually got me interested in San Francisco State College. I had been only eleven years old when I had started to baby-sit with her kids. It was Gustine who helped connect me with a minorities educational-opportunities program. Once I checked it out, I decided to enroll.

It was a little overwhelming when I first started classes at San Francisco State because it was so much bigger than Skyline Junior College. One of the first things I did was to make sure I had all the resources necessary to "go the distance." I went directly to the library and found someone to show me how to use the material correctly. Then I read all I could find about taking proper notes and conducting research. I even took a minicourse in root words so I could expand my vocabulary and learn word origins.

Once I began to become more independent, more active with school and in the community, it became increasingly difficult to keep my marriage together. Before that, Hugo had viewed me as someone he had rescued from a very bad life. When I showed my independence, he felt as if he could no longer maintain his role as my savior. This was the man who had introduced me to so many things. He had showed me so many places. We took trips in this country and he took me to visit his home in Ecuador. We flew to Europe and spent time in Rome.

But things soured between my husband and me as I exerted my autonomy. Hugo could see that I did not fit his mold anymore, but he kept trying. When he finally resigned himself to the fact that I was going back to school and he saw that I liked my literature courses, he bought me books and a typewriter. When he became aware that I liked music, he bought me a guitar. He hoped those things would keep me at home.

My world was supposed to be within the confines of our home and social life, a world strictly defined by Hugo. But that would no longer do for me. I wanted to set my own limits and control my destiny. I began to have dreams about more freedom and independence, and I finally came to understand that I did not have to live a life based on someone else's dreams.

> *No girl child born today should responsibly be brought up to be a housewife. Too much has been made of defining human personality and destiny in terms of the sex organs. After all, we share the human brain.*
>
> Betty Friedan, 1968

Frequently, 1968 has been called a turning point, and the year that shaped a generation. Both statements are probably true. Those twelve months started with the shock of the Viet Cong launching the Tet offensive. That invasion not only shattered the lunar New Year truce but all hope for a quick end to the Vietnam carnage, which already had earned the dubious distinction of being the longest war in United States history.

In those early months of 1968, new battle strategies also were being drawn by small bands of daring women liberationists who congregated in cities around the nation. In San Francisco, I eventually discovered that many of those women were wives, mothers, students, bright dropouts, and others who met to discuss their sexuality, employment opportunities, and male tyranny. Certainly one of the high-water marks of the year was the growth of the women's movement, which ushered in a new era of feminism, transforming our culture and greatly influencing my life and the lives of a multitude of others.

In 1968, the past had been severed from the future. Any time that kind of dislocation happens, there is bound to be pain. In this case, the cut was deep, so there was a great deal of hurt. A third phrase is often used to sum up 1968. Some people call it the worst year of the century. Obviously, for many of us involved in the issues of the day, that remained to be seen, but few can forget the horrors we bore witness to during those 365 days.

Recall with me for one chilling moment what took place near the close of Tet, when 567 unarmed Vietnamese civilians were massacred at the hamlet of My Lai. This atrocity by a platoon of U.S. soldiers was reminiscent of the brutality displayed at Wounded Knee in 1890 and in other slaughters of native people. The American public would not learn about My Lai until the following year, but there was more than enough sorrow and fury to go around.

University campuses, including my own San Francisco State, were in turmoil, and some were even shut down by protesting students. When Martin Luther King, Jr., the most eloquent leader of nonviolence, was assassinated in April, massive rioting exploded in scores of cities. Then in June came another needless death—Senator Robert Kennedy was shot and killed in Los Angeles.

I was even more caught up in the idealism and promise of this man than I had been with his older brother. When Bobby Kennedy made his run for president—a race I am confident he would have won—I truly became interested in mainstream politics. Just before he was shot, Kennedy told a throng of loyal supporters at the Ambassador Hotel, "We can end the division within the United States, the violence." His death was painful. He was a person who had spoken to the issues that were important to me and to many other Native Americans. He had visited Cherokee communities in 1968. He had traveled the country exposing the severity and degradation of poverty among native people, and the failure of the nation to help.

> . . . a national tragedy and a national disgrace.
>
> Robert Kennedy's description of the federal
> government's treatment of Native Americans

Only seconds before they entered a dark passageway in the hotel kitchen where death lurked, Bobby Kennedy tried to reassure a worried bodyguard. "It's all right," he said. But he was wrong. It was not all right. It was not all right for Bobby Kennedy or for the rest of us. The balance was off.

Later that summer, the world tuned into Chicago, where the Democratic convention boiled over in division because of the war. Outside on the streets, demonstrators and bystanders were clubbed, gassed, and maced by police using Gestapolike tactics.

No, it was not all right.

On November 8, 1968, Richard M. Nixon and Spiro T. Agnew edged out the Democratic ticket, headed by Hubert Humphrey. America's voters had chosen them to run the nation.

It was not all right. So much was wrong. It was as though the country was still mired in the bloody rice paddies of Vietnam, caught in the choking clouds of tear gas in Chicago, stuck in the darkness and death at the Ambassador Hotel. We had to find a way out. We had to discover the light and go on. We had to shatter the stifling silence nurtured by the Establishment. The songs of Janis Joplin, Jimi Hendrix, the Stones, Credence Clearwater Revival, and the music that would become Woodstock, still a year away, furnished a cadence. Tribes of spirited women, longhaired kids, poor people, students, workers, blacks, and Hispanics provided the courage.

> *[Those] phony intellectuals . . . don't understand what we mean by hard work and patriotism. . . . If you've seen one ghetto area, you've seen them all.*
>
> *Spiro T. Agnew, 1968*
>
> *The great silent majority supports us.*
>
> *Richard M. Nixon, 1969*

The torch of protest and change was grasped by Native Americans. In 1969, the rage that helped to give a voice and spirit to other minority groups spread through native people like a springtime prairie fire. And just as the tall grass thrives and new life bursts forth after the passage of those indispensable flames, we too were given a renewal of energy and purpose.

For my family and other native people whom we befriended in San Francisco, the federal termination and relocation programs dating from the 1950s had failed. Termination certainly never even came close to liberating anyone. If anything, those policies had only increased the misfortune and despair among native people. Whether they would admit it or not, government officials also must have been disappointed. Although thousands of American Indians had been relocated, the relocation act's goal of abolishing ties to tribal lands was never realized—thank goodness. A large percentage of native people who had been removed to urban areas ultimately moved back to their original homes.

Just after astronaut Neil Armstrong walked on the moon in July of 1969, a popular yarn started going around the Indian community in San Francisco. According to this story, the government wanted to put a human on the moon. The scientists had come up with the technology to do that, but they were not sure just how to get the person back to earth. Then they had another brilliant idea. Why not put an Indian in the rocket ship and tell him he was being relocated? Once that Indian got to the moon, he would figure out his own way home and return without costing the government a single cent.

Among Native Americans, there was more than jokes being cracked in 1969. Old notions of how we could really make a difference and improve our lives were cast aside faster than pecan shells at harvest. Like the pivotal year which preceded it, 1969 became a crucial time for all native people, especially when it concerned self-awareness, social up-heaval, and finding solutions for the problems of inequity and bigotry.

A new era of Indian militancy had begun in 1968 with the inception of the American Indian Movement, known as AIM, founded in Minnesota by Clyde Bellecourt, a Chippewa. Other AIM chapters soon appeared on reservations and in cities across the country. AIM members staged dem-onstrations and sit-ins to protest the loss of tribal property and resources. They vigorously called attention to the long list of human-rights issues that had been denied to us.

My family had always kept its ties with the American Indian Center in San Francisco, and in the late 1960s, I renewed my relationship with old friends there. The center was a hotbed of sedition, fortunately. Al-though many native people were leaving the Bay area and Los Angeles to return to their homes or reservations, California's Indian population remained substantial. Those of us who were still in California began to find a new sense of self-esteem. The center was an important place for us to go to discuss the issues and formulate our plans. It also helped to give us direction and boost our pride. Soon, delegations of native people were appearing before the state board of education to demand fairer treatment of Native Americans in textbooks and curricula. In San Fran-cisco, an Indian Historical Society was formed and began to publish a journal.

Bobby Kennedy's last words to his bodyguard were coming true after all. Perhaps it *would* be all right. I was caught up in the idealism, the social movements, the unrest. I finally felt like a person who belonged to the time, yet I wanted to become more involved and was not quite sure how or what to do.

Then something happened that gave me the focus I was searching for. It all started in November of 1969, when a group of Native Americans representing more than twenty tribes seized a deserted island in the midst of San Francisco's glittering bay. Citing a forgotten clause in treaty agreements that said any unused federal lands must revert to Indian use, they took over the twelve-acre island to attract attention to the government's gross mistreatment of generations of native people. They did it to remind the whites that the land was *ours* before it was *theirs*.

Maybe the *Nuñnehi*, those Immortals from the old story, had come to this place to help not only the Cherokees but all other native people. Maybe those Immortals would dwell there until the balance was returned.

The name of the island is Alcatraz. It changed me forever.

CHAPTER 10

SEARCHING FOR
BALANCE

A long time ago, a man had a dog which began to go down to the river every day and look at the water and howl. At last the man was angry and scolded the dog, which then said to him, "Very soon there is going to be a great freshet, and the water will come so high that everybody will be drowned; but if you will make a raft to get upon when the rain comes, you can be saved, but you must first throw me into the water."

The man did not believe it, and the dog said, "If you want a sign that I speak the truth, look at the back of my neck." The man looked and saw that the skin on the dog's neck had worn off so that the bones stuck out.

Then he believed the dog, and began to build a raft. Soon the rain came and the man took his family, with plenty of provisions, and they all got on the raft. It rained for a long time, and the water rose until the mountains were covered and all the people in the world were drowned. Then the rain stopped and the waters went down again, until at last it was safe to come off the raft.

Now there was no one alive but the man and his family, but one day they heard a sound of dancing and shouting on the other side of the ridge. The man climbed to the top and looked over; everything was still, but along the valley he saw great piles of bones of the people who had been drowned, and then he knew that the ghosts had been dancing.

There is only a little irony in the knowledge that Alcatraz, the tiny island in San Francisco Bay that propelled me and so many others into the current of Native American awareness, had served originally as a prison. A large number of native people had been subjected to what was hardly better than prison conditions for a long time, so using Alcatraz as a symbol seemed entirely appropriate.

By the final days of the 1960s, various tribal activists felt the time had arrived for all of us to change our behavior. For too many years, most native people had lived as if they were being held hostage in a land their ancestors had cherished for eons before the Europeans ever came ashore.

Our experience with whites revealed that they could not be trusted. We would always remember the long line of treaties and promises. Most were as worthless as the politicians who drafted them. They were only pieces of paper filled with empty words as hypocritical as most of the white men's promises.

> All of our people all over the country—except the pure-blooded Indians—are immigrants or descendants of immigrants, including even those who came over here on the Mayflower.
>
> *Franklin Delano Roosevelt, 1944*

> My ancestors didn't come on the Mayflower but they met the boat.
>
> *Will Rogers*

> I am not so sweet on old Andy [Andrew Jackson]. He is the one that run us Cherokees out of Georgia and North Carolina. . . .
>
> [The native people] had a treaty that said, "You shall have this land as long as grass grows and water flows." It was not only a good rhyme but looked like a pretty good treaty, and it was till they struck oil. Then the government took it away from us again.
>
> So the Indians lost another bet.
>
> *Will Rogers*

By the time Oklahoma became a state in 1907, the Cherokee people had become quite used to the rhetoric and rhymes of the white men's treaties. In my view, Oklahoma statehood was a very dark page, not only in Cherokee history but in the history of the United States. The harm heaped on our people during that span of years from 1893 to 1907 was tremendous. That was the termination period, highlighted by the passage of the Curtis Act, the establishment of the Dawes Commission, and distribution of tribal lands.

Besides our schools being closed down, our judicial system halted, and our central form of government almost destroyed, the land we had always held in common was divided into individual allotments. Although some of the mixed-blood leaders had long accepted the view that individual ownership of land and even of slaves was acceptable, the main body of the Cherokee people did not share that opinion. Statehood did nothing to change their way of thinking.

I have always felt that the thought of many Cherokees at the time was expressed best by W. A. Duncan in a letter published in the *Cherokee Advocate* on October 5, 1892. Duncan wrote, "The term 'allotment' as used among us is simply another word for title in severalty to our lands. If the system of owning land in severalty has the effect to exclude so many people among the whites from the enjoyment of a home, it seems to me that the same system among the Cherokees would soon have the effect to render many of them homeless. Business knows no pity, and cares for justice only when justice is seen to be better policy. If it had power to control the elements, it would grasp in its iron clutches the waters, sunshine and air and resell them by measure, and at exorbitant prices to the millions of famished men, women and children. I do not want to see our Cherokee people without homes. The title in common to our lands is the strongest guarantee against the homelessness of many of our people."

For the Cherokee Nation and the others of the Five Tribes, statehood meant only the heartbreaking conclusion to decades spent fighting attempts to transform Indian Territory into a white commonwealth. Even though the Cherokee Nation supposedly ceased to exist after Oklahoma statehood, two important factors kept our people intact. One was the complexity of the land transfers. The other was the tenacity of the Cherokee people. Many whites believed that through the years, all Cherokees had fully embraced the Anglo-Saxon way of life.

> *The Cherokees, known as one of the "five civilized tribes," are probably the most intelligent Indian nation and the one farthest advanced in civilization. For years the Cherokees have been at least nominally Christians. For these reasons the Gov-*

ernment's treatment of them is particularly instructive as it is unobscured by many of the difficulties which tend to befog the main issue. We have here a tribe with a government similar to that of the United States; with its newspapers, with its schools, churches, asylums; with its leaders comparable in ability with many of the leading men of the United States.

Thomas Valentine Parker, Ph.D., 1907

The Cherokee are a bright intelligent race, better fitted to "follow the white man's road" than any other Indians.

Theodore Roosevelt

The white professors and anthropologists thought they knew our people so well, but they did not. Neither did the United States government. The federal bureaucrats had not planned for the difficult legal complications required to destroy a nation. Many documents required signatures to make them legal and binding, a function which Chief W. C. Rogers served.

In 1914, the year my father was born in rural Oklahoma, the year W. A. Duncan's prophecy printed in the *Advocate* in 1892 came true, the Bureau of Indian Affairs set out to run the affairs of our tribe as an administrative dictatorship. That was to continue for decades. In 1976, when the unlawful conduct of the BIA officials came under review, a federal court said the attitude of government officials "can only be characterized as bureaucratic imperialism."

Some things never change. Almost since its inception, there have been many attempts to reform the BIA. I guess I agree with former Creek Chief Claude Cox of Oklahoma, who said reforming the BIA was kind of like rotating four bald tires on an old car. The net result would be no change.

Many Cherokees opposed allotment, including the leaders of the intertribal Four Mothers Society and the Keetoowah Society. One of them was a charismatic leader, Redbird Smith, who was born in 1850 near Fort Smith, Arkansas, while his parents were en route to Indian Territory. When he was a young boy, his father, Pig Redbird Smith, dedicated Redbird to the service of the Cherokee people in accordance with ancient customs. The elder Smith played a key role in the organization of the Keetoowahs prior to the Civil War. He saw to it that when

My close friend, Gustine Moppin, Klamath, matriarch of the Alcatraz Island occupation, with my brother James Mankiller, Alcatraz, 1970.

ABOVE: My sister, Vanessa Mankiller, during the Alcatraz Island occupation near San Francisco, 1970.

LEFT: My sister Linda and brother Richard at Alcatraz Island during the occupation, 1970.

LEFT: On one of my visits to a meeting or to see family during the occupation of Alcatraz, 1970.

OPPOSITE BELOW: My daughter, Gina Olaya, with pipe, her friend Kimberly Contrares on the right, and an unidentified adult on the left at American Indian Community School, Oakland, California, 1974.

OPPOSITE ABOVE: Bill Wahpapah, Kickapoo and Sac and Fox activists, with me about the time we co-founded the American Indian Community School, Oakland, California, 1974.

BELOW: Bay Area Indian Community members gathered around the drum in Oakland, California, 1975. I am third from right in the back row; Felicia is in the middle row on the far left.

Sisters Debbie and Peanut Steele with baby Chemasi at Kashia Rancheria, mid-1970s.

BELOW: A Hopi traditional leader and I at the federal courthouse in San Francisco. She had ridden in the back of a pickup from her home in the Southwest to provide moral support for lawyers in a federal Hopi rights case, San Francisco, mid-1970s.

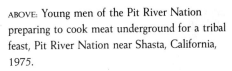

ABOVE: Young men of the Pit River Nation preparing to cook meat underground for a tribal feast, Pit River Nation near Shasta, California, 1975.

BELOW: Sherry Morris, pensive and twirling her hair, as was her habit when in deep, deep thought. Stilwell, Oklahoma, 1979. Photo by Elray DeRoin. *(Courtesy Michael and Meghan Morris.)*

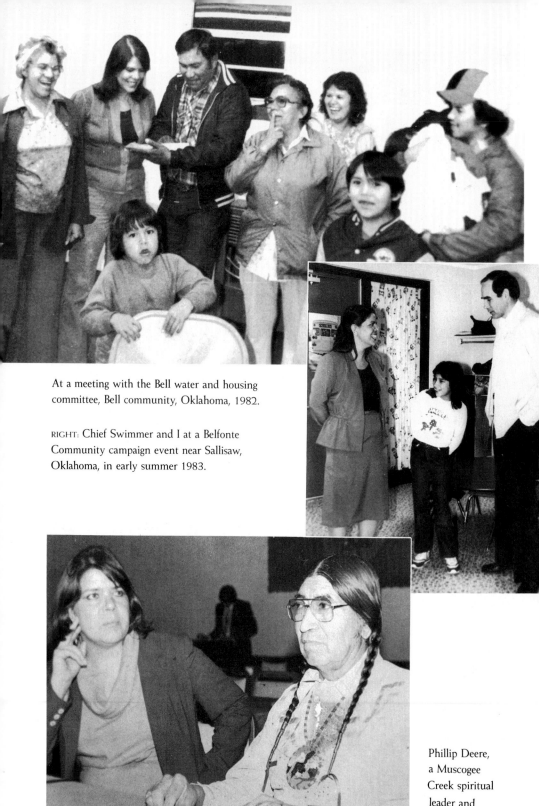

At a meeting with the Bell water and housing committee, Bell community, Oklahoma, 1982.

RIGHT: Chief Swimmer and I at a Belfonte Community campaign event near Sallisaw, Oklahoma, in early summer 1983.

Phillip Deere, a Muscogee Creek spiritual leader and a personal mentor, Tahlequah, 1984.

Taking the oath of office for deputy chief on inauguration day,
August 14, 1983, Tahlequah, Oklahoma.

ABOVE: My mother, daughters, and I at Oklahoma Women's Hall of Fame, Oklahoma City, 1986.

RIGHT: Mary Ross, an engineer and educator, a lineal descendant of Chief John Ross, with me at age nine, CERT Education Dinner, Denver, Colorado, 1987.

Charlie Soap at a powwow in Spavinaw, Oklahoma, May 1986.

RIGHT: Charlie Soap and I in traditional dress at a powwow honoring my ascension to principal chief, Tahlequah, 1986. Bertha Alsenay is in the background.

Deputy Chief John Ketcher and I on inauguration day,
August 14, 1987. Tom Bearpaw is in the background.

OPPOSITE BELOW: Leaders of the Intertribal Council of the Five Tribes. Left to right: Choctaw Chief Hollis Roberts, Muscogee Creek Chief Claude Cox, me, Seminole Chief Ed Tanyan, and Chickasaw Governor Overton James, Tahlequah, 1987.

ABOVE: My return to San Francisco State for Alumni of the Year award, 1988.

A prominent Cherokee midwife, Cherokee, North Carolina, 1988. *(Courtesy of the Smithsonian Institution.)*

Receiving an honorary doctorate from Yale University, New Haven, Connecticut, May 1990. *(Courtesy Yale University.)*

Wrapping up the 1991 election campaign for principal chief with campaign workers. Left to right: Lynn Howard, Gwen Grayson and her daughter, Mary Charlotte.

Headed for yet another community meeting, near Sallisaw, Oklahoma, 1989.

Completing the Cherokee Nation's first bond issue in 1992, Tulsa, Oklahoma.

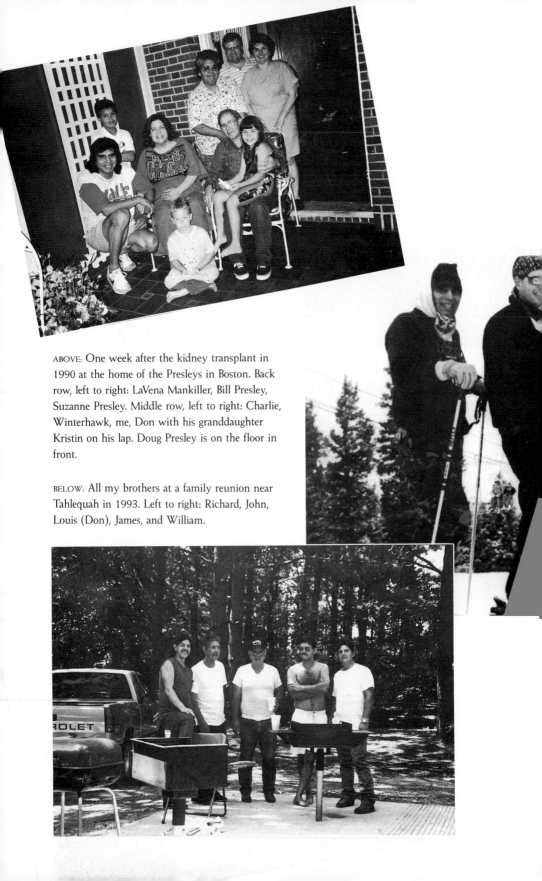

ABOVE: One week after the kidney transplant in 1990 at the home of the Presleys in Boston. Back row, left to right: LaVena Mankiller, Bill Presley, Suzanne Presley. Middle row, left to right: Charlie, Winterhawk, me, Don with his granddaughter Kristin on his lap. Doug Presley is on the floor in front.

BELOW: All my brothers at a family reunion near Tahlequah in 1993. Left to right: Richard, John, Louis (Don), James, and William.

I am presenting the traditional "state of the nation" address at the old Cherokee Capitol, Tahlequah, September 1992.

CENTER: Charlie Soap and his sons on a ski trip. Left to right: Charlie, Chris, Cobey, and Winterhawk. Angel Fire, New Mexico, 1991.

Preparing to rearrange household art. Left to right: Winterhawk, Gina, me, Charlie, and my grandson Kellen in front.

Three of my four grandchildren. Back row: Aaron Swake; front row: Jaron and Breanna Swake. Stilwell, Oklahoma, 1993.

Redbird was only ten years old, he received instruction at the council fires. Later, Redbird, an ardent traditionalist, followed his father's ways, and joined the Keetoowahs.

In our own times, the Cherokee Nation continues to enjoy a good relationship with the members and leaders of the Keetoowah Society. I am a frequent participant in its activities, including all-night dances at the society's ceremonial grounds. The Keetoowah Society is still very well respected among our people, especially among those who understand its historic role in the Cherokee Nation and the importance of continuing our tribal traditions such as ceremonial dances.

Even the revered Keetoowah Society has not been immune to factionalism, however. That has been the case for a good many years. Besides the original Keetoowah Society, there also are smaller groups, including a federally recognized tribal group called the United Keetoowah Band. This band has asserted that it, not the Cherokee Nation of Oklahoma, should represent the interests of Western Cherokees. The band also has been mistakenly associated with the original Keetoowah Society, which has made it clear in public pronouncements and in an amicus curiae brief that it has no association with the United Keetoowah Band.

It was during the 1890s when Redbird Smith was chosen to guide a branch of the Keetoowah Society called the Nighthawk Keetoowahs. This faction, whose members were known as Nighthawks because they met after dark and sent messengers to the various "fires," or ceremonial grounds, of the Cherokees, continued to oppose property distribution and dissolution of the tribal government until a few years after Oklahoma became a state. Smith was arrested by federal marshals and spent some time behind bars after he refused to enroll for allotment. The more traditional Keetoowahs retreated into the hills of eastern Oklahoma to pursue their spiritual beliefs. They refused to take up residence on assigned property or to sign up for allotments. They believed their sole hope for survival was through the power that lives behind the sun.

In 1908, Smith's position as chairman was officially changed to that of chief by the Nighthawk Keetoowah Council. He was unanimously elected by the membership to serve in that capacity for life. He remained a steadfast and capable leader of the Nighthawk Keetoowahs until his death on November 8, 1918. In the last years of his life, Smith was obsessed with building a spirit of cooperation among all the factions of the Cherokee people. He wished to reawaken a racial pride. He encouraged those Cherokees who were better off financially to help those less fortunate.

> *After my selection as a Chief, I awakened to the grave and great responsibilities of a leader of men. I looked about and saw that I had led my people down a long and steep mountain side, now it was my duty to turn and lead them back upward and save them. The unfortunate thing in the mistake and errors of leaders of governments is the penalty the innocent and loyal followers have to pay. My greatest ambition has always been to think right and do right. It is my belief that this is the fulfilling of the law of the Great Creator. In the upbuilding of my people it is my purpose that we shall be spiritually right and industrially strong.*
>
> *I have always believed that the Great Creator had a great design for my people, the Cherokees. I have been taught that from my childhood up and now in my mature manhood I recognize it as a great truth. Our forces have been dissipated by the external forces, perhaps it has been just a training, but we must now get together as a race and render our contribution to mankind.*
>
> *We are endowed with intelligence, we are industrious, we are loyal, and we are spiritual but we are overlooking the particular Cherokee mission on earth, for no man nor race is endowed with these qualifications without a designed purpose. Work and right training is the solution of my following. We as a group are still groping in darkness in many things, but this we know, we must work. A kindly man cannot help his neighbor in need unless he have a surplus and he cannot have a surplus unless he works. It is so simple and yet we have to continually remind our people of this.*
>
> *Our Mixed-bloods should not be overlooked in this program of a racial awakening. Our pride in our ancestral heritage is our great incentive for handing something worthwhile to our posterity. It is this pride in ancestry that makes men strong and loyal for their principle in life. It is the same pride that makes men give up their all for their Government.*
>
> *Redbird Smith*

In 1917, after the death of W. C. Rogers, the officially elected principal chief of the Cherokees, the federal government stipulated that the president of the United States would have sole authority to appoint a Cherokee chief in the future. In the next twenty years, during various presidential administrations, that is just what the government tried to do.

Several principal chiefs were appointed when needed, mostly serving only long enough to sign legal documents. A. B. Cunningham was appointed in 1917, followed by Ed M. Frye in 1923, Richard B. Choate in 1925, Charles J. Hunt in 1928, Oliver P. Brewer in 1931, and W. W. Hastings in 1936.

But our traditional people would not abide by this federal interference. They continued grass-roots efforts to unify the Cherokees and to resist the initiatives of the federal government to bring about total assimilation of the Cherokee people.

During this time, there were no democratically elected tribal representatives. Without a central Cherokee government, our people, especially the children, were preyed upon by greedy charlatans eager to acquire our land. In the old days, the great Cherokee republic had passed laws and developed programs to support and protect the children. An extensive educational system was built, and even an orphanage to house survivors whose lives were devastated by the Civil War. Now the skeleton of the Cherokee Nation could do little to combat the wholesale theft of the land and future of so many Cherokee children.

Redbird Smith's group, along with other Cherokee individuals and organizations, fought hard to protect our land and families, but ultimately, the efforts were in vain. Yet they were successful in some areas. In a time when the pressure to assimilate was tremendous, quite a number of Cherokees, including Smith's followers, managed to preserve the old Cherokee spirituality, ceremonial dances, and the idea that land should be held in common for the general use of everyone. They also perpetuated belief in personal responsibility and community interdependence. Stoke Smith, son of Redbird Smith and chief of the Nighthawk Keetoowah Society, continued the tradition of rejecting assimilationist policies. In 1948, he stated, "We cannot accept their religion or their plan of action. We are content to remain here as we are and will not be a party to any agreement to change our way of living or endanger our homes."

In addition to the actions of those involved in the grass-roots effort, the Cherokee Executive Council proceeded to conduct governmental meetings and to pursue claims against the United States. The U.S. government, of course, refused officially to recognize the council, and continued to operate with its own system of presidential appointees.

The decades following statehood brought more misery to Oklahoma's Native Americans. Angie Debo, the astute writer and lecturer who did so much to expose the mistreatment of native people, described how those who came before us—our grandparents and elders—had been forced "to accept the perilous gift of American citizenship." Debo's careful writing exposed the government's liquidation of the assets of the independent native republics, the Cherokees, Choctaws, Chickasaws, Creeks, and Seminoles, for exactly what it was—nothing but a sweeping betrayal.

In return for becoming federal and state citizens, the tribal population of Oklahoma became entrapped in what Debo called an "orgy of exploitation." Within a single generation, many native people in the state were stripped of their holdings and preyed upon by swindlers. Many came to depend on public charity for their very survival.

> *Unquestionably the policy of destroying the Indians' institutions and suppressing the traits that once made them strong has degraded an overwhelming majority of the fullblood group. But the waves of white influence that flooded the lowlands will almost certainly reach these isolated hills; and the Indians' chance of survival still depends upon their ability to face the inundation. If the present attempt to understand and use their genius for collective effort, the revival of racial selfconsciousness through free consultation rather than arbitrary rulings, and instruction in the white man's economic techniques will restore the hope and confidence of former days, the lost fullbloods in the hills may yet be saved.*
>
> Angie Debo
> And Still the Waters Run, *1940*

There were very few improvements in general conditions and little good news for the Cherokees during the two decades between my father's birth in 1914 and 1934, when the Indian Reorganization Act was passed, putting a stop to further land allotments. Unscrupulous individuals who claimed they wanted to protect individual Cherokees managed to connive away more of our people's property and estates through fraud and deceit. Even children were fair game to these scoundrels.

Because our tribal school system had come to an end by 1913, many Cherokee boys and girls, such as my father and his sister, were gathered up and sent to boarding schools to learn more of the white man's ways. Some children were at the mercy of professional guardians who supposedly had their charges' best interest in mind. But too many times, that was not the case. There was no public outcry for action, or much support or even talk of reform measures. Neither were there many public officials who truly were concerned about the welfare of those youngsters. But there was at least one person who did care, someone who wanted the suffering stopped. She was a truly remarkable woman. Her name was Kate Barnard.

As Oklahoma's commissioner of charities and corrections, Barnard was one of the few public officials who dared to cry out against the abuse of Native American children. From territorial days until her retirement because of illness in 1915, this frail but energetic woman championed the rights of exploited orphans and took a firm stand against the wrongs suffered by native people.

Kate Barnard traveled the state, appealing for reforms, cajoling when necessary, but poised to threaten if appropriate. Like other white institutions, most of the state's press was part of the conspiracy of silence. It simply did not acknowledge the existence of native people's woes. Aware of that fact, Barnard relied on her stirring speeches to reach the public and convince the political powers of the need for increased federal protection for all the members of the Five Tribes.

> *I have been compelled to see orphans robbed, starved, and buried for money. I have named the men and accused them and furnished the records and affidavits to convict them, but with no result. I decided long ago that Oklahoma had no citizen who cared whether or not an orphan is robbed or starved or killed—because his dead claim is easier to handle than if he were alive.*
>
> Kate Barnard

Besides Kate Barnard and those Cherokees who were able to rally to the cause of our people during the first part of the twentieth century, there were only a few enlightened individuals. From that unhappy period, marked by the end of the Great War and the onset of the Great Depression, came only a few shining moments when it appeared that our people might have regained at least some of their balance.

In 1924, Congress passed the Indian Citizenship Act. It provided that "all noncitizen Indians born within the territorial limits of the United States be, and they are hereby, declared to be citizens of the United States: Provided, that the granting of such citizenship shall not in any manner impair or otherwise affect the right of any Indian to tribal or other property."

This meant that by law, Native Americans did not give up their tribal rights and citizenship just because they were made United States citizens. As a result, native people were officially citizens of three sovereign entities—their tribe, the state where they lived, and the United States. Not all native people celebrated passage of the citizenship act. In fact, there was little lobbying for or against the measure, with one notable exception. Some of the Iroquois nations actively lobbied against the legislation, arguing that the citizenship act was being arbitrarily forced on them against their will. They contended that it violated their own tribal citizenship and form of government. Their protests had little effect.

Despite successful passage of the act, many states refused to stop their blatant discriminatory practices against native people, especially when it came to testifying in courts of law, jury duty, and voting. Some of those problems would not be cleared up until the 1960s civil-rights revolution.

In 1926, just two years after the citizenship legislation became law, the United States government finally began to recognize that federal policies concerning Native Americans had been failing since the late nineteenth century. A two-year government study was ordered to be conducted by the Institute for Government Research, known today as the Brookings Institution. The eye-opening results of that exhaustive study of the social and economic conditions among native people was made public in 1928. Called the Merriam Report, the survey signaled the beginning of change in the federal government's thinking about Native Americans.

For the first time in memory, the white government grudgingly acknowledged that native people had not been allowed any real voice in the control of their own destiny. The culture and values of our people had to be preserved and nurtured, rather than neglected and destroyed. The report uncovered the many problems that tribal people had been experiencing for years, including malnutrition, disease, poverty, and dissatisfaction with our living conditions. Immediately, a call went out to humanize the boarding schools and to reform the Bureau of Indian Affairs, especially in education and health care. It was determined that a solution had to be found to the allotment process, which quickly was turning Native Americans into a population of paupers. So many of us were on the verge of becoming people with no hope, but only empty eyes and weak hearts. That trend had to be reversed.

On the heels of the Merriam Report, the stock-market crash of 1929 plunged the nation into economic mayhem. Several years earlier, the depression had already come to roost in rural Oklahoma, so the stock crash affected us less severely. A large number of native people suffered from disease and malnutrition and had a short life expectancy. Then in 1932, after three long years of extreme economic suffering, the presidential election of Franklin D. Roosevelt brought hope to destitute Americans and the promise of sweeping reform. Among the many transitions was an important change of command at the Bureau of Indian Affairs. On April 21, 1933, just seven weeks after Roosevelt took office, he chose John Collier for the job of commissioner of Indian affairs. Collier was a vigorous and reform-minded man.

A former social worker and a close friend of the Navajos and the Pueblo people, Collier proved to be a man of strong convictions. He had an abiding respect for all native people. Because of his associations with various tribes, Collier encouraged the native arts and was a strong proponent of preserving our religious traditions and culture.

A crusader and an outspoken idealist, Collier heard our cries of distress. He proved to be a forceful leader interested in positive change as well as the welfare of Native Americans, whose property, held in trust by the government, was quickly shrinking. It was John Collier who tried to ensure that Roosevelt's New Deal reached the Cherokees and other native people.

Collier created the climate for cultural and civil freedom, and worked hard to attain vital educational improvements. He wished to revolutionize the BIA and rid the system of what he referred to as the "old evils." Early on, he led the campaign for the passage of the important Indian Reorganization Act (IRA), the first major piece of legislation to counter the oppressive federal Indian policies established in the late nineteenth century. In particular, the new law was drafted to help curtail the pattern of economic destruction among Native Americans that resulted from the Dawes Act of 1887. Some critics maintain that despite good intentions, the act failed to achieve that specific goal.

Those same critics also contend that after its passage in 1934, the IRA did little to revitalize native people. However, most would agree that it did help to end the disastrous allotment system. The IRA was intended to strengthen tribal self-government through constitutions, but it also established a system whereby the secretary of the interior gained a considerable degree of control over tribal elections and governmental functions. This benchmark measure also opened new doors by establishing Native American preference in hiring within the BIA. It also authorized a student loan fund so native people could receive training at colleges and trade schools.

Sometimes known as the Wheeler-Howard Act, this legislation had ambitious goals, but was plagued with its share of problems. For example, a fund for land acquisition was never established, and by the mid-1970s, forty years after passage of the IRA, tribes had gained 595,157 acres, while government agencies had condemned 1,811,010 acres of tribal land.

The IRA gave the Bureau of Indian Affairs more, not less, authority over the affairs of native people. In all fairness, given the era in which it was passed, the IRA was a real attempt at reform. However, it would certainly have been far more effective if its original intentions had been kept and a land-acquisition program had been fully funded.

Even though the IRA helped to usher in a new era of optimism for Native Americans in our relationship with the federal government, not everyone was supportive, including a formidable number of white Oklahomans and some Cherokees. Part of the problem was that people were mixed about Commissioner John Collier. At the start of Roosevelt's tenure, Oklahoma Democrats had hoped he would name someone from their state as commissioner of Indian affairs. But when the Democrats could not come to any consensus about a candidate, the nod went to Collier.

Members of Oklahoma's congressional delegation generally worked together in opposition to the IRA. Our former tribal attorney, W. W. Hastings—a Cherokee who entered Congress in 1915 and, as Angie Debo pointed out, "had achieved distinction in a mixed society"—saw no need for the changes called for in the reform legislation. After studying the measure, he concluded that it would make our people feel inferior and further prevent our assimilation.

The Oklahoma press joined big business and prominent ranchers in vehemently opposing the bill, as did several Christian groups and religious zealots. Their objections resulted from Collier's support of native religion, which the missionaries and preachers thought was pagan. Nonetheless, large numbers of Choctaws, Chickasaws, Creeks, and members of other tribes approved of the IRA, as did several thousand Cherokees.

Ultimately, implementation of the IRA was delayed by a combination of political infighting and lack of endorsement from some skeptical tribal leaders and assimilated mixed-bloods. Vicious assaults by angry white businessmen, ranchers, and farmers did not help. Even attempts to change the bill to appease all sides met with angry opposition in Oklahoma, where state lawmakers passed resolutions condemning key provisions. Extreme right-wingers and pseudopatriots sullied Collier's reputation by calling him an atheist and a "Red"—as in communist—for many years the worst label anyone in this nation could be given. In 1935, Collier was obliged to refute those bogus charges during appearances before the House Indian Affairs Committee.

Finally, in 1936, after the addition of excessive amendments to comply with the objections of its Oklahoma enemies, a bill was passed by Congress known as the Oklahoma Indian Welfare Act. This law, like the IRA, allowed tribes to adopt constitutions and secure corporate charters giving native people in the state the right to engage in business, administer tribal property, and elect officers. The Cherokee Nation did not organize under the Oklahoma Indian Welfare Act of 1936 because of our historical relationship with the United States and our belief in our inherent sovereignty as a nation.

Ignoring the federal government's system of appointing what some of our people called "chiefs for a day" as token leaders, a council made up of several Cherokee organizations met in 1938 and chose its own candidate. The council elected J. Bartley Milam of Claremore, Oklahoma, as our tribe's new principal chief. History was in the making. On April 16, 1941, President Roosevelt solidified the relationship between the two governments by appointing Milam as chief of the Cherokee Nation. For the first time ever, the elected chief of the council and the presidentially appointed chief were one and the same. And this time it was not just temporary. Chief Milam, subsequently reappointed by Roosevelt and later by President Harry Truman, would remain our leader until his death in 1949, when we returned to chiefs by presidential appointment for some time.

Although World War II brought about a severe cut in domestic spending, especially for the New Deal Indian programs, Chief Milam proved to be fully committed to the revitalization of our tribe. During the first several years of his tenure, attention was focused on the events transpiring in war-torn Europe and in the Pacific, but Milam forced the

United States to continue to deal with the Cherokees on other issues of importance. This was vital, since much of the energy of reform was lost in the war effort.

In addition to the administrative side of his role as principal chief, Milam also took a strong interest in Cherokee culture, history, and education. He was instrumental in establishing Cherokee-language classes at several institutions. Milam also played a key part in the creation of the Cherokee National Historical Society. He initiated negotiations for the purchase of the site of the old Cherokee National Female Seminary to develop a national heritage center for all of our people.

Just as we did during World War I, the Cherokee Nation again responded to the call of the United States in World War II. Many Cherokees enlisted in the armed forces and fought bravely in North Africa, Sicily, and the Pacific. One of our best-known soldiers was Thomas Bearpaw, a Cherokee from Stilwell, who served with Darby's Rangers, an elite U.S. Army commando unit. He was captured during the Battle of Anzio Beach in 1943, transported to Poland and then to northern Italy, where he was held prisoner until 1944. Bearpaw received the Bronze Star, the Oklahoma Medal of Valor, and several other decorations.

The experience of traveling across the seas to new and strange lands had a profound impact on our young Cherokees as they met people of other races and ethnic backgrounds.

On the home front, many tribal leaders from across the nation recognized that Native Americans were still in a precarious position when it came to basic human rights. In response to those concerns, many of those leaders met in Denver in 1944 to form the National Congress of American Indians. One of those in attendance to help with the founding was Chief Milam. Now considered to be the oldest and most representative national organization for native people, the NCAI was established to help Native Americans protect their land and treaty rights, and to preserve cultural values.

> *We, the members of the Indian tribes of the United States of America invoking the Divine guidance of Almighty God in order to secure to ourselves—the Indians of the United States and the Natives of Alaska—and our descendants the rights and benefits to which we are entitled under the laws of the United States, and the several states thereof; to enlighten the public toward the better understanding of the Indian*

> *people, to preserve rights under Indian treaties or agreements with the United States, to promote the common welfare of the American Indian and to foster the loyalty and allegiance of American Indians to the flag of the United States do establish this organization and adopt the following Constitution and By-laws.*
>
> Preamble to National Congress of
> American Indians Constitution

Returning to Oklahoma after the historic founding of the NCAI, Chief Milam worked toward the establishment of an elected tribal council for the Cherokee Nation, to further legitimize our government and to make it more responsive to the needs of the Cherokee people.

With John Collier's resignation as head of the BIA in 1944, an era drew to a close. Any advancements that had been made under the Indian Reorganization Act began to be hobbled by the changing political climate. In 1946, in an attempt to counteract the continuing loss of land, Milam began to purchase property to be held in trust for the Cherokee Nation. By year's end, he had purchased 21,453 acres. Aware of our previous dealings with the government, Milam was correct to make such a move. Previous reform measures were being ignored. The resurgence of tribal governments that Collier had fought for would not become a reality until after the termination policy and federal relocation program of the 1950s proved to be disastrous for Native Americans.

On July 30, 1948, after receiving the approval of our "protectors" at the BIA, Milam called a national convention at Tahlequah. The meeting was controversial; there were charges that it was dominated by white attorneys. As a result of the dissatisfaction with how the convention was conducted, Milam was expelled from membership in the Keetoowah Society during a special session called on August 13, 1948.

At the July convention, a standing committee of eleven members, with the principal chief as an ex officio member, had been elected. The representatives were chosen from each of the nine districts of the old Cherokee Nation. There was also a member at large, and one representative from the Texas Cherokees. This was a major step toward the return of the tribal-council form of government for the Cherokee Nation. It was also one of Milam's last significant acts as principal chief. On May 8, 1949, Bartley Milam died.

Later that year, President Harry Truman appointed William Wayne

Keeler, an affluent mixed-blood oil executive, to succeed Milam as chief of the Cherokee Nation. Keeler would be reappointed by succeeding presidents until 1971, when at last the *entire* Cherokee tribe would be permitted for the first time since statehood to elect its own chief.

The grandson of George Keeler and of Nelson Carr, prominent white Indian Territory pioneers who had married one-eighth Cherokee women, Keeler grew up in the Bartlesville area in eastern Oklahoma. In those parts, it was well known that Keeler's paternal grandfather, George Keeler, had brought in the first commercial oil well in Indian Territory, in 1897. The gusher was dubbed the Nellie Johnstone, after the wife of one of Keeler's business partners.

In understanding the significance of Keeler, it is important to note that his background contrasted strongly with that of his predecessors. Born in Dalhart, Texas, while his parents were on a business trip, Keeler was reared in the "oil patch." He graduated as valedictorian of his high school class, and studied engineering at the University of Kansas on a Harry E. Sinclair science scholarship. When Sinclair Oil became enmeshed in the infamous Teapot Dome scandal, the scholarship money was suddenly cut off, forcing Keeler to drop out of the university. In 1929, he went to work full time for Phillips Petroleum Company, one of the foremost oil companies in the country, with its corporate headquarters in Keeler's hometown of Bartlesville.

Twenty years later, when Truman first appointed him as Cherokee chief, Keeler was a vice-president of the refining department at Phillips and one of the firm's rising stars. He climbed rapidly through the corporate ranks at Phillips. After several key promotions, Keeler became executive vice-president in 1956, chairman of the executive committee in 1962, and president and chief executive officer in 1968. He hobnobbed with several United States presidents and foreign dignitaries, and served on many prestigious boards and councils. In the 1950s and 1960s, Keeler also chaired his share of task forces commissioned to study BIA operations, discuss native land rights, or tackle the gamut of problems experienced by contemporary Native Americans trying to survive the termination and relocation policies of the federal government.

Although his countless fans like to point out that, for the most part, he continued to pursue the same causes and concerns that had interested his predecessor, Chief Milam, Keeler also has attracted his share of detractors. Some of them prefer to ignore his achievements, and instead claim that Keeler's considerable white heritage, as well as his strong connections to the white Establishment, were negatives as far as the Cherokee Nation was concerned. They enjoy claiming that W. W. Keeler was much more comfortable on the golf course or at a cocktail party than he was attending a traditional dance at an isolated ceremonial ground. I recall an article published in *Ramparts* in 1971 which spoke of Keeler as being only one-sixteenth Cherokee and more "the descendant in spirit and fact of the whites who overran Indian Territory and took away from the Indians, to whom it had been given in payment, sacred lands where their ancestors were buried."

My own traditional relatives, however, are very respectful of Bill Keeler. And many elders in rural areas remember when Keeler came to visit their communities.

> *History is a great teacher. It must be questioned, it must be pierced with an analytical eye; but it can never be dismissed.*
>
> William Wayne Keeler
>
> *The protection of our land and water and other natural resources are of utmost importance to us. Our culture not only exists in time but in space as well. If we lose our land we are adrift like a leaf on a lake, which will float aimlessly and then dissolve and disappear.*
>
> *Our land is more than the ground on which we stand and sleep, and in which we bury our dead. The land is our spiritual mother whom we can no easier sell than our physical mother.*
>
> *We are products of the poverty, despair, and discrimination pushed on our people from the outside. We are the products of chaos. Chaos in our tribes. Chaos in our personal lives.*
>
> *We are also products of a rich and ancient culture which supersedes and makes bearable any oppressions we are forced to bear. We believe that one's basic identity should be with his tribe. We believe in tribalism, we believe that tribalism is what has caused us to endure.*
>
> National Indian Youth Conference policy statement, 1961

Throughout the twentieth century, there have always been many full-blooded Cherokees and those of half or more Cherokee blood who have pursued our more traditional ways and culture. Some of them were members of my family; others were good friends of my grandfather and father. They lived on isolated tracts of rocky land and in small communities dotting the hills of eastern Oklahoma. None of those communities was incorporated, and most did not appear on any maps. Some were not even visible to motorists who may have strayed from the beaten path and driven down the dirt roads snaking through those hidden hills.

Generally, the more traditional Cherokees maintained their individual allotments and depended on seasonal work to supplement meager incomes. They also counted on their gardens and on hunting and fishing. On special occasions, they congregated at the nearest church, school, or ceremonial ground. Most of them spoke Cherokee as their first language. Some spoke nothing but Cherokee. Besides maintaining our language, many Cherokees preserved a sense of community in more than one hundred distinct Cherokee settlements scattered throughout our Nation. People shared what little they had with one another. They found humor and joy even in seemingly small things. The Cherokee medicine and ceremonies continued despite everything that happened around us.

Tribal elders talked about those times. They spoke of when some folks in Washington made serious efforts to help us out. Yet for too long, our tribal leaders were still being appointed by the federal government.

Tribal elders told me that when they were young and trying to make a go of it, no one ever gave up the dream of a revitalized Cherokee Nation. People would walk to one another's homes in those rural communities and sit on the porches and discuss ways to keep the Cherokee culture and Cherokee government alive. People rode horses over the hills to attend community meetings. Men and women got together just to talk about how best to retain our traditions. They spoke of the old days of our tribe, and they told stories to keep our Cherokee spirit strong.

Some of them repeated the old stories that teach us lessons. They may have told the story of the deluge, the one about the big flood and the dog that warned the man, or the story of the ghosts dancing after the waters had disappeared. It is a story that has been passed down through time.

One story tells of the dog with the bones protruding from its neck. Another version tells of a star with a fiery tail falling from the heavens. That star becomes a man with long hair, and he is the one who warns the people of the coming deluge. Similar stories of the earth being flooded can be found among many other native tribes. Sometimes, in those other stories, the warning of the rising waters comes from cranes, sometimes from wolves.

There are people who probably think that at least part of the flood story sounds as if it came from the Bible. But others know that the great deluge that caused the people to float around aimlessly in our Cherokee story is quite different. It was a phenomenon brought on by an upheaval and tilting of the earth, so that the waters flowed over the land and covered everything. Chaos resulted. The flood came because the earth had lost its balance.

CHAPTER 11

FULL CIRCLE

A long time ago, several young men made up their minds to find the place where the Sun lives and see what the Sun is like. They got ready their bows and arrows, their parched corn and extra moccasins, and started out toward the east. At first, they met tribes they knew, then they came to tribes they had only heard about, and at last to others of which they had never heard.

They found a tribe of root eaters and another of acorn eaters, with great piles of acorn shells near their houses. In one tribe, the young men found a sick man who was dying, and they were told it was the custom there when a man died to bury his wife in the same grave with him. They waited until he was dead, when they saw his friends lower the body into a great pit, so deep and dark that from the top they could not see the bottom. Then a rope was tied around the woman's body, together with a bundle of pine knots, with a lighted pine knot in her hand. She was lowered into the pit to die in the darkness after the last pine knot had burned.

The young men traveled on until they came at last to the sunrise place where the sky reaches down to the ground. They found that the sky was an arch, or vault, of solid rock hung above the earth. It was always swinging up and down, so that when it went up, there was an open place like a door between the sky and ground, and when it swung back, the door was shut. The Sun came out of this door from the east and climbed along on the inside of the arch. It had a human figure, but was too bright for them to see clearly and too hot to come very near. They waited until the Sun had come out, and then tried to get through while the door was still open, but just as the first *young man was in the doorway, the rock came down and crushed him. The other six were afraid to try it. Because they were now at the end of the world, they turned around and started back again, but they had traveled so far that they were old men when they reached home.*

It was on Alcatraz, that irregular oblong hump of barren sandstone stuck in the bay waters between San Francisco and Sausalito, where at long last some Native Americans, including me, truly began to regain our balance.

Alcatraz was a most appropriate site for that watershed event because the earliest people to look on the place were the Ohlones, from the Costanoan family. Long before any Europeans sailed into the bay, the Ohlones and other coastal tribes frequently had paused at the island to get their bearings while navigating choppy seawaters in sleek canoes. Native people did not use the island for a burial site, or build their domed bark and hide houses on the rugged surface. Instead, they saw that it was a place better suited for the ocean birds to rest and preen in the sun.

When the Spaniards came, they found other uses for the island. They fortified it with the guns of conquest. In the late 1700s, they also gave it a name—*Isla de los Alcatraces*, or "Island of the Pelicans," after the big white birds that congregated there. Many years later when Anglo settlers took over California, the United States Army turned Alcatraz, as they called it, into a military prison and disciplinary barracks. It was not just for Confederate captives and convict soldiers, but also for the native people whom the whites enslaved.

In the early 1870s, two of those people brought in shackles to the island had fought in the Modoc War, in northern California. Their tribal chief, named Kintpuash, known to the whites as Captain Jack, had led his people in a futile struggle to prevent their removal to a reservation. On Good Friday, April 11, 1873, Captain Jack shot and killed the only general in the U.S. Army to die in the so-called "Indian wars." For this deed, Captain Jack was hanged along with three of his headmen. The two teenage Modocs sentenced to Alcatraz had been spared the hangman's noose, but being sent to the island was almost a worse fate. One of them soon died of tuberculosis, and the other no doubt wished he were dead.

Besides illness and foul conditions on the island, the prison guards could be deadly. During the late 1800s, many native people of California were locked away on Alcatraz. So were Paiute people and Chiricahua

Apaches, including a friend of Geronimo's. It is said that to this day, the Apaches of Arizona keep alive a woeful dirge that tells the story of one of their brave warriors who dared go against the white man and was taken manacled to Alka-taz, the lonely island.

In the aftermath of the 1906 San Francisco earthquake, the city jail population was shipped to Alcatraz for safekeeping. During World War I, conscientious objectors sent from Fort Leavenworth, Kansas, took up residence in the island's honeycomb of cellblocks. Then in 1933, when the army had no more use for the place, Alcatraz was transferred to the Federal Bureau of Prisons. It was transformed into a high-security penitentiary to house the nation's most incorrigible convicts—those who were regarded as being monstrous, depraved, and beyond all redemption. The first batch arrived in the autumn of 1934. Celebrity inmates included Al Capone, Alvin Karpis, "Machine Gun" Kelly, and Robert Stroud, the famed "Birdman of Alcatraz."

They were well known to the outside world, but like all the others on "the Rock," as Alcatraz was commonly called, they were given no special treatment. They had no recreation, no rehabilitation. Most inmates never had a visitor. They spent an average of sixteen to twenty-three hours each day in a cell that measured only five feet by nine feet. Punishment for the slightest violation was immediate and severe. Swift currents of frigid bay water made escape practically impossible, although some convicts who became desperate enough tried to reach the mainland. Three who supposedly escaped the island were never heard of again.

Once a sanctuary for gulls and pelicans, Alcatraz had become an inhumane warehouse for the living dead. It was an island of hate. Because of mounting financial problems and public pressure, Attorney General Robert Kennedy ordered the federal prison to be closed in 1963. For a year after the last inmate was removed, Alcatraz sat like an aging derelict surrounded by water, a symbol of past punishment and acts of brute force. Visitors to San Francisco stood on Fisherman's Wharf and gazed at "the Rock." Some of them circled it in tour boats. In the dying sunlight when the fog moved in, it seemed to be only a mirage. The island was no longer as it had been centuries before, when free-spirited native people stopped there as nature's guests.

On a brisk November day in 1969, it was on this ancient island of mean rock and ruined cellblocks that Native Americans made a stand. Our time in the sun had arrived.

There had been a few victories for native people earlier in the decade, when the winds of change came with the civil-rights movement, and the mood of the nation shifted. Slowly, ever so slowly, it seemed that the white population was beginning to understand that Native Americans also had concerns and needs. By the early sixties, the tribal termination policy had been fully discredited. The suffering of tribes that had been obliged to participate became apparent.

> *During the present century we have been moving steadily away from all the pervasive paternalism of the 1880's and '90's toward a more wholesome respect for the human dignity of individual Indians as well as the values of age-old tribal cultures.*
>
> > *Phillieo Nash, commissioner of Indian affairs*
> > *December 6, 1962*
>
> *I have a dream that my four little children will one day live in a nation where they will not be judged by the color of their skin, but by the content of their character.*
>
> > *Martin Luther King, Jr., August 28, 1963*

A significant piece of progressive legislation during that decade was the Economic Opportunity Act of 1965. This new law allowed Native American organizations and tribes to bypass the BIA while they planned, developed, and implemented their own social, educational, and economic initiatives. For some native communities and reservations, it was the beginning of economic self-determination.

The passage of more reform legislation and judicial action soon followed. Then on March 6, 1968, President Lyndon Johnson, inspired by promises made in the Kennedy years, delivered the first message to Congress on Native American affairs in more than a century. He spoke of providing native people with the freedom "to remain in their homelands, *if* they choose, without surrendering their dignity; an opportunity to move to the towns and cities of America, *if* they choose, equipped with the skills to live in equality and dignity."

Johnson pointed out that the housing situation for most native people was inadequate. He noted that unemployment among native people had reached an astonishing 40 percent, and only half of our youngsters graduated from high school. He called us the forgotten Americans. He stressed that instead of more paternalistic practices, the federal government needed to allow freedom of choice and to protect "the rights of the first Americans to remain Indians while exercising their rights as Americans."

Congress responded by passing the Indian Civil Rights Act of 1968, which brought further federal intervention into tribal governments and courts. Ostensibly, the act extended the protection of the United States Bill of Rights to Native Americans, but mostly as those rights related to citizens under tribal governments, not the government of the United States.

The wheels of bureaucracy never turn fast enough. Some elements of the bill were not legislated for more than a decade. Individual Native Americans secured the promise of new rights in the 1960s, but it took many more legal triumphs in the 1970s to win completely the right of self-government that we all were so anxious to obtain. Federal Indian policy still had a long way to go. Endless delays increased our anger and frustration. Before any balance or harmony could be achieved, the archaic federal system that dominated our lives had to be fully rehabilitated. That reform needed to come from within. We wanted to make sure that the government knew this simple fact, and that we had its undivided attention.

Native American activism became more militant for many of those reasons. That is why the native protests and marches of the 1960s were so important. That is why native people seized Alcatraz.

A takeover of the island had been under consideration for some time. In 1964, just one year after the Alcatraz prison operations had been halted, five Sioux people living in the Bay area had made a run at it. Dressed in their full tribal regalia, they landed on Alcatraz and claimed title to the island for their people. Federal marshals quickly moved in, and the "squatters" were forced to leave.

During the years following that first takeover attempt, San Francisco's Board of Supervisors was deluged by proposals for commercial developments on Alcatraz. They included resort hotels, patriotic memorials, public parks, and gambling casinos. One party suggested turning the island into a cemetery. Of the more than five hundred schemes the city officials reviewed, the one that caught the officials' collective eye was from Texas oil tycoon Lamar Hunt. He offered to pay a reported $2 million for the island in hopes of erecting a shopping and tourist complex, complete with manicured gardens, an underground space museum, and a futuristic tower topped by a revolving restaurant. Hunt said he would preserve the main cellblock for tourists' enjoyment. In late September of 1969, the supervisors gave Hunt's proposal their stamp of approval.

That action incensed our local Native American community, especially those involved with the Bay Area United Native American Council and others associated with the American Indian Center. Both of those entities had helped to sponsor the failed occupation of the island in 1964. Alcatraz still had great symbolic value. Almost immediately, planning got under way to launch another occupation. The target date was the summer of 1970.

Before a preliminary course of action could be considered, more disaster struck. On the evening of October 28, 1969, a four-alarm fire of mysterious origin gutted our beloved American Indian Center building in the Mission District. For almost a dozen years, this center had been a home away from home for many of us, perhaps for as many as thirty thousand native people.

Just weeks after the fire, while Alcatraz was returning to the headlines, government officials began to scramble for ways to placate us. They offered available space at the Presidio, the sprawling U.S. military reservation, as a perfect spot for the reestablishment of the Indian Center. I suppose they did not realize the irony of Native Americans retreating to an army fort. The offer was declined, and a temporary center was soon established elsewhere in the Mission District. Although our original building—its entire physical structure—had been decimated, the spirit of the Indian Center could not be destroyed.

The fire had a galvanizing effect on everyone in the local Native American community. Time was of the essence. A statement had to be delivered. It would require action and not mere words. We could not sit in the ashes and weep. We had to pick ourselves up and go on. We could not afford to wait for the next summer. The occupation of Alcatraz had to occur as soon as possible. And it did.

On November 9, 1969, fourteen native people hitched a ride with Sausalito yachtsmen on a charter boat headed to Alcatraz Island. Most of them were students from Berkeley, Santa Cruz, and San Francisco State College. They were led by a visionary young Mohawk man named Richard Oakes and by Adam Nordwell, a Chippewa from Minnesota.

They landed at about six o'clock in the evening and claimed the island "in the name of Indians of All Tribes." To them, "the Rock" symbolized our lost lands. They declared it Indian property under the terms of the Fort Laramie Treaty of 1868. That document contained a provision allowing any male Native American older than eighteen whose tribe was party to the treaty to file for a homestead on abandoned or unused federal property. It was the same argument the five Sioux had made when they went to the island in 1964.

Beyond the terms of the treaty, the activists even offered to buy Alcatraz from the government. To do that, they tapped into the sixty dollars that made up the kitty of the San Francisco State College Native American studies program. Then they purchased twenty-four dollars' worth of glass beads and red cloth to offer in fair exchange for the island. After all, they reasoned, the white men had made a similar offer when purchasing a larger island they had named Manhattan more than three hundred years before.

This time, there were were no takers. After nineteen hours, Coast Guard cutters pulled alongside the island docks, and the native people were escorted from Alcatraz.

But they did not stay away. They could not do that. They had to go back to "the Rock." In the early hours of November 20, eighty-nine native people—men, women, and children from a variety of tribes—returned to Alcatraz Island. They brought with them tangible items such as food, water, and sleeping bags, and intangible ones such as the hopes, aspirations, and dreams of all of us from the Native American community who remained behind. They also took along plenty of resolve.

This time, their stay would last not nineteen hours, but nineteen months. The island population sometimes swelled to as many as one thousand. All sorts of people came. They came from tiny Alaskan native villages, from the great Iroquois Nation, the Northwest Coast, from Oklahoma, South Dakota, Montana, the surrounding California native communities, and every region of the United States. Some came bearing gifts of fresh salmon or dried meat. Others came bearing the gift of a special song, ceremony, or prayer. Vine Deloria, Jr., the Sioux who wrote the book which became our Indian manifesto, *Custer Died for Your Sins*, was a visitor. So were Anthony Quinn, Jane Fonda, Jonathan Winters, Ed Ames, and Merv Griffin. Candice Bergen brought her sleeping bag and spent a night on the floor of the clinic. There were boats loaded with politicians, reporters, photographers, and curiosity seekers running the Coast Guard blockades. Donations of food and clothing and offers of support came from churches and synagogues, women's organizations, labor unions, and the Black Panthers. Troops of Girl Scouts and Boy Scouts visited the island, bringing with them Christmas toys for the native children.

Although Alcatraz ultimately would not remain a sovereign Indian nation, the incredible publicity generated by the occupation served all of us well by dramatizing the injustices that the modern Native Americans have endured at the hands of white America. The Alcatraz experience nurtured a sense among us that anything was possible—even, perhaps, justice for native people.

> *We will give to the inhabitants of this island a portion of the land for their own to be held in trust by the American Indian Affairs and by the Bureau of Caucasian Affairs to hold in perpetuity—for as long as the sun shall rise and the rivers go down to the sea. We will further guide the inhabitants in the proper way of living. We will offer them our religion, our education, our life-ways, in order to help them achieve our level of civilization and thus raise them and all their white brothers up from their savage and unhappy state. We offer this treaty in good faith and wish to be fair and honorable in our dealings with all white men.*
>
> Proclamation from Alcatraz Indians to the United States
> November 20, 1969

Before it was over, four of my brothers and sisters and their children had joined the original band on the island. I, too, would become totally engulfed by the Native American movement, largely because of the impact that the Alcatraz occupation made on me. Ironically, the occupation of Alcatraz—a former prison—was extremely liberating for me. As a result, I consciously took a path I still find myself on today as I continue to work for the revitalization of tribal communities

From those unforgettable events that flashed like bright comets years ago, I have tried to retain valuable chunks of experience along with some of youth's raw courage. It is my hope that those idealistic moments have blended with the perspective that luckily comes with maturity. It makes for a vintage mixture that has helped to sustain me against all odds, against real and imaginary foes, and even against death itself.

Still, no matter where my path leads me, I must always remember where the journey started. It was in San Francisco—at Alcatraz, and at the American Indian Center, and in my own home where, starting about the time of the Alcatraz takeover, native people often came to sip coffee, make plans, and build indestructible dreams. The occupation of Alcatraz excited me like nothing ever had before. It helped to center me and caused me to focus on my own rich and valuable Cherokee heritage.

My brother Richard, six years my junior, was the first of the Mankiller siblings who joined the other native people at Alcatraz. He later served on the Alcatraz Council, the panel of men and women who tried to maintain a semblance of order on the island. After Richard, the next ones to go were my younger sister Vanessa and our little brother James.

Finally, my sister Linda wanted to go out and be with the others. Only twenty years old, Linda already had three small children, and she was separated from her husband. She and her kids were temporarily staying with Hugo and me. When she made up her mind to go, I accompanied Linda and her children to the island. At the docks, we saw a lot of people we knew. We rode out together in a boat supplied by Credence Clearwater Revival that was called the *Clearwater*. Of the four Mankillers who went to Alcatraz, Linda ended up staying there the longest. She remained until June of 1971, when federal marshals finally removed the last few native occupants.

I will always be very proud of my brothers and sisters for going to Alcatraz. I did not stay there, but always returned to the mainland, where I felt I could be of more service by remaining active in the various support efforts. I found myself spending more time at the new home of the American Indian Center. It was a key command post where much of the fund-raising activities for Alcatraz took place, and almost all of the communications were funneled to and from the island.

The entire Alcatraz occupation was such an important period for me. Every day that passed seemed to give me more self-respect and sense of pride. Much of the credit for that awakening has to go to the young men and women who first went to Alcatraz and helped so many of us return to the correct way of thinking. One of the most influential was Richard Oakes.

Oakes was a student at San Francisco State. Formerly an ironworker in New York, he moved to California, where he drove a truck. He then worked at Warren's, an Indian bar in the Mission District, while he went back to college. He was instrumental in starting the Native American studies program at San Francisco State, and he soon became one of the strongest voices of activism and social protest at the American Indian Center.

I became well acquainted with Richard Oakes during the occupation, and I found him to be one of our most articulate leaders. Although only in his late twenties when I met him, Richard spoke persuasively about treaty rights and the need for America to honor its legal commitments to native people. He spoke of the various tribal histories and diverse cultures, and of the many contributions Native Americans have made to contemporary society. His words, considered so radical in the 1970s, are strikingly similar to the language of many of the relatively moderate tribal leaders of today.

> *Alcatraz was symbolic to a lot of people, and it meant something real to a lot of people. There are many old prophecies that speak of the younger people rising up and finding a way for the People to live. The Hopi, the spiritual leaders of the Indian people, have a prophecy that is at least 1,200 years old. It says that the People would be pushed off their land from the East to the West, and when they reached the Westernmost tip of America, they would begin to take back the land that was stolen from them.*
>
> *There was one old man who came on the island. He must have been eighty or ninety years old. When he stepped up on the dock, he was overjoyed. He stood there for a minute and then said, "At last, I am free."*
>
> *Alcatraz was a place where thousands of people had been imprisoned, some of them Indians. We sensed the spirits of the prisoners. At times it was spooky, but mostly the spirit of mercy was in the air. The spirits were free. They mingled with the spirits of the Indians that came on the island and hoped for a better future.*
>
> Richard Oakes, 1972
> from Ramparts, *written shortly before his death*

Richard and his wife, Anne, a Pomo woman, had five young children and took care of several others. In January of 1970, after they had resided on the island for almost three months, one of their daughters, Yvonne, was playing in a deserted prison building when she fell down a three-story stairwell. She was rushed to the mainland, but she died two days later. Annie had had a premonition that something bad was going to happen to her family.

The girl's death cast a veil of sorrow over the island. Although Richard explained that even in death his daughter was still within the circle of life, the grief was too much. He and Annie packed up their few possessions and left with their other children. Later that year, Richard helped the Pit River Indians in their struggle over land rights with a powerful utility company. He endured tear gas, billy clubs, and getting tossed in jail, only to end up in a bar brawl back in San Francisco where two men beat him to a pulp with pool cues. Richard survived, but he was never able to return to his earlier level of activism. He moved farther north to settle in the Pomo country near Santa Rosa. In September of 1972, a caretaker of a YMCA camp claimed that Richard had threatened him with a knife. The white man pulled a gun and shot Richard Oakes dead. He was in his thirtieth year.

Annie floundered after Richard's death. I made it a point to visit her several times at her home. Gradually, she began to withdraw more and more from community work, and finally we lost touch. But whenever I hear the name Annie or see a Cherokee woman whose demeanor reminds me of my friend, I think of that resilient Pomo woman and of her children and of the daughter who fell to her death on Alcatraz, and I always feel profoundly sad. I pray that Annie is doing well. I also think of Richard Oakes, the visionary young man whose turbulence helped us all find harmony.

> *We did a lot of singing in those days. I remember the fires at nighttime, the cold of the night, the singing around the campfire of the songs that aren't shared by the white people . . . the songs of friendship, the songs of understanding. We did a lot of singing. We sang into the early hours of the morning. It was beautiful to behold and beautiful to listen to.*
>
> *Richard Oakes, 1972*

Another of the eloquent native leaders to emerge from the Alcatraz Island experience was John Trudell, a wiry young Lakota man—one of the best thinkers I have ever met. Immensely creative and irreverent, Trudell is still absolutely committed to whatever he is doing. That has not changed.

John and his wife Lou and their two daughters, Maurie and Tara, came up from Los Angeles to join the Indians of All Tribes, as the group at Alcatraz was called. I thought they were the most incompatible couple I had ever met. John was hyperactive and serious, while Lou was level and steady but with a great sense of humor. She became the consummate earth mother on the island and later for the entire East Bay Indian community. John and Lou did have one common interest—a great love of politics. Their third child, a son they named Wovoka after the Paiute medicine man who had originated the Ghost Dance, was born on Alcatraz.

During the occupation, John served as the announcer on Radio Free Alcatraz, which was beamed for thirty minutes each evening over Berkeley's radio station KPFA. He often spoke of creating a complex on Alcatraz that would include an educational center for Native American studies, a historical archives and museum, and a spiritual center. Grace Thorpe, a Sac and Fox and the daughter of all-time Olympic hero Jim Thorpe of Oklahoma, was a guest on his program, as were many other activists.

Lou became a close friend of mine, and I always have maintained a great deal of affection and respect for John. Even when the federal government rejected all Native American claims to Alcatraz and suggested that the island be used as a park, John and the others would not budge.

> We will no longer be museum pieces, tourist attractions and politicians' playthings. There will be no park on this island, because it changes the whole meaning of what we are here for.
>
> John Trudell
> New York Times, April 9, 1970

Throughout the Alcatraz experience and afterward, I met so many people from other tribes who had a major and enduring effect on me. They changed how I perceived myself as a woman and as a Cherokee.

Gustine Moppin—the Klamath woman whom I had known since I was a young girl, the person who had convinced me to continue my education—was a true inspiration. Gustine was the personification of the Cherokee concept of "having a good mind." Unfailingly cheerful even in the worst of circumstances, she devoted every waking moment to helping others.

Gustine thought I had the potential to do something with my life. She encouraged and supported me through those years as my marriage eroded and I struggled for independence. I appreciated that. I was always happy that we reconnected during the Alcatraz experience. Years later when she developed diabetes, we had many talks about the toll this dreaded disease takes on native people. She lost an arm to diabetes and then had to undergo dialysis when her kidneys failed. Ultimately, she was confined to a wheelchair. When I last saw her in the winter of 1990, Gustine was quite frail, but she had not stopped helping people. She was busy counseling other amputees on independent living. She still served on the boards of several Indian agencies. Soon after that visit, Gustine passed into the other world. I lost a sister. The Bay area Native American community lost its matriarch.

Another California relocatee from those bittersweet years whom I stayed in contact with was Bill Wahpepah, who was Kickapoo and Sac and Fox. I worked very closely with Bill on several projects, including an alternative school, youth services, and an Indian adult education center. He brought some of the primary AIM leaders—Dennis Banks, Carter Camp, and Vernon and Clyde Bellecourt—to his home. Clyde Bellecourt, one of AIM's founders, was especially likable. He came to the Bay area with an entourage of native children. It was obvious how much he cared about them and how hard he worked to help them.

Leonard Crow Dog, a vital cog in the Native American movement, also came to Wahpepah's place. I liked him quite well. He maintained a certain presence that reminded me of the Cherokee elders I knew when I was a little girl back in Oklahoma. On one occasion, Leonard led an impressive Lakota ceremony in the adult education building in Oakland. He and his wife, Mary, their young son, and other people traveled in a large truck. They carried a sacred buffalo skull with them wherever they went.

Bill Wahpepah was always there for us. He opened his home to everyone, especially the Indian children. Most of them were second-generation relocatees who would have been out on the streets without Bill's guidance. I saw Bill weep in utter frustration over a young man who continued to sniff paint. I knew those tears were real. They came from a man who had survived alcoholism and heroin addiction to emerge in the 1970s as one of our finest spokespersons for native rights. He traveled all over the world, telling anyone who would listen about the problems of Native Americans, while he searched for answers and solutions.

Bill, whose life had been hard, died much too young. He was in his late forties and at the height of his activism when he walked into spirit country after a sudden illness. Like so many others who had been relocated, Bill had always spoken of someday returning to live among his people in Oklahoma. That was not to be. He was taken home to Shawnee, Oklahoma, for a tribal burial.

The same was true for my own father. Only in death did he return to the place where he was born.

My father's death tore through my spirit like a blade of lightning. It came during the Alcatraz occupation. By that time, my parents had long since left San Francisco and Hunter's Point. The spice company my father worked for had relocated, so my folks had moved farther south, down the coast to a small town not too far from Salinas and Monterey, places that John Steinbeck had immortalized in his books. Life had finally leveled out for my father and mother. It was the best period of their life together. At last, they had a decent place to live. Most of their kids were grown and making their ways in the world, and several of us were deeply involved in the Native American rights movement.

Just when it appeared that all was well, more misfortune came calling. My father began to experience high blood pressure and severe kidney problems. The diagnosis was not good—end-stage polycystic kidney disease. At that time, the options for treatment were quite limited. Kidney transplants, which are widely performed today, were experimental and not available at all to persons older than fifty-five. That meant my father was just barely eliminated from consideration. Dialysis, although readily available, was not nearly as efficient as it is now.

We were only starting to adjust to the shock of my father's illness when I experienced more health problems of my own. Once again, I began to have urinary-tract infections and the discomfort associated with kidney problems, just as I had when I was pregnant with my first daughter. After extensive testing to find out why I continued to be plagued with the infections, I also was diagnosed with polycystic kidney disease. I had inherited it from my father. All of us were stunned.

The physicians told me that this genetic condition is characterized by the appearance of many cysts on the kidneys which may continue to grow and overcome the healthy tissue until the kidneys fail. They said that in mild cases of the disease, total kidney loss is certainly not inevitable. In fact, some people live out their lives without even knowing they have the disease because it has produced no symptoms.

But further tests revealed that just like my father, I had a severe form of the disease. In both of our cases, the disease was progressive and incurable. Mine was not nearly as advanced as it was with my father, but all predictions were that I could expect to experience kidney failure by the time I reached my early to mid-thirties, sometime in the 1980s. I reacted to the diagnosis almost with relief. At least I finally had an explanation for the repeated infections, which sometimes required days of hospitalization.

My doctor asked me to limit my protein intake, have my kidney functions monitored regularly, and rest as much as possible. Afterward, the woman in the hospital bed next to mine, who had overheard the discussion, asked if there was anything she could do for me. I told her yes she could, and I asked her for a cigarette. I had not smoked for about a year, but from that moment forward, it became a habit again until I stopped once and for all in 1980.

Because of the hereditary question, I immediately had my two girls, Gina and Felicia, tested for any possible signs of kidney disease. Thankfully, the results were negative, and both of them were clear of any symptoms. Then I arranged for a tubal ligation. I considered it unfair to risk having another child who might end up with a deadly illness.

Dad's health steadily declined, but we tried to make him as comfortable as possible. His approval and support were always very important to me, even after I was a grown woman with children of my own. We had always shared an interest in political debate, in the community around us, and in books. Now we shared this family disease.

It was so difficult to watch my father slowly leave us. He hated being sick, he hated having to give up his job, and he hated taking medicine. My mother practically had to force him to see the doctor for regular visits. We all went to see him as often as we could. He understood our involvement in Alcatraz—that we were fighting for native rights. A conservative Cherokee full-blood, Dad was pleased that his children were taking a stand. I have a strong memory of a Thanksgiving visit with my dad. He was bedfast, and while the rest of the family was busy out in the kitchen getting all the little ones fed, I brought him a plate of food. We ate together, just the two of us, a rare treat in a family as large as ours. He smiled at me and told me he was proud to have a daughter who had become a revolutionary. As it turned out, that was to be his final Thanksgiving dinner.

The end was very sad. Because my parents had no health insurance, we children brought Dad to San Francisco General Hospital, where he could be placed on dialysis. His reaction to the procedure was not at all good. He had to undergo cardiac surgery to remove fluid that was gathering in his chest. Afterward, I went to his room and walked over to his bed. A huge scar and dressing were across his heart. My father looked up and said, "Look what they have done to me now."

After undergoing that surgery, he failed very quickly. We sent the boat out to Alcatraz to retrieve my brothers and sisters. The good doctors worked ever so hard to save him. They ran up and down the halls and did all they could. It was not enough. With his children and his wife gathered around his bed, my father died. He was fifty-six years old. It was February of 1971.

We never even considered leaving him in California. We brought Charley Mankiller back home to his everlasting hills of Oklahoma. My brother Don and my mother made the arrangements. Some of us flew back to Oklahoma, others drove across country to get there. Even though the lives of my brothers and sisters had taken different paths, my father's death brought us together. We took him to Echota Cemetery, just a few miles from where I now live. Waiting for him were the graves and spirits of his parents, grandparents, cousins, aunts, and old friends, all of them long departed to the other world. It was a cold February day. We formed a line of cars and pickups and followed the hearse from the funeral home in Stilwell out to the graveyard.

Even in my grief, the countryside looked so familiar to me. I was back home again. Rocky Mountain is sparsely populated, but as our procession of vehicles wound slowly down the road to the cemetery, people came outside and stood in their yards to watch us pass. You could almost hear them saying, "There goes Charley Mankiller. They are bringing Charley Mankiller home."

Death will come, always out of season.

Omaha Chief Big Elk

Our immortality comes from our relationship with Mother Earth. We are a part of the land in every real sense. Our ancestors were buried in the land and became part of the earth. We grew up among the dust of our ancestors. Our struggle to preserve the Indian ways is tied up with our struggle to preserve the ecological balance. The two things are almost the same.

Carter Camp, AIM leader
Oklahoma Today, May–June *1992*

Most people who spoke or sang at my father's funeral service did so in our Cherokee language. Some people literally walked out of the woods to attend the service. Others came from as far away as Kansas and North Carolina. He was buried beside his parents and a child my mother had miscarried between my birth and Linda's. There was something very natural about laying him to rest in that ground near people he loved. It was so peaceful, and I knew the trees would protect him.

Still, as we left and made our way back to California, we were all numb. The anchor that had always kept our family together was gone. In many ways, none of us would ever be the same again.

For my mother, it was a most terrible time. Part of her spirit went with my father. They had jointly fought for his life. Now that he was gone, she looked as if she had waged her last great battle. From then on, life for her would never be the same. They were so connected. She had done her best to prepare for his loss, but the transition was difficult. She had been married to him since she was a fifteen-year-old girl, and over the course of more than thirty years, they had gone through so much together. They had raised a family, buried children, and gone through the trials of relocation. Besides loving him, my mother truly respected and liked my father. Watching someone you care so much about suffer through such indignity and dehumanization is not easy. But she made the necessary adjustments and, like the rest of us, she persevered.

I returned to Native American issues for my comfort. The Alcatraz occupation came to a halt a few months after my father's death. Then I became even more involved with community work. I knew for sure that I could no longer remain content as a housewife.

Hugo was not at all in favor of my involvement in Alcatraz or any of the other projects I became associated with in the Bay area. During that period of my awakening, he was most unhappy whenever I held meetings at our home. He also opposed the idea of my traveling anywhere without him, even if only for a short time. Of course, he neglected to remember that a few years earlier, when he had got itchy feet and was gone for weeks at a stretch traveling around the world with his cousins in the merchant marine, I had learned to adjust.

Times for the two of us had changed so radically. I had become a much stronger person and was more than ready to assert my independence. So when Hugo informed me that I could not have a car, I did not acquiesce. Instead, I went straight to the bank, withdrew some money, and bought an inexpensive Mazda. It took a little bit of doing, but I figured out how to operate the stick shift on those terrific San Francisco hills.

Buying that little red car without my husband's consent or knowledge was my first act of rebellion against a lifestyle that I had come to believe was too narrow and confining for me. I wanted to break free to experience all the changes going on around me—the politics, literature, art, music, and the role of women. But until I bought that little red Mazda, I was unwilling to take any risks to achieve more independence. Once I had the car, I traveled to many tribal events throughout California and even in Oregon and Washington.

> *Eliminating the patriarchal and racist base of the existing social system requires a revolution, not a reform.*
>
> *Premier issue of* Ms. *magazine,* 1971

All around me, there was so much going on. There was a great deal to accomplish. One task I took on was acting as director of the Native American Youth Center in East Oakland. I literally discovered the building that housed the organization, on the corner of Fruitvale and East Fourteenth streets. I drafted some volunteers to slap fresh paint on the place, pulled together some school curricula and a cultural program, and opened the doors. My experience at the San Francisco Indian Center was put to good use. Some of the young people who made their way to this new youth center were dropouts. Others came there at the end of the school day.

I suppose there is much to be said for ignorance. I had no idea what I was doing when I became involved at the youth center, but I learned quickly—on the job. My enthusiasm seemed to make up for any lack of skills. There were field trips to plan and coordinate, and visits to various tribal functions all over northern California. At the center, while the kids did their homework after school, they listened to the music of Paul Ortega,

Jim Pepper, or some of the other talented native singers and musicians who came there. All the while, we tried to instill pride in our Native American heritage and history, and to encourage our young people to use that pride as a source of strength to survive the tough streets of East Oakland.

We also worked on basic educational needs. I worked very hard with a young Klamath girl to get her to return to school. I scraped up a little bit of money to pay her, and she helped me with the center's office work. She was just fine with running errands, but when it came to jotting down telephone messages or filing, she became terrified. Finally, she broke down and admitted that she had absolutely no reading skills at all. I immediately got her into a literacy program.

At the youth center, I also learned valuable lessons about self-help. When I had no clue where I was going to come up with the money needed for a renovation project, I went to a bar about a block from the center called Chicken's Place. The sister of my friend Gustine was the owner, and many of the native people of East Oakland went there. I stepped inside and asked for volunteers. Suddenly, to my great surprise and delight, I had several people on their feet, all ready to get to work. I was even more amazed by their ability and commitment. From then on, whenever we needed funds for a field trip or warm bodies to do some work, I went straight to Chicken's Place. The folks there never let me down.

A little of that absolute faith in our ability to get things done by helping one another sustained me later when I returned to Oklahoma. But it was in Oakland where I formed a belief that poor people, particularly poor American Indian people, have a lot more potential and many more answers to problems than they are ever given a chance to realize.

Beyond the youth center, I also became a volunteer worker for the Pit River people in their fierce legal battle with the powerful Pacific Gas and Electric Company over the rights to millions of acres of the tribe's northern California land. This was the tribe that my old friend Richard Oakes had tried to help. I saw a story on the six o'clock television news about the tribe's efforts to reclaim ancestral lands. They were rural people—a very gutsy tribe just trying to get back what was rightfully theirs. Something about them reminded me of the Cherokees. I heard their lawyer speaking on the news, and afterward I called him up and said that I would like to volunteer my services. He said that would be just fine, and I began an almost five-year association with that tribe. It lasted until the mid-1970s, when I finally left Hugo and California behind.

During the time I volunteered for the Pit River people, I absorbed a great deal of the history and culture of the native tribes in California. Most of the time, I stayed quite busy at the tribe's legal offices in San Francisco, where I helped to organize a legal defense fund. But frequently, my daughters and I would visit the traditional leaders out on their land. Whenever we went to Pit River country, we stayed in a small cabin not far from the home of Raymond and Marie Lego.

Raymond was a traditional tribal leader, and the Lego home became the center of activity for those of us taking part in the land fight. Often in the evening, we sat on the front porch, and Raymond and Marie told us about their long struggle to get back the land. Sometimes Raymond would bring out an old cardboard box filled with tribal letters and documents, which he treated as though they were sacred objects. We were privileged to be able to see those things and to spend that time with such people. I felt at home there. The Legos grew a garden. They hunted, and lived a simple life. The demeanor and lifestyle of the Pit River people put me in mind of my own people back in eastern Oklahoma.

From my time with the Pit River tribe, I came away with so much information I would later use. I learned about treaty rights and international law. Everywhere my girls and I went during the 1970s in California, we received an education. Those were fine trips. We drove to Mendocino on the northern shore of a half-moon-shaped bay. We followed the Pacific coast. We visited with Pomo people I had met at Alcatraz, and we gathered seaweed with them along the shore. Collecting seaweed was one of their seasonal rituals, and we placed what we found in special baskets that were family heirlooms. The seaweed was quickly fried in very hot grease and wrapped in thick bread. It was delicious.

We went to Kashia, a Pomo *rancheria* in the mountains near Santa Rosa. Only about five acres in size, Kashia is where some of the activists sought refuge after the 1973 AIM takeover at the hamlet of Wounded Knee on the Pine Ridge Reservation in South Dakota. Wounded Knee was the site of the 1890 massacre where, it is said, the Lakota Nation's sacred hoop was broken and where many dreams died with the slaughtered native people. Some of the soldiers who participated in the killings even received medals from the United States government. Russell Means, John Trudell, and other strong activists went to Wounded Knee in 1973 to demand reforms. Their seventy-two-day standoff with the FBI ended in a shoot-out and deaths on both sides, but it focused more attention on the injustices in Indian life.

My brother Richard was at Wounded Knee. After Alcatraz, he had worked at a television station in San Francisco, but he left to go to Wounded Knee because he felt it was important. My mother was so worried that he would end up getting shot, but he was not hurt. Like many other young native men of that time, Richard heard the call to help the people at Pine Ridge, and he went. Whether the occupation of Wounded Knee helped or hurt Pine Ridge continues to be the subject of debate among the people most affected—those who live on Pine Ridge Reservation.

There was still much talk of the bloodshed at Wounded Knee when my girls and I camped at Kashia. We stayed with the parents of my friend Maxine Steele. Her brother Charles had gone to Wounded Knee. We cooked our meals outside, and we talked. We felt it was a magical place. It still is today. There are several Indian doctors there, mostly women. We attended dances in the traditional Pomo round house. Under the stars, we listened to stories of history, medicine, and ceremonies.

All of it was a remarkable experience. All of those trips and visits. All of the music and dancing. All of the hard, hard work. All of the time spent in the fight for Alcatraz, at the youth center, with the Pit River people gave me precious knowledge. All of the people I encountered—the militants, the wise elders, the keepers of the medicine, the story-tellers—were my teachers, my best teachers. I knew my education would never be complete. In a way, it was only beginning. I felt like a newborn whose eyes have just opened to the first light.

More and more, I found my eyes turning away from the sea and the setting sun. I looked to the east, where the sun begins its daily journey. That was where I had to go, not to heal for a few weeks after a marital squabble, not to lay a loved one to rest and then leave again—I had to go back to stay. Back to the land of my birth, back to the soil and trees my grandfather had touched, back to the animals and birds whose calls I had memorized as a girl when we packed our things and left on a westbound train so very long ago. The circle had to be completed. It was so simple, so easy.

I was going home.

CHAPTER 12

HOMEWARD BOUND

*I*n the times before the Cherokees learned the ways of others, they paid extraordinary respect to women.

So when a man married, he took up residence with the clan of his wife. The women of each of the seven clans elected their own leaders. These leaders convened as the Women's Council, and sometimes raised their voices in judgment to override the authority of the chiefs when the women believed the welfare of the tribe demanded such an action. It was common custom among the ancient Cherokees that any important questions relating to war and peace were left to a vote of the women.

There were brave Cherokee women who followed their husbands and brothers into battle. These female warriors were called *War Women* or *Pretty Women*, and they were considered dignitaries of the tribe, many of them being as powerful in council as in battle.

The Cherokees also had a custom of assigning to a certain woman the task of declaring whether pardon or punishment should be inflicted on great offenders. This woman also was called the *Pretty Woman*, but she was sometimes known as *Most Honored Woman* or *Beloved Woman*.

It was the belief of the Cherokees that the Great Spirit sent messages through their Beloved Woman. So great was her power that she could commute the sentence of a person condemned to death by the council.

The Ghigau, known by her later name of Nancy Ward, is often called the last Beloved Woman. She earned her title, the highest honor that a Cherokee woman could *achieve, by rallying the Cherokees in a pitched battle against the Creeks in 1755. As a War Woman of the Wolf Clan, she accompanied her first husband, Kingfisher, into battle. In the field, she prepared food for him and chewed his bullets to cause fatal damage when they struck their marks. When Kingfisher was killed in the heat of the fray, she raised his weapon and fought so valiantly that the Cherokees rose behind her leadership and defeated the Creeks.*

In recognition of her courage in war, Nancy was given her prestigious title. She spent the remainder of her life as a devoted advocate of peace between the Cherokees and all others.

It is wise to learn from the past while keeping an eye peeled on tomorrow. But often it is best not to know everything that the future holds. All the while I volunteered with the Pit River tribe, took my courses at San Francisco State, and feasted on the harvest of seaweed near Kashia, I had no inkling of what lay ahead.

Some life events are predictable. Divorce from Hugo was unquestionably imminent. But unknown to me, additional pain lurked just around the bend. There would be more close encounters with death and with dying. An equitable share of happiness and fulfillment also waited. Still, since I am no soothsayer or medicine person, I could not be sure just what to expect. But sometimes I caught glimpses of harbingers.

Little did I realize, in the middle of the 1970s, that in less than a decade I would not only be back in Oklahoma working for my tribe, but I would be principal chief of the Cherokee Nation. I later learned that others did have that knowledge. Years before I was honored to become the first Cherokee woman chief, a Cherokee spiritual leader saw it all in visions as clear as spring water.

I am a spiritual person, born with a gift inherited from my forefathers.... One of our prophets is a woman, the First Woman ... a woman came out from the place where the holy spirit had gone into. She was an ideal woman, an ideal Cherokee woman, and she was nice and she smiled. And I thought, I'm not dealing with gods now. This is a human, I can talk to her.

At that moment, as she smiled at me, I knew that she was the Red Lady of the Eternal Flame. That she was in the third form of our deities, our ancient deities.... Then we moved from that scene to a higher ground where I observed a large arbor all made of natural material. And under that arbor were all people that had passed us. They didn't have a care in the world. . . . And then she smiled. I was again talking to a spiritual representative. And at that point, I woke up from that vision, or dream. . . . I knew right then and there, five years ahead of time, that she, Wilma Mankiller, was going to be chief. With experience of this nature, we could only say that she is a special gift. She is somebody special.

A Cherokee spiritual leader, speaking of a vision

This spiritual leader later told me that when we first met, he was startled because he recognized me from the vision.

I would not return permanently to Oklahoma until 1977, about the time of that vision. I went home one year before, but it was more of a time for scouting old haunts. After a little while, I returned to California. In the summer of 1977, my daughters and I finally came home to stay.

Those last years in California were hectic and sometimes disturbing. My marriage to Hugo had completely unraveled. I recall looking across the room at this handsome man I had married when I was barely out of high school, the father of my children, the man who had liberated me from Hunter's Point, and thinking how he had smothered me. We had grown so far apart. I knew I could not be content to stay in the marriage any longer. I could no longer simply turn on the radio, hum to music, and mentally fly away.

For a while, I found refuge at the home of Lou Trudell. She and her three kids lived in a housing complex on East Fourteenth Street in Oakland. Their house was close to an alternative school operated by the Black Panther Party, and just a couple of blocks from the site of the Indian Adult Education Program, which was a popular gathering place for Indian activists.

Lou and John's differences had finally caught up with them, and they had divorced. He eventually married a bright Paiute woman named Tina Manning. After they had been together for a while, John and Tina and their children would visit the Bay area and stay in Oakland with Lou and the older Trudell brood.

When I finally did leave California to go home to Oklahoma, one of the last stops I made was at Lou's place, and John and Tina were there with her. They made some sandwiches for us to eat on the trip.

I had not been back in Oklahoma very long when I received word that Tina Manning Trudell, who was pregnant with John's child, along with three of their children—Ricarda, age six, Sunshine, three, and Eli, one— had been killed in a mysterious fire on the Paiute people's Duck Valley Reservation in Nevada. Tina's mother, Leah Manning, also was killed in the fire. Tina's father, Arthur Manning, a former tribal chairman, was severely burned. John was attending a demonstration in Washington, D.C. To this day, he and many others contend that the fire was arson. John has repeatedly stated that he strongly suspects FBI involvement.

I know that the pain John experienced is impossible to understand. After a time, he used his immense talent and energy to create music and poetry. One of the many ballads he wrote and recorded is "Tina Smiled." He has also collaborated with Robert Redford in the making of the fine documentary *Incident at Oglala*, and he played a leading role in *Thunderheart*. This popular motion picture was loosely based on the life of Leonard Peltier, a Native American activist serving a life sentence for supposedly having murdered two FBI agents in 1975. Many native people believe Peltier is a political prisoner who should be released or, at the very minimum, receive a new trial. I am one of them. For a long time, I have kept a poster which reads, "Free Peltier."

In more recent years, John Trudell came to visit me in Oklahoma. He showed up at our Cherokee Nation tribal headquarters. I have a great deal of genuine love for John, and it was good to be able to spend time with him again. He still lives life on his own terms. He was barefoot, had a sort of half Mohawk haircut, and wore a long silver earring dangling from one of his ears. When we sat down for coffee, I told him that he had to be one of my most bizarre friends. John laughed at that comment. "You have the nerve to sit there and tell me that I'm bizarre?" he asked. "Here you are in this complex running a great big bureaucratic organization. What about you? I think you're the one who is bizarre." On days when the political headaches of my job as chief become almost surreal, I recall John's words and I smile. I also remember the old times in Oakland with John and his two wives, our time together at Lou's place. John's friendship continues to be very important to me.

Everyone who showed up in those days in Oakland found Lou warm, witty, and very generous. Her house was a place of comfort. I especially liked her kitchen. Lou and I gathered there with some other women at least once a week to share our thoughts. It was a most eclectic circle of women.

There was my old Klamath friend, Gustine Moppin, always optimistic even if her latest lover had just run off or if she was without a penny for her rent. Gustine just smiled and said somebody else better was in store for her, or she would somehow come up with enough rent money before an eviction notice arrived. As if by magic, Gustine was always right.

There was Susie Steel Regimbal, my self-assured Pomo friend with a biting wit. Susie came from a people whose spiritual leaders were women. From her, I learned of the tribal concepts of traditional female leadership and the belief that indigenous value systems far exceed those of Western society.

Then there was Linda Aaronaydo, a Creek and Filipina. She was the youngest in our group of five women. A preschool teacher, Linda had the demeanor and looks of the stereotypical country schoolmarm, but the heart of an anarchist. She regaled us with stories of her experiences on the social-protest front, including the 1968 Poor People's March to Washington, D.C.

We talked about many subjects. We discussed our children, the emerging women's movement, the role of Native American women, indigenous rights, the environment, and politics. We also spoke of men, and we told each other things that we would never share with a man. We spoke of our innermost angers, fears, and vulnerabilities. We spoke of dreams—our secret dreams. These were shared only when we were all together in Lou's kitchen.

Occasionally we would go on picnics, to activist meetings, to a rather raunchy bar in East Oakland, or to powwows. Mostly, we just got together at Lou's house to talk and sing and dream. None of us was quite sure where we were headed, but we all knew there was no turning back. The outward foundations of our lives had already crumbled, and we had to move on.

And that is what we did. We took a variety of paths from Lou's kitchen to reach new places none of us had ever been to before.

Gustine, who inspired so many others, stayed active in Indian affairs in the Bay area until 1990, when she walked into spirit country. Susie entered into a wonderful partnership with a Creek man named Kenneth Tiger, who shared her love of books, art, music, health food, and the Pomo culture. She became the first female tribal chairperson of her Pomo band just before she died of stomach cancer in late 1992. Linda ended up becoming a physician and established a practice in Santa Rosa, where she raised her children and devoted more time to learning about her Creek history and heritage. Lou is now a nurse-practitioner in rural New Mexico. She lives near her ancestral home, with a clear view of the mountains and an even clearer view of her future.

The three of us from that group who remain—Lou, Linda, and I—see one another only occasionally. I visited with Lou at a Farm Aid concert in 1992 in Texas, and we fell into easy conversation, as we always do. We also talk on the telephone and correspond. No matter how much time passes or what happens, that special bond between us is still there. I have heard people speak of a bond that develops between survivors, people who have come through some sort of threatening experience together. I suppose that is what our bond is like. We are survivors of a battle to gain control of our own lives and create our own paths instead of following someone else's. And because our lives are still evolving, it will be interesting to see where and when we will complete the journey that began so long ago in that sanctuary, Lou's kitchen.

The future belongs to those who believe in the beauty of their dreams.

Eleanor Roosevelt

In that last fleeting period before I left California for Oklahoma, I instituted some important changes in my life. In 1974, I finally asked Hugo for a divorce because we no longer had any kind of reasonable life together. We had always been so very different. Our lifestyles and aspirations were worlds apart.

At first, Hugo resisted my request for a divorce, but finally he went along with my wishes. After the divorce, I resumed my own name, a part of my Cherokee heritage. I was Wilma Mankiller again.

Sometimes Hugo helped us financially, but mostly it was up to me, a college student with a limited income, to feed two daughters and survive in one of the nation's most expensive cities. Later that year, I moved to Oakland because the cost of living was much cheaper. Even though I was consciously planning my return to Oklahoma, I still needed to pay bills, put groceries on the table, and earn a grubstake so we could move. To accomplish all that, I took a job as a social worker with the Urban Indian Resource Center while continuing with my various volunteer duties in the Native American community.

But there was another very good reason why I could not immediately leave the West Coast for Oklahoma. It had to do with Hugo and Gina, our nine-year-old daughter.

It began one day before we moved to Oakland, while we were still living in San Francisco, when Hugo came to our place to pick up Gina. He was taking her to see a circus performance at the Cow Palace in San Francisco. Late that evening, I received a phone call from Hugo informing me that he had decided to keep Gina with him and go on a trip. I told him not to do that, and he responded that he would bring Gina home on one condition—that I tell him I loved him.

I flatly refused. So Hugo kept Gina and did not return her to me for almost one whole year. It was a horrible time, an unbelievably horrible time. Hugo called periodically to tell me that Gina was OK, and then he would always ask about our getting back together. I was frantic and very worried about Gina, but I could not give in and go back to the kind of life I had had with Hugo.

During the time Hugo had Gina with him, using her as some sort of bargaining chip, they went to Chicago to see his snobbish relatives, whom we had visited on our honeymoon in 1963. Then he took her to live in Berkeley for a while, and from there, they traveled abroad and ended up at his family's home in Ecuador. Gina was sent to school, learned Spanish, and was given all sorts of presents and fancy dresses. Although she was generally spoiled by her father and his family and, I am sure, loved all the attention, she was not really a happy little girl. She missed being with her sister and me. Eventually, Gina began to lose her pretty hair, and she developed an ulcer.

Finally, Hugo and Gina returned to the United States, and they came to San Francisco for a visit. When he brought her by the first time, I saw that she was different. She acted very formal at first, but by the end of the day, she was back to her old self. I took a chance and let Hugo return for her, because he promised to bring her back again the following week. I held my breath and waited, and sure enough, the next week, there was Gina.

This time I asked her how she felt about staying with her sister and me. Her birthday was coming up, and they were going to have a big party for her in Ecuador with lots of gifts and such, and I am sure all of that was on her mind. But ultimately Gina said she felt good about not going back with her father. She wanted to stay with us. I picked up the phone and called Hugo. I told him of Gina's decision, and he was quite angry.

Even though I had my two daughters back together, I was worried because Hugo had kept all our passports. I was not sure just what he might try. I was so afraid he would try to take Gina again. I knew I could not stay with her twenty-four hours a day. That is when I decided we had to spend some time in Oklahoma, at least for a little while.

We came back to visit during the summer of 1976. We did not stay very long. I was just happy to get away from the Bay area for a while, and from Hugo once and for all. He had quit sending any support payments on a regular basis even before he took Gina, and after she returned to me, everything was cut off. That did not bother me. Money had always been an issue in his family, but not in mine. I was glad just to be free of him.

That first return trip was an orientation visit for us, especially for my daughters. I had not lived in eastern Oklahoma for some time, and I had to reconnect with my past. I immediately became involved in the ceremonial dances again. On the first Saturday of every month from April to October, the members of the Four Mothers Society and friends would gather. The men tested their skill with bow and arrow by shooting at bales of hay. Families watched while comfortably seated on blankets and quilts on the ground. Later there would be a stickball game, then the evening meal. In summer when vegetables and fruit were in season, the dinners were sumptuous. Meals usually included sliced tomatoes and cucumbers, corn harvested that day, green beans, okra, freshly dug potatoes, and onions. Dessert was fresh blueberries, huckleberries, or peaches, cobblers made from those fruits. Later, when the time was right, the evening ceremonial dances began. They sometimes lasted until sunup.

Aunt Maude Wolfe, my father's cousin, told us about an empty cabin near one of the ceremonial dance grounds. That was where we stayed for most of the visit. There was electricity, but no running water. It was quite a dramatic change for the girls. In some ways, it must have been as strange for them as when I went to San Francisco as a child. The girls had had some experience getting along with few amenities when we had gone to Pit River or visited some of the other rural tribes in California, but they were not prepared for such living on a daily basis. After a few weeks, we returned to California. But my mind was made up—we would move back to Oklahoma permanently the following summer.

When the time arrived for the big move, I decided to rely on a well-used pickup truck I had bought. I rented a trailer, hitched it on the back, and got some friends to cram it full of my old appliances and furniture. Next I convinced my sister Frances to use her vacation time to keep us company. It was an undaunted crew—Frances and I, Felicia, Gina, our pet dog, and a guinea pig. Just ten blocks out on the freeway, we realized we had made a mistake. The refrigerator and load of furniture started to move all around the trailer bed. Then the rains came. Frances had to clear the windshield with her hands because the wipers did not work. By that time, the load had shifted so much that the pickup was starting to slide sideways down the road. We turned around and went back to Oakland. By the time I got rid of the truck and figured out a new game plan, Frances had run out of vacation time.

Feeling a little like Okies going back home, the two girls and I and our trusty animal friends left once again. This time, we were in a well-packed U-Haul truck, and we had that sack of sandwiches from Lou's kitchen. Many friends sent with us their blessings and a lifetime of memories. We drove the truck east to Oklahoma. We covered some of the same territory my family had traveled across twenty years before when we had been relocated by the federal government. When we arrived at my mother's place, I had twenty dollars to my name, no car, no job, and few, if any, prospects. But we were happy. At last I was home to stay.

My mother had already moved back home to Adair County a short time ahead of us. She rented a house not very far from Mankiller Flats, and we crowded in with her until we found our own place and I could hunt a job and bring in some money. Later on, after things settled down, I built my own house, where I live now, and I helped arrange for a house to be built for my mother and my youngest brother, Bill, just up the road a ways. Our old house, which we had left in the 1950s, was gone. So was the smokehouse, and there were few traces of the old gardens. But the spring, where my grandfather and my father had drunk and where I had drunk when I was just a little girl, was still there. So were the trees and the hills, and all the birds and animals. We knew we could bring our old homeplace back to life. That is what we did.

Gradually, most of my brothers and sisters also came home to live in Oklahoma. Frieda lived in Tulsa, never having moved away from Oklahoma. Vanessa had returned before I did. Richard, my brother who had gone to Wounded Knee, and Frances and Linda all followed. One by one, with their families in tow, all of them drifted back—all of them but Don and John, two of my older brothers. They stayed. Don has a ranch to run near Yosemite, and grandchildren to fuss over. Johnny remains in San Francisco, kind of an unofficial caretaker of the Mankiller legacy we left behind in California.

When we first moved back, I felt as though folks welcomed us, but for a while, they seemed to treat us more like company than family. Little by little, they warmed up. I suppose they finally saw that we meant to stay put. I recall the day I knew I was really and truly home. It was some time after our return. I went into Stilwell to take care of some business. I was walking across the lawn of the Adair County Courthouse, and I spied some old Cherokee men sitting on the benches. They were chewing tobacco and talking over the world's most important problems, just as old Cherokee men have done in Stilwell for a long, long time. As I walked by them, I heard one of them say to the others, "There goes John Mankiller's granddaughter." Those five simple words were sweet to hear. Out in California, beyond my own family and our extended tribal family, I really did not have any true sense of community or lineage. I missed that very much. But when I heard the old man say, "There goes John Mankiller's granddaughter," it was as though I were a ten-year-old girl again on my way to the picture show. It was as if I had never been away.

Much of my time was spent looking for work. It was a tough time, but I was very determined. I tried to keep myself in a positive frame of mind by playing my guitar and sewing. I made ribbon shirts and clothes for my brothers and sisters, and school clothes for Mitchell, my sister Linda's youngest son. The music and sewing were soothing after a day spent job hunting. I did not allow myself to get discouraged.

Then, at last, during that first autumn after our return, in October of 1977, I found a job. I went to work for the Cherokee Nation of

Oklahoma. Based on all my experience with various tribes and Native American issues in California, it seemed so logical for me to finally do something on behalf of my own people. At first, I had a difficult time getting a position. Whenever I went to the tribal headquarters to inquire about the various jobs being advertised, I was told that I was overly qualified or, for some reason, just did not fit. Finally, I got fed up with hearing that, so I walked right into the office and said, "I want to work! Whatever you have, please let me try it. I need to go to work!"

Apparently that approach was effective. I was hired as an economic stimulus coordinator at a salary of about $11,000 a year, a pretty fair sum for a low-level management job. The cost of living was so much lower in Oklahoma than in the Bay area that I felt a little bit rich. To celebrate, I went right out and bought a used station wagon.

Basically, my primary assignment as an economic stimulus coordinator was to get as many native people as possible trained at the university level in environmental science and health, and then help to integrate them back into their communities. It seemed like a nice enough job title. But when I started to work for the tribe, I had very mixed feelings. For so long, I had been involved with the nitty-gritty issues of Indian activism, and I soon found that things were not done in quite the same way in the Cherokee Nation. It all seemed like a huge bureaucracy, and I was hard-pressed to find anyone with any beliefs in grass-roots democracy. Still, I knew that such people were there, and I would eventually find them or they would find me.

The tribal power base was dominated by men, but it was refreshing to see that at least a rebirth of our government, which the federal government had tried to suppress for seventy years, was in full swing. Our tribe—the nation's second largest, surpassed only by the Navajos—was once again electing its own chief, and it had a brand-new constitution.

Former Principal Chief William W. Keeler was the one who had started things up with the constitutional revision in the early 1970s, when he appointed a committee to draft a new governing document. Keeler had been appointed in 1949 to head the Cherokees, and in 1971 he became the first chief elected by *all* of the Cherokee people since 1903. After serving a four-year term, Keeler withdrew from active participation in politics and retired to take care of his ranch and his many business interests.

Keeler was succeeded by Ross O. Swimmer in August of 1975. An attorney and the president of First National Bank of Tahlequah, Swimmer was elected principal chief by a narrow margin out of a field of ten candidates. A staunch Republican, a graduate of the University of Oklahoma, and a High Church Episcopalian, Swimmer had begun his service to the Cherokee Nation in 1972 as tribal attorney.

After taking office as chief, Swimmer immediately saw to it that the new constitution drafted during Keeler's term was modified and finally passed. Swimmer was quick to move for the adoption of a new constitution because the election for principal chief had been so close and contentious. It was his hope that the constitution would have a unifying effect. It would also show our people that he did not intend to usurp the government, but rather to lead as an executive with the power of the tribe divided among three separate entities.

Under the terms of the newly adopted constitution, a principal chief and deputy principal chief were to be elected every four years. A fifteen-member tribal council would act as the legislative branch, and a three-member judicial appeals tribunal as the judiciary branch. The constitution promised "speedy and certain remedy" to all Cherokees who suffered wrong and injury. It also established a check-and-balance system within our tribal government, and allowed for all registered Cherokees to vote in tribal elections. After federal approval of the constitution by the U.S. Department of the Interior, our people ratified it in June of 1976.

The constitution, which was supposed to unify the Cherokees, did not do so. Regarding tribal membership, many people thought a requirement of one-quarter blood quantum should have been instituted. Others thought the Cherokees who lived outside the Cherokee Nation should not be allowed to vote in tribal elections. Some people objected to the inclusion of the Delawares and Shawnees as Cherokee tribal members. Others objected to the exclusion of the Cherokee freedmen and intermarried whites.

I met Chief Swimmer not too long after I started working for the tribe, but we had little contact at first. I was quite busy at my job, and when I finished my assignments, I would look around to see what else needed to be done. After all that time I had spent trying to raise money for various Native American causes and projects in Oakland and San

Francisco, one thing I definitely knew how to do was write a fairly good grant proposal.

My five years spent with the Pit River people alone were invaluable when it came time for me to work on behalf of my own tribe. At Pit River, I had learned a great deal about treaty rights and the government-to-government relationship between Indian nations and the United States. When folks at the Cherokee Nation discovered that I possessed some ability, I was kept very busy churning out proposals. By 1979, I was made a program development specialist for the Nation, a job I would hold for two years. When a couple of the grant proposals received funding and I started to earn some fairly good revenue for the tribe, I came to the attention of Chief Swimmer and the council.

It was also in 1979 that I decided to finish my college work by picking up a few remaining course credits for my bachelor of science degree in social work. I took the Graduate Record Examination and selected the University of Arkansas at Fayetteville for my graduate work in community planning. Located in northwestern Arkansas not very far from the Oklahoma line, Fayetteville is a picturesque city with rolling hills and shady residential streets. Although the university campus was a drive of about an hour and fifteen minutes each way, I enjoyed the daily commute from my home. It gave me a chance to think and make plans—and even dream about my future. I was able to arrange for a graduate assistantship to help defer some of the expense, and I never did have to take a formal leave of absence from my post with the Cherokee Nation. That gave me peace of mind, because I had the understanding that I could come back to my full-time job as a program specialist whenever I wished.

My daughters were busy with their own schoolwork and new friends. We were building a home and becoming reacquainted with our ancestral land. Everything appeared to be in order. I was very pleased with my work at the University of Arkansas, and the direction my life was taking since we had returned to Mankiller Flats. I also enjoyed renewing old acquaintances with various folks and family members from my past, and making new friends in the community, including many nonnative persons. In fact, two of my very best friends were a white couple, Mike and Sherry Morris. Along with their little girl, Meagan, they had moved to eastern Oklahoma a couple of years before. In 1979,

Mike accepted a position with the Cherokee Nation as our director of education.

Sherry and I were about the same age, but other than that simple fact, there were very few similarities between us—at least on the surface. For example, Sherry came from the Deep South, a totally different background, lifestyle, and culture than mine. A strikingly beautiful woman, she had been concerned with her physical looks as a girl and young woman. But even though she was a former beauty queen and had been a first runner-up for Miss Mississippi, we hit it right off when we met. Sherry became one of my best friends.

Sherry was just beginning to come into her own as a person. She had finally stopped being so concerned with her physical self, and was starting to turn inside as well as looking beyond at the world around her. Over time, rural health-care issues and early child development became her primary interests. She also was so great with Meagan, her exceptional three-year-old daughter. It was good to see how Sherry nurtured her child. As someone who had experienced my own evolution into a more independent woman, I felt privileged to be able to watch Sherry grow and find her own path.

Then something happened. Something beyond tragedy occurred. It took place on November 8, 1979, a Thursday. A sign, an omen that calamity was approaching had showed up at my house the night before.

That evening, my second cousin Byrd Wolfe and his wife, Paggy, came to visit me at Mankiller Flats. Byrd was very active at the Flint ceremonial grounds in our community, and Paggy was a shell shaker at our ceremonial dances. We sat and talked of the world of Cherokee medicine—a special world that few outsiders realize still exists to this day. The Cherokee Nation and our people have a well-known reputation for being able to adapt to the non-Indian world and of running a well-organized tribal government. But what people do not realize is that we live within two realities, and the two are very different. One reality is the acceptance of and ability to deal with the non-Indian world around us, and the other reality is our being able to hold onto and retain our ancient Cherokee belief systems, values, customs, and rituals.

An essential part of our belief system in some communities is the belief in the power of medicine people. That evening at my home, we discussed those practitioners. We sat around the fire burning in my stove, and we talked about how medicine people usually practice two kinds of old medicine. One type requires the use of herbs, roots, and other gifts of creation for curing, for something as simple as a headache or as complex as a blood ailment. The other type draws on ancient tribal rituals and customs, which sometimes include songs, incantations, and other thoughts or acts. Many of the prescriptions and rituals are preserved in medicine books written in Cherokee and passed down from medicine person to medicine person.

That November evening, our conversation turned to the use of medicine to settle disputes or cause harm. As time passed, the gist of our talk centered on how, even in contemporary Cherokee society, some of our people still use medicine to "settle scores."

As the three of us sat near the fire and continued to talk about medicine, we became aware of a presence outside my house. We heard sounds coming from the darkness, and we looked out the windows into the night. There were movements in the trees. Then we saw the owls— some were in flight, and others were sitting in the branches. We heard their voices.

Some Cherokees, including my own family, are taught to beware of owls. We were told that a *dedonsek*, "one who makes bad medicine," could change into an owl and travel through the night skies to visit Cherokee homes. That usually brought bad luck. I had heard stories that if owls came close to the house, it often meant bad news was coming. Just the hooting of an owl could make some people wary. In eastern Oklahoma, there are still Cherokee tales of *Estekene*, the Owl, who can change shape to appear in almost any form. Other native peoples also consider the owl to be a powerful figure of death in their tribal legends. They throw rocks and sticks at owls that gather near their homes.

That November evening, my house was surrounded by owls. They were everywhere. Despite what I had been taught as a child, owls normally do not bother me as long as they keep some distance. But these owls did not do that. They came very close to my house, and made all sorts of loud noises. All of the owl activity, coupled with our conversation, made me feel very uneasy. Later, after my cousin and his wife had left and I was alone with my two daughters, the owls were still there.

> *The Indian knows his village and feels for his village as no white man for his country, his town, or even his own bit of land. His village is not the strip of land*

four miles long and three miles wide that is his as long as the sun rises and the moon sets. The myths are the village, and the winds and rains. The rain is the village, and . . . the talking bird, the owl, who calls the name of the man who is going to die.

Margaret Craven
I Heard the Owl Call My Name, *1973*

I am not someone who experiences premonitions or visions. But even though I did not have a feeling that something bad was going to happen, a kind of uneasiness did wash over me. It was very unsettling.

The next morning, I arose and prepared to go to Tahlequah. I had not missed any classes prior to that time, so I planned to take the day off from college to speak to the personnel director at the Cherokee Nation about working on a study to pick up some extra cash. At the time, I was living on about three hundred dollars per month from my graduate assistantship, a few grants, and food given to me by my Cheyenne friend, Jerri Warledo. I needed the extra money for necessities.

Just as I headed out the front door, something on the television caught my eye, and I stopped for a few minutes to watch. I cannot even recall exactly what it was. The hostage crisis in Iran had just erupted, so perhaps it was a newscast that made me stop. Much later, I thought about how my stopping to watch television threw my routine off and changed my timing slightly, although it did not cause me to hurry.

I left my home and got on the road. As I always did, I drove my station wagon up the backcountry roads until I reached Highway 100. Everything seemed perfectly normal. I was only about three miles from my house, going up a slight grade. On the other side of the hill, a car headed for Stilwell pulled out to pass two other cars that were going slowly. There was a blind spot at that point, and the driver of that other car did not see me. I did not see the other car until it was too late. I came up to the top of the hill, and there was that car in my lane bearing down on me. In a split second, I realized we were about to collide. I tried to veer to the right, but it did no good. Our automobiles crashed head-on.

I have little recollection of what happened after the collision. I faintly remember people screaming at each other, trying to figure out how to extract me from the wreckage of my car. The front of my auto was pushed back so far that the edge of the hood cut into my neck. My face was literally crushed. My right leg was very severely crushed, and my left leg and ankles were broken. So were many of my ribs. There was blood all over the place, pouring from cuts and abrasions. Death was very near. I felt it.

Two ambulances tore down the two-lane asphalt highway to the scene of the crash. Of course, I had no way of knowing it at the time, but there was only one person from the other vehicle involved in the accident. Only much later would I find out that the other victim was also a woman. Her car was much smaller than my station wagon, and sustained even more damage. She lived only a short time. Unbelievably, she was someone I knew. She was my friend—my very good friend. The woman who died was Sherry Morris.

The odds of two friends crashing into each other on a rural road had to be quite low. I had seen Sherry earlier that week. We had made plans to go together to Arkansas to hunt for antiques. She was anxious to find an oak table. Her husband, Mike, was away at an educational conference. Fortunately, their daughter, Meagan, was not with Sherry on that fateful ride when our cars collided.

One of the ambulances carried Sherry to Tahlequah, but her neck was broken, and they knew she was dead before arrival at the hospital. I was taken to Stilwell, where I was stabilized. From there, they quickly transported me to a larger hospital in Fort Smith. I faded in and out of consciousness. As the ambulance sped down the highway, I believe I was really trying to die. It was such a wonderful feeling! That is the best way to describe what I felt. I was dying, yet it was all so beautiful and spiritual. I experienced a tremendous sense of peacefulness and warmth. It was probably the most profound experience I have ever had. All these years later, I can still recall how it felt, but it is difficult to explain. It was overwhelming and powerful. It was a feeling that was better than anything that had ever happened to me. It was better than falling in love.

I had this feeling all the while the ambulance raced me to the hospital. There was a woman there in the ambulance. I later learned she straddled me and tried to stop me from dying. She fought to keep me alive. But there was this tremendous pull toward what seemed to be an overpowering love. The woman was pulling me back toward life.

I recall that while I was in that condition, Felicia and Gina came into my mind. Then I made an unconscious choice to return to life. I did not see any tunnels or white lights. There was none of that. It was more as if I came to fully understand that death is beautiful and spiritual. It is part of life, and when I finally came out of it, I vowed to hang onto that experience. I wished to retain that feeling, and I did so. As a result, I have lost any fear of death. I began to think of death as walking into spirit country rather than as a frightening event. Even though more brushes with death were ahead, the idea of dying no longer frightened me.

That first day, right after the accident, I was in surgery for six hours. Then I was taken into intensive care. Some of the people who were at the scene of the accident told me later that when I was pulled from the car, I was so badly mutilated they did not know if I was a man or a woman. I did not really wake up until a couple of days later. Then I realized I had been in an accident, and immediately I asked if there had been others involved, and my friends and family assured me that everything was OK. They wanted to shield me from the news about Sherry. For three weeks, I did not know what had happened. People would come into my hospital room, and I would ask about the other driver.

Friends and relatives came to visit, including Mike Morris, but I did not see Sherry, and I thought that was odd. I asked about her and was told that she was busy with something or other, but that did not seem to make much sense. She and Mike were close friends of mine, and I wondered why she was not with me. Then one day Mike spoke to my family and the doctors, and he asked to visit with me alone. He wanted to tell me the truth. Mike came into my room and said he had something to tell me. I thought it was going to be about his work or the mysterious project that was keeping Sherry away. But it was not. Instead he told me that the woman in the other car was Sherry, and that she was dead.

It was awful—truly awful. I do not remember much of what happened after that, but Mike says the shock and emotional pain were so severe that I began to cry uncontrollably, and then I began to hemorrhage from the many wounds in my face. Nurses and doctors rushed to the room to stop the bleeding.

My sister, who was waiting in the hall outside my room, said that a few minutes after Mike went into my room, she heard me scream. Much later that day, she visited me, but I did not acknowledge her presence for several hours. When she left, I asked her, "Did you go to her funeral?" She said, "Yes." I returned to my silent mourning.

Having to deal with the shock of Sherry's death, coupled with my own physical pain, made the suffering almost unbearable. For a very long time, I carried around my share of survivor's guilt. My relationship with Mike was difficult, but he had little or no emotional support, so I tried to be there for him and his daughter. He had a very hard time moving forward and escaping his deep depression.

Finally, Mike did get on his feet. There were bumpy times, but our friendship survived. He and little Meagan stayed on in Oklahoma for several years. Ultimately, they moved to Maine, where Mike became a dean at the University of New England. Later, he moved to New Mexico to pursue his career as a professional educator and to launch a multicultural university. Meagan joined her father in Albuquerque. She has grown into a bright, energetic young woman. During the George Bush years, Meagan was right there at Kennebunkport, picketing the Bush residence to protest the so-called Gulf War of 1991. That was a very brave thing for her to do, but Meagan is as socially conscious and as involved with issues as her mother was. Mike is proud of her, and I know Sherry is too.

Meanwhile, I had to keep moving forward. My own struggle with the many debilitating injuries was difficult, to say the least. My initial stay in the hospital lasted for more than eight weeks. During that time, there were many surgeries to put my face and shattered bones back together. Before it was all over, I would have to endure seventeen operations, mostly on my right leg. At one point, the doctors thought I would not walk again, and they even considered amputation. The pain was unbelievable, and I had to wear full casts on both legs. I was confined to a wheelchair for some time, and would be somewhat incapacitated for almost a year. I could not even go to the bathroom or brush my teeth without assistance. To this day, I am not sure how I managed to regain mobility.

But throughout the entire ordeal, I never allowed myself to become depressed—not once. I had faced death, and I had survived. I would not permit myself to sink into a negative state. Recovering at my home, I had the time to examine my life in a new way—to reevaluate and refocus.

The entire family was a big help to me during those troubled times. My sister Linda came to my house every day for about six months. I will always be indebted to her. Mother also helped to care for my daughters, and our friends pitched in to see that our basic needs were fulfilled. I was so proud of my girls. They rolled with the punches. They did not allow the chaos in our lives to best them.

During the long healing process, I fell back on my Cherokee ways and adopted what our elders call "a Cherokee approach" to life. They say it is "being of good mind." That means one has to think positively, to take what is handed out and turn it into a better path. At the beginning of some Cherokee traditional prayers and healing ceremonies, everyone is asked to remove all negative things from the mind, to have a pure mind and heart for the prayer and the ceremony ahead. I tried to do that in the process of healing.

That accident changed my life. I had experienced death, felt its presence, touched it, and then let it go. It was a very spiritual thing, a rare natural gift. From that point on, I have always thought of myself as the woman who lived before and the woman who lives afterward.

Throughout the recuperation process, I made steady progress. I read and made plans and worked very hard at improving my physical self. I was determined not to have to wear leg braces. My goal was to get out and walk a quarter of a mile to the mailbox and back. At first, I could not even get out of my yard without tumbling onto the ground. I would become frustrated and angry at my helplessness, but I went back the next day and tried again. I started to make some real progress. Week by week, I got a little farther.

But my trials were far from over. I was to experience even more physical woes before I could even become weaned off the crutches from the automobile accident. All of this came just a few months after my first encounter with death. It was in early 1980, and I began to experience muscle problems. At first, it was relatively minor. For instance, I had a little trouble peeling a grapefruit and holding a pencil. Then it became worse. I dropped my hairbrush constantly and lost my grip. Before long, I could not even hold my toothbrush. Then I started to experience severe double vision. My sister Linda took me to several physicians, including an optometrist and neurologist. They did not help. They could not confirm any specific disease or ailment.

My strength was leaving me. I was growing weaker and weaker. Before too long, I lost control of my fingers, my hands, my arms. Then I could no longer stand up, even on my crutches. I would rise and then crumble and fall. I could speak only for short periods of time because my throat muscles would give out. My breathing became labored, and I could not hold my head up. I lost the ability to chew except for very short periods of time. Soon, I had lost forty pounds. I was afraid to drink water because it would come out of my nose. Some days I could not keep my eyes open for very long, so I would just lie down and keep my eyes closed. That became my existence.

For someone who absorbed life visually, loved to read, and was always on the go, the inability to see things around me and to move about freely was particularly difficult. During that terrible period, Linda took me to Oklahoma City to visit Mary Barksdale, an activist lawyer and good friend. I lay on the back seat of the car all the way there to conserve my strength. When we drove up to Mary's house, Linda helped me out of the car with my crutches. As I started to walk toward the front door, my muscles suddenly gave out and I fell straight forward on the sidewalk. I broke my nose again, and blood gushed all over me. I began to choke. It was so awful.

After that experience, I came to the conclusion that I was destined to continue to erode until death took me. I clearly remember one night at my house when I was lying there on the couch and several of my brothers and sisters had come to visit. My breathing became more and more strained. I felt my old friend death approach me. Somehow, I knew what to do. I found that if I relaxed and closed my eyes, everything would get better, and that is what I did that night. I lay there absolutely still, and the moment passed.

Almost ten months after the automobile accident and seven months after my muscle problems started, I found out what was causing my condition. This revelation came on Labor Day in 1980. I was watching the television, and switched on the "Jerry Lewis Muscular Dystrophy Telethon." A woman appeared and described her muscle problems, and how she had come to be dependent on a respirator. As she talked, I began to think that her symptoms sounded so familiar. She spoke of subtle signs such as the drooping of an eyelid, difficulty with chewing, and immobility. Then it struck me—"My God! That is what I have!"

The woman was describing myasthenia gravis, a form of muscular dystrophy that can lead to paralysis. Finally, I knew what was causing my awful problems.

The following week, Linda took me to Tulsa, and I met with the staff at the local Muscular Dystrophy Association and their physicians, and they conducted tests. My fears were well founded. I was immediately diagnosed with systemic myasthenia gravis.

I went to my sister's car and wept quietly. I was spent. I needed to collect my thoughts before proceeding. I thought about how I had somehow managed to get through the trauma of the automobile accident and Sherry's death, and then had faced the continuing problems with my legs and regaining use of my limbs. Now this had happened to me. I was stricken with a disease that most people had never even heard of. I was very discouraged, but I knew I could not give in. I went home and prepared to battle this latest assault on my physical self and spirit. I could feel the anger running through my body. I was determined to win. I drew on the strength of my ancestors and of present-day Cherokee medicine people, and on my own internal resolve to remove all negative factors from my life so I could focus on healing.

In November of 1980, I checked into a hospital in Tulsa and went through more tests and procedures. I quit smoking and worked very hard to prepare my body and mind for what lay ahead of me. The physicians presented me with various treatment options, including chest surgery to remove my thymus. I also understood that I would need to endure further treatment through high doses of steroids. Although this approach seemed drastic, it made complete sense. I did not want merely to cope with this disease—*I wanted to beat it.* I wanted to rid myself of it. I wanted it to go into total remission. That is why I opted for surgery.

The operation was successful. I felt a surge of strength when I woke up on a respirator after the surgery. Within less than a week after my surgery, I was up. I wanted to wash my hair and take care of myself. I was anxious to get on with living and my work. The surgery and the intensive drug program truly worked miracles. Although the drugs had side effects, such as causing a significant weight gain, the worst of my symptoms were completely gone within four to six weeks after the operation. I continued to experience moderate muscle dysfunction, but even that was under control in less than two years after the surgery. The drug therapy continued until late in 1985, yet I was able to return to my post with the Cherokee Nation in January of 1981.

Within only a very few years, I would became first of all deputy chief and then principal chief of the Cherokee Nation. That vision of the spiritual leader would come true. But none of that would have happened if it had not been for the ordeals I had survived in the first place. After that, I realized I could survive anything. I had faced adversity and turned it into a positive experience—a better path. I had found the way to be of good mind.

DANCING ALONG THE
EDGE OF THE ROOF

Among the many revered Cherokee formulas, there is one for the treatment of ordeal diseases. Ayunini, from whom this formula was obtained so very long ago, said the disease is often sent to someone by a friend or even a parent, to test the afflicted person's endurance and knowledge of counterspells.

The prayer is addressed to the Black, Red, Blue, and White ravens, which are each in turn declared to have put the disease into a crevice in Sanigilagi—the Cherokee name of Whiteside Mountain, at the head of Tuckasegee River, in North Carolina. The term is used figuratively for any high precipitous mountain. The word adawehi, which is used several times in the formula, refers to a magician or supernatural being.

Translated into English, the entire prayer goes like this:

Listen! Ha! Now you have drawn near to hearken and are resting directly overhead. O Black Raven, you never fail in anything. Ha! Now you are brought down. Ha! There shall be left no more than a trace upon the ground where you have been. It is an ancestral ghost. You have now put it into a crevice in Sanigilagi, that it may never find the way back. You have put it to rest in the Darkening Land, so that it may never return. Let relief come.

Listen! Ha! Now you have drawn near to hearken, O Red Raven, most powerful adawehi. Ha! You never fail in anything, for it was ordained of you. Ha! You are resting directly overhead. Ha! Now you are brought down. There shall remain but a *trace upon the ground where you have been. It is an ancestral ghost. Ha! You have put the Intruder into a crevice of Sanigilagi and now the relief shall come. It [the Intruder] is sent to the Darkening Land. You have put it to rest in the Darkening Land. Let the relief come.*

Listen! Ha! Now you have drawn near to hearken, O Blue Raven; you are resting directly overhead, adawehi. *You never fail in anything, for it was ordained of you. Ha! Now you are brought down. There shall be left but a trace upon the ground where you have been. You have put the Intruder into a crevice in Sanigilagi, that it may never find the way back. You have put it to rest in the Darkening Land, so that it may never return. Let the relief come.*

Listen! Ha! Now you have drawn near to hearken; you repose on high on Wahili, O White Raven, adawehi. *You never fail in anything. Ha! Now you are brought down. There shall be left but a trace upon the ground where you have been. Ha! Now you have taken it up. You have put the Intruder into a crevice in Sanigilagi, that it may never find the way back. You have put it to rest in the Darkening Land, never to return. Let the relief come.*

In 1981, as I went back to my old job of writing grant proposals on behalf of the Cherokee Nation, I found I was still angry. But it was a healthy anger and not destructive. My rage came mainly from the frustration caused by the way I feel about Western medicine, the way it generally dehumanizes patients. At least, that had been my experience during my long recovery process.

To help channel the anger and to maintain a good mind, I decided to write a short story that would address this issue of cultural clashes. It was the story of the aging Ahniwake, a kind of Cherokee "everywoman" who found herself at the mercy of the American system of medicine after a lifetime of turning to traditional Cherokee doctors in her ailments. Another character in my story was a young woman named Pearl, the older woman's granddaughter, who was trying to guide Ahniwake through unfamiliar surroundings in the ways of white people.

I called the story "Keeping Pace with the Rest of the World." It did not appear in print until 1985, in *Southern Exposure*, a publication of the Institute for Southern Studies. That issue was called "We Are Here Forever: Indians of the South." That story was my first published piece, and it helped me deal with the trauma I had to endure. It was pure fiction, but it was filled with the stark truth.

"[The doctor] did not know how to heal an illness, only how to cut it out." . . .
*More to herself than to Pearl, Abniwake added, "He did not know my clan, my
family, my history. How could he possibly know how to heal me?"*

> Wilma Mankiller, from the story
> *"Keeping Pace with the Rest of the World,"*
> Southern Exposure, *1985*

During my months and months of rehabilitation, I was able to do
some writing and reading. I also studied various tribal issues. I came to
realize that I had been given a chance to think about what I wanted to
do with my life. When the reality of how frail life is dawned on me, I
set about to begin projects that I could not have tackled otherwise.
Fortunately, Chief Ross Swimmer was willing to allow me to go back to
my position with the tribe. I was still in my recovery phase when I hobbled
into his bank in Tahlequah and asked him if I could return to my job.
He did not hesitate for a second, and for that I am grateful.

When I returned to my duties with the Cherokee Nation, I did so
with a fury. I was not particularly anxious to move up the ladder of
hierarchy in my tribe. My work was my main priority. I was determined
to work closely with self-help projects and program development. I wanted
to see to it that our people, especially those living in rural areas, had the
chance to express their own special needs. I was determined to do this
by using the "good mind" approach.

In 1981, I helped to found and subsequently was named the first
director of the Cherokee Nation Community Development Department.
I did not necessarily seek the job. In fact, I first headed a national search
to locate a director before I finally decided to accept the position myself.
Immediately, we set out to identify new ways to implement renewal
projects in rural Cherokee communities. This department grew from important development work carried out in the tiny Adair County community named Bell. As this project evolved, we needed a new department
so we would be eligible to receive grants.

I had assumed that Swimmer and his consultants had located some
funding for the project. Not so. We immediately put together several
federal and foundation grants. We also recruited many volunteers to allow
local citizens to construct a sixteen-mile water line and to revitalize several
of their homes.

Bell was a poor community with about 350 people, of which 95 percent were Cherokee. Most of them spoke Cherokee. In my mind, the Bell project remains a shining example of community self-help at its very best. The local residents were able to build on our Cherokee *gadugi* tradition of a physical sharing of tasks and working collectively, at the same time restoring confidence in their own ability to solve problems.

We established a partnership between the Cherokee people living at Bell and the Cherokee Nation. Our goal was to bring members of the community together so they could solve their common problems. From the beginning, the Bell residents realized they were responsible for the success or failure of the project. They knew they were expected not only to develop long-range plans, but also to implement their community renewal, with our staff members acting only as facilitators and funding brokers.

It turned into a massive community-renewal effort using local labor and talent and about a million dollars in hard costs, funded by grants. When we started out at Bell, it was a community in utter decline. At least a quarter of the people living there had to haul in water for household use, and almost half of the homes fell well below minimum housing standards. The mean family income in Bell was very low. Many of the young people were leaving the community to find jobs elsewhere.

But instead of surrendering to defeat, the people of Bell became involved in their project. They proudly met the challenge. In the end, they were able to complete everything they had set out to accomplish. The new rural water system that brought the town its first running water was installed by community volunteers—the men and women of Bell. The rehabilitation work on the twenty homes and the dilapidated community center was carried out by the homeowners themselves. The construction of twenty-five new energy-efficient residences was accomplished with resources of the Cherokee Housing Authority. The local people served as their own labor force.

> *Though failure had been the unanimous prediction of Bell's neighbors, people from surrounding communities came to see what was happening. So did several foundation executives who viewed this renewal project as an example of Third World development; certainly few places in the world were poorer than Bell. When a local CBS television crew—attracted by Bell's reliable scenes of poverty—came to film powerlessness, they played an inadvertent role in changing the situation by letting*

residents see themselves on the evening news and begin to feel less isolated. Soon, even the non-Indian residents of Bell were saying positive things about this water project in the newspapers, and the Indian community began to feel visible for the first time. Most important, they had become visible through something they were doing for themselves.

The next fourteen months encompassed a novel's worth of personal change and problem-solving, but by the end, the water system was complete. The CBS crew returned to document success, and the seven-minute story that resulted appeared on "CBS Sunday Morning" with Charles Kuralt. Now known as "the town film," it is often replayed with pride.

. . . for Wilma, watching individual people flower was the greatest reward.

Gloria Steinem
Revolution from Within, 1992

Bell is only about ten miles from Mankiller Flats, and from the very start I was aware of the obvious similarities between the two places. That is why the project and its overwhelming success were important to me. Bell meant so much to me, and in so many different ways. Bell represented success where everyone else had anticipated failure. For me, the Bell project also validated a lot of the things that I believed about our people. I have always known that Cherokee people—particularly those in more traditional communities—have retained a great sense of interdependence, and a willingness to pitch in and help one another. I also knew that we had the capacity to solve our own problems, given the right set of circumstances and resources. The Bell project affirmed those beliefs.

On a more personal level, the Bell community project was very important to me because during it I came to know a man who proved to be very crucial in my life. I am proud to say this man eventually became my husband. His name is Charlie Lee Soap. He is a full-blooded, bilingual Cherokee, and probably the most well-adjusted male I have ever met.

I had first encountered Charlie Soap in 1977, not long after my daughters and I moved back to Oklahoma. At that time, he was working with the Cherokee Housing Authority, and I consulted him about a housing matter. Charlie had a reputation as someone who could get things done in the housing office. He was quiet, but very positive and very efficient.

I had also heard the comments of the women who worked at the housing authority office. They mentioned that Charlie, a tall and handsome man, was a skillful Plains-style dancer, and when he was in college, he had learned to do many different tribal war dances in full regalia—complete with a colorful eagle-feather bustle and Angora leggings. His dancing prowess at powwows was known throughout Oklahoma. I was told that Charlie could walk into a school filled with children and captivate his audience. They would watch spellbound as he danced, with his long black hair flying. Afterwards, the children would crowd around him to ask questions, and reach out to touch a feather. Later, when I really got to know him, I saw that Charlie is indeed like a Pied Piper, particularly with children and young people. They love him and his stories, and he enjoys working with them to help them build self-esteem and to encourage them to remain in school.

During the Bell project, Charlie was assigned to work with me as a co-organizer. That is when I really came to know him. I was impressed from the very start. After some of our lengthy meetings in Bell, Charlie would drive me home to Mankiller Flats. We would sit in his pickup outside my house and talk at length, not only about the Bell project but also about our own dreams and aspirations. I came to learn a lot about this man, and found that Charlie Soap was much more than just another skilled dancer.

We discovered we are about the same age. Charlie is a bit older. He was born on March 25, 1945, at Stilwell. His mother's name was Florence Fourkiller Soap, and his father was Walter Soap, a farmer who also worked for the railroad. After his father died, Charlie's mother eventually remarried, and her name is now Florence Hummingbird. Both of Charlie's parents could trace their family lines back to our people's old homelands in the Southeast. Like my own family, Charlie also came from a family with eleven children. He had one sister and nine brothers, including two half brothers. Charlie was right about in the middle.

He learned as a boy how to work hard and pull his own weight. He and his siblings cut railroad ties, cleared land for crops, picked strawberries and beans, and hauled hay. His family lived in the Bell community and then moved to a nearby community called Starr. They lived as traditional Cherokees, and at one time, Charlie's father was very active in the Keetoowah Society. Cherokee was the Soap family's primary language.

Charlie mostly attended country schools. He became an accomplished athlete, and later played basketball at college and during a hitch in the navy. Charlie had been married twice before. He had three sons from his first marriage—Chris and Cobey, and another son who had died during heart surgery as an infant. Charlie's youngest son, Winterhawk, was from his second marriage. When I met Charlie, that marriage was in trouble and was soon to end.

At the time, I was quite happy, living near Rocky Mountain on my ancestral land with my two daughters. They were busy with schoolwork and friends, and I had my tribal duties, not to mention my concerns about recovering my health. It had been several years since my marriage had broken up, but I was not particularly interested in more than a casual relationship with a man. At any rate, Charlie was still wrapped up in his own problems. We simply did not pay much attention to each other on a personal level until later, after the Bell project was concluded. Instead, we first developed a fine working relationship, and that led to a solid and strong friendship. That proved to be the best foundation for us when we finally realized we were in love.

From the very start, Charlie and I found that we worked very well together. Many of our values were the same. We also complemented each other in different ways. I think I was able to provide Charlie with some self-confidence, and he helped me to understand how to get things done within a bureaucratic system. He has taught me so much, because he knows quite a lot about Cherokee medicine and many of the old stories that have been handed down through the generations.

On the other hand, we were not afraid of our differences, and enjoyed debating various issues with one another. Some of the issues we wrestled with concerned religion and spirituality. Charlie had been raised in the church, and even had taught Sunday school for a while. I had had some exposure to Christianity, but had never even read the Bible. Despite our different religious experiences, Charlie and I are both highly spiritual people. Today, we attend church regularly, as well as ceremonial activities. We enjoy doing both.

Charlie's marriage ended in 1983, but we did not marry for three more years, until October of 1986. Our relationship as a couple developed very slowly. It evolved as we grew more comfortable with each other, but we remained wary and cautious. I recall very well a day when Charlie stopped by my house for a cup of coffee. We had been sitting there in the kitchen talking when he kissed me. It was so unexpected. We embraced and kissed again. Both of us were wondering what was going on. For about a week or so after that, we shied away from each other, but that did not last. We missed being with each other too much.

From the onset, our relationship was as solid as a rock. It all stemmed from a deep respect. It is the strongest love I have ever known. We genuinely like each other. We never seem to get bored, and I think we continue to bring out each other's strengths. That is so important. It has been said that when someone asks Charlie or me to name our personal heroes, we start our lists by naming each other. It's true.

Now that I am principal chief of the Cherokee Nation, Charlie remains constant. He is a secure male. He is neither intimidated nor threatened by strong women or by other strong men. He still is one of the most unusual persons I have ever met. He is bright, never pretentious, and he genuinely enjoys helping people. He is free from all traces of racism and sexism. He likes children and is respectful of old people. Charlie Soap is a comfortable man. He is comfortable to be with, and he is comfortable with himself. He is guileless. He is my best friend.

> *I know who I am, what I am, and what I can do or cannot do. I am a Cherokee and I am proud of it. There is no one who can take that away from me.*
>
> Charlie Soap, 1992

Those first few years in the early 1980s were some of the most pivotal in my life. Everything about the Bell experience was positive. My daughters were doing well in their schoolwork, and were learning more each day about their Cherokee heritage. Many members of my family were living within easy reach. My work was very satisfying. I was beginning to feel complete.

After enduring two back-to-back assaults on my physical self, that period was comforting to my mind and soul. It was the best medicine. Serving as the principal organizer and enabler at the Bell community marked the first time I had been given any real power within the tribe. I enjoyed the tasks and eagerly asked for more. Chief Swimmer was generous in his response to my requests. I was able to use federal grants to finance my people's dreams.

Then in 1983, history was made when Ross Swimmer asked me to run as his deputy chief in the next election. Just the year before, he had been deserted by most of his closest political supporters, partly because he had been diagnosed with lymphatic cancer. Those supposed allies of Swimmer's had little courage or loyalty. One of the reasons they decided to challenge him as chief was because they considered that he was too ill to remain in office, since he was out much of the time taking chemotherapy treatments. They wrote him off as a dead man. So the following year when the time came for Swimmer to announce his bid for reelection for another four-year term, he remembered me. I suppose he trusted me, and was satisfied with my work and my allegiance to the tribe. He asked me if I would consider being on the ticket as his deputy.

By that time, Swimmer had recovered much of his health. The chemotherapy treatments had been effective. His prognosis was good, but he had also chosen to seek internal Cherokee healing from William Smith, a traditional medicine person, and from the Seven Medicine Men at the ceremonial grounds. He stepped inside the circle and asked for their help. I recall that Chief Swimmer made the point that he did not seek the traditional Cherokee healing as a symbolic gesture, but because he believed in its power.

> *I know just from my own knowledge that most, or many, contemporary medicines are derived from the natural medicines that the Indians developed years ago and . . . the folks there certainly have a handle on those medicinal roots and herbs and things. They might well have a lot of the answers to common illnesses. A lot of those roots and herbs have been synthesized into drugs today, and combined with some other chemicals that make them more potent, still serve the same purpose.*
>
> *. . . in my ancestry, one of the Swimmers was a medicine man and listed all the herbs and the roots and the mushrooms and everything else that were used medicinally and many of them are extracted today and used in everyday medicine. So, I was fairly confident that [Cherokee traditional medicine] certainly wasn't going to hurt me and if anything it might hold some secret to helping.*
>
> *Former Cherokee Chief Ross Swimmer*

Unquestionably, Swimmer was taking a great chance by bypassing his male friends to select me as his running mate. I suppose he saw me as an effective leader and manager. He must have forgotten that I am also a liberal Democrat.

I was greatly flattered by Swimmer's selection of me, but I thought the whole idea was totally ludicrous. Because our tribe is so large, running for tribal office is much like running for Congress, or even a national political post. It is very much a mainstream process, complete with print and broadcast advertising, campaign billboards, rallies, and all that sort of thing. I honestly believed I could not possibly get elected. I realized that I had successfully developed and managed tribal programs and had much experience, including my years in California, but I simply could not picture myself in high tribal office. I told Chief Swimmer I was honored that he had chosen me, but my answer was a polite no. I had to decline.

But almost immediately after I gave him my answer, I started to think about what was transpiring around me. I then gave Chief Swimmer's offer more thought. I went out among some of our rural communities in eastern Oklahoma where we were facilitating development projects. In one small community, I came upon three of our people living in an abandoned bus without any roof. Their few extra clothes were hanging on a line. They had few other possessions. It was a very sad scene. It burned into my mind.

I knew this was not an isolated situation. Many Cherokees were forced to put up with poor housing, rising medical costs, and educational deficits. I realized I was being given an opportunity to create change for Cherokee families such as those living in the old bus. I knew that if I did not act, I would no longer have any right to talk about or criticize the people who held tribal offices.

The visit to that small community had a major impact on me. I drove straight to Ross Swimmer's home. I told him I had reconsidered, and I would run for election as deputy chief in the 1983 election. I quit my job with the Cherokee Nation so there would be no conflict of interest, and I filed for office.

From the start, I figured most people would be bothered about my ideas on grass-roots democracy and the fact that I had a fairly extensive activist background. I adhered to a different political philosophy than many people living in the area. But I was wrong. No one challenged me on those issues, not once. Instead, I was challenged mostly because of one fact—I am female. The election became an issue of gender. It was one of the first times I had ever really encountered overt sexism. I recalled that my first real experience with sexism had occurred in California. I had once slugged a boss during a Christmas party in San Francisco when he came up behind me and tried to kiss me. He did not fire me, but I do believe he got the message that I did not want to be mauled. The memory of that time came back to me during the 1983 campaign.

I heard all sorts of things—some people claimed that my running for office was an affront to God. Others said having a female run our tribe would make the Cherokees the laughingstock of the tribal world. I heard it all. Every time I was given yet another silly reason why I should not help run our government, I was certain that I had made the correct decision.

The reaction to my candidacy stunned me. It was a very low time in my life, but I would not be swayed. I figured the best tactic was to ignore my opponents. I remembered a saying I had once read on the back of a tea box. It said something like this—if you argue with a fool, someone passing by will not be able to tell who is the fool and who is not. I did not wish to be taken for a fool.

I built my run for office on a positive and cheerful foundation to counter the incredible hostility and great opposition I encountered. To say that the campaign was heated would be the understatement of all times. Most of the negative acts did not originate with my opponents for office, but with those who did not want a woman in office. I even had foes *within* the Swimmer-Mankiller team. Toward the end of the campaign, some of them openly supported one of my opponents.

Occasionally, the actions of those who were out to stop my election were violent. I received hate mail, including several death threats. After one evening rally, I returned to my car and discovered that all four tires had been slashed. On other occasions, there were threatening messages over the telephone. Once I picked up my ringing telephone and heard the sound of a rifle bolt being slammed shut on the other end of the line.

I also had a chilling experience while riding in a parade. I was waving and laughing and smiling at the crowd along the street when I spied someone in the back of the crowd. I saw a young man, and he had his hand cocked and his fingers pointed at me as if he were holding a pistol. Then he drew his hand back, firing an imaginary gun. I never even blinked. I just calmly looked away. The parade continued. No matter how disturbing those incidents were, the scare tactics did not work. One consolation was that the people in Bell and other rural Cherokee communities where I had worked were very supportive.

My two opponents for office were J. B. Dreadfulwater, a popular gospel singer and former member of the tribal council, and Agnes Cowan, the first woman to serve on the tribal council. She was older than I was, and already established in our tribal government. They were worthy opponents who lliked to criticize me for having no experience in tribal politics. In truth, I had a great deal of applicable experience, but I did have much to learn about political campaigning.

Some of the early experiences were painful. For example, we sent invitations for the first campaign event and made a lot of preparations. That particular evening arrived, and everything was laid out beautifully. Only five people, however, came to hear me speak, and three of them were related to me. But I smiled and realized it could only get better from there.

I think my opponents ignored the fact that I had a great deal of experience as a community organizer. I had learned a long time ago, at the Indian Center in San Francisco, how to reach large groups of people and bring them together. That is just what I did. I went door to door and campaigned. I attended every event and rally. I kept encountering opposition as a female candidate, but I did not use it as an issue in my campaign. Gradually, I saw some changes, but they were very few and far between.

Finally, election day arrived. When the ballots had been counted, Ross Swimmer was reelected, to his third term. I beat out Dreadfulwater in that first election, but had to face Cowan in a July runoff. In a tough battle, I defeated her and was able to claim ultimate victory. It was truly a moment to remember forever. The people of my tribe had selected me to serve as the first woman deputy chief in Cherokee history. I took office on August 14, 1983. As one of my supporters put it, at long last a daughter of the people had been chosen for high tribal office.

> *Women can help turn the world right side up. We bring a more collaborative approach to government. And if we do not participate, then decisions will be made without us.*
>
> Wilma Mankiller, Denver, September 1984

My two years as deputy chief proved to be difficult—very difficult. I had inherited many people on Ross Swimmer's staff, and would not have my own people aboard for some time to come. Although Swimmer had chosen me as deputy and had stuck with me through the tough campaign, there were major differences between us. He was a Republican banker with a very conservative viewpoint, and I was a Democratic social worker and community planner who had organized and worked for Indian civil and treaty rights. Also, I had been elected along with a fifteen-member tribal council that, for the most part, did not support me. In fact, they had mostly worked against my election. Suddenly they were confronted with this young idealist woman, this veteran of Alcatraz, who was not only the newly elected deputy chief of the tribe but also acted as president of the council. I was shocked by how petty and political some of them behaved, even after my election.

Serving as president of a council that, at the start, did not support me was an interesting experience. Several members were almost hostile, but what surprised me the most was the lack of support I received from the three women on the council. Of course, they had also opposed my election, but I had naively assumed that once I was in office, we would all work together. But the situation did not get any better. In the subsequent election, two of the women supported my opponent, and the third did not seek reelection. I suppose that throughout those first few months, I felt a real lack of personal power. I had all the responsibility with none of the authority. Mostly, I just coped.

Gradually, I learned to adjust, and so did many of the council members. Still, it took all of us a while to figure out individual styles and ways of doing business. I stayed very busy as deputy chief, helping to govern an Indian nation spread over fourteen counties in northeastern Oklahoma. Despite our differences, Swimmer and I shared an absolute commitment to the rebuilding and revitalizing of our rural communities. As deputy chief, I helped to supervise the daily operations of the tribe. Those included more than forty tribally operated programs ranging from health clinics to day care, elderly assistance to water projects, Head Start classes to housing construction.

Then in September of 1985—just a little more than two years after I took office—there was more sudden change to deal with. Chief Swimmer was asked to go to Washington to head the BIA when he was nominated by President Ronald Reagan to serve as assistant secretary of the interior for Indian affairs. To assume the top Indian affairs post in the federal government, with fourteen thousand employees and a $1 billion annual budget, was an offer that Swimmer, then forty-one, did not want to refuse. The offer came at about the time other tribal officials and I had just about gotten used to each other.

Although it had never been invoked before, Article Six of our Cherokee Nation Constitution, ratified in 1976, provided for the replacement of a principal chief who leaves before the expiration of a term of office. According to this constitutional provision, the deputy principal chief automatically replaced the resigning chief. Legislation passed by the Cherokee Nation tribal council called for that body then to elect, from within its ranks, a new deputy principal chief. Members of the council would then recommend a name to fill the vacancy on the council, after which the nominee would be confirmed by the full tribal council.

When I first learned about Swimmer's upcoming departure, I was somewhat concerned that I would go through the same ordeal as before, when I ran for deputy chief. I immediately began to prepare myself— spiritually and emotionally—for the onslaught. But remarkably, the transition was not that difficult. I suppose many people who were opposed to me thought they could live with the tribal laws and wait for two years until the next election, when they could clobber me at the polls. My problem seemed clear. I had to serve the balance of Ross Swimmer's term—from 1985 to 1987—without any real mandate from the people.

Swimmer's presidential nomination was ultimately confirmed by the United States Senate, and on December 5, 1985, I was sworn in as principal chief of the Cherokee Nation in a private ceremony. Formal ceremonies were held on December 14 at the tribal headquarters. Right before I took the oath of office, Ross Swimmer called me to offer his best.

Memories of my public inauguration will stay with me as long as I live. It was not the happiest of occasions. Swimmer had had little time to prepare me for all the complex issues we were facing. His staff members and many other people felt that the Cherokee Nation would crash and burn with a woman in charge. I was very wary. I knew full well what was ahead.

For the ceremony, I wore a dark suit and white blouse. There was snow on the ground, but the sky was clear and blue and cloudless. So many people came to me with hugs and smiles and good wishes. There were tears of happiness. I recall sitting behind the chief's desk for the first time for an official photo, and someone in the office said, "You look very natural sitting there. It's very becoming."

The council chamber was packed. There were many photographers, reporters, and guests. At the proper time, I stepped forward and placed my hand on a Bible. I raised my other hand to take the oath of office. It is a very straightforward pledge:

"I, Wilma P. Mankiller, do solemnly swear, or affirm, that I will faithfully execute the duties of Principal Chief of the Cherokee Nation. And will, to the best of my abilities, preserve, protect, and defend the Constitutions of the Cherokee Nation and the United States of America. I swear, or affirm, further that I will do everything within my power to promote the culture, heritage, and tradition of the Cherokee Nation."

Thunderous applause followed when I finished the oath and stepped up to the podium. As the crowd became still, the sound of camera shutters clicking continued until I spoke. I thanked everyone in attendance, and all of my friends, family, and supporters. I spoke of the deep honor of assuming the position of chief. I complimented Ross Swimmer for his leadership, and I talked of the many tasks before me.

> . . . I think there's a bit of nervousness in the Cherokee Nation. I think any time there's a change, people wonder what's going to happen, is there going to be some kind of major change. And my political adversaries like to spread around rumors that there's going to be a purge of employees. That's just not the case. I like what's going on at the Cherokee Nation. There will be very little that will change. The only thing that will change is that there will be more of an emphasis on the development of the economy.
>
> Wilma Mankiller, inaugural speech, 1985

By the time I took the oath of office, my eldest daughter, Felicia, had married, and I had my first grandchild, Aaron Swake. I was a forty-year-old grandmother, as well as the first woman to serve as chief of a major tribe. I told the reporters, who seemed to materialize from out of nowhere, that the only people who were really worried about my serving as chief were members of my family. That was because all of them knew very well how much time I tended to devote to my job. My daughters were, of course, concerned about my health. But my little grandson thought it was great that his grandma was the chief.

I'll have to do extra well because I am the first woman.

Wilma Mankiller, People *magazine, 1985*

One thing that I never tried to become as chief was "one of the boys," nor am I a "good ol' girl." I never will be. That goes against my grain. I do know how to be political and to get the job done, but I do not believe that one must sacrifice one's principles. Gradually, I noticed changes within the tribe and especially within the council.

Rural development was, and still remains, a high priority on my list of goals. For me, the rewards came from attempting to break the circle of poverty. My feeling is that the Cherokee people, by and large, are incredibly tenacious. We have survived so many major political and social upheavals, yet we have kept the Cherokee government alive. I feel confident that we will march into the twenty-first century on our own terms.

We are staffed with professionals—educators, physicians, attorneys, business leaders. Already, in the 1800s, we fought many of our wars with lawsuits, and it was in the courts where many of our battles were won. Today, we are helping to erase the stereotypes created by media and by western films of the drunken Indian on a horse, chasing wagon trains across the prairie. I suppose some people still think that all native people live in tepees and wear tribal garb every day. They do not realize that many of us wear business suits and drive station wagons. The beauty of society today is that young Cherokee men and women can pursue any professional fields they want and remain true to traditional values. It all comes back to our heritage and our roots. It is so vital that we retain that sense of culture, history, and tribal identity.

We also are returning the balance to the role of women in our tribe. Prior to my becoming chief, young Cherokee girls never thought they might be able to grow up and become chief themselves. That has definitely changed. From the start of my administration, the impact on the younger women of the Cherokee Nation was noticeable. I feel certain that more women will assume leadership roles in tribal communities.

In 1992, I attended a meeting in the Midwest. My keynote presentation had been well publicized in the region. After my presentation, a native man told me he had an important message for me. He told me he was an Oneida, and one of the prophecies he had heard was that this time period is the time of the women—a time for women to take on a more important role in society. He described this as "the time of the butterfly."

When I read recently of Judge Ruth Bader Ginsburg's nomination to the Supreme Court, Hillary Rodham Clinton's work on health-care reform, the appointment of Ada Deer as assistant secretary of the interior in charge of the BIA, and the election of a female Canadian prime minister, I smiled and thought about the prophecy of the anonymous Oneida man who had driven all day to pass along his message to me.

> *I had negative thoughts [about women leading the tribe] before. But I have had the opportunity to work with her [Mankiller]. I have been impressed with her leadership.*
>
> J. B. Dreadfulwater, *former political opponent of Wilma Mankiller's*
> New York Times, *December 15, 1985*

In 1987, after I had fulfilled the balance of Ross Swimmer's term as chief, I made the decision to run on my own and to win a four-year term of office. It was not an easy decision. I knew the campaign would be most difficult. I talked to my family and to my people. I spent long hours discussing the issues with Charlie Soap, whom I had married in 1986. Charlie had contracted with private foundations to continue development work with low-income native community projects. His counsel to me was excellent. He encouraged me to run. So did many other people.

But there were others who were opposed to my continuing as chief. Even some of my friends and advisers told me they believed the Cherokee people would accept me only as deputy, not as an elected principal chief. Some of those people came to our home at Mankiller Flats. I would look out the window and see them coming down the dirt road to tell me that I should give up any idea of running for chief. Finally, I told Charlie that if one more family came down that road and told me not to run, I was going to run for sure. That is just what happened.

I made my official announcement in early 1987, calling for a "positive, forward-thinking campaign." I chose John A. Ketcher, a member of the tribal council since 1983, as my running mate for the June 20 election. In 1985, John had been elected by the council to succeed me as deputy chief when I became principal chief. An eleven-sixteenths bilingual Cherokee, John was born in southern Mayes County in 1922. A veteran of World War II and a graduate of Northeastern State University in Tahlequah, Ketcher, as I do, considered unity and economic development to be the two priorities for the Cherokee Nation. He still does. John has remained deputy chief to this day, and is a great asset to the Cherokee people.

> *After we debate issues, we remain friends and support each other. We are all Cherokees. The same blood that flows in the full-bloods flows in the part-bloods. We all have things we would like to see happen, but if we argue over issues or candidates the four years between tribal elections, we wouldn't be able to get anything done for those who need it and those we serve—the Cherokee people.*
>
> Deputy Principal Chief John A. Ketcher

I drew three opponents in the race for principal chief. I had to face Dave Whitekiller, a postal assistant from the small community of Cookson and a former councilman; William McKee, deputy administrator at W.W. Hastings Indian Hospital, in Tahlequah; and Perry Wheeler, a former deputy chief and a funeral home director from Sallisaw, in Sequoyah County.

From the beginning, the best description of the campaign came from someone on the council, who said there was an "undercurrent of viciousness." I ignored things that were going on around me. I did the same thing I had always done—went out to the communities and talked to as many of the Cherokee people as possible about the issues. I tried to answer all their questions. My critics claimed that I had failed to properly manage and direct the Cherokee Nation, which was obviously false. Our revenue for 1986 was up $6 million, higher than it had ever been to that point. I was not about to lose focus by warring with my opponents.

The election eliminated all the candidates except for Perry Wheeler and me. None of us had received more than 50 percent of the votes. I had polled 45 percent to Wheeler's 29 percent. We had to face each other in a July runoff. My supporters worked very hard during those last few weeks. Charlie was one of my main champions. On my behalf, Charlie visited many rural homes where English is a second language to remind the people that prior to the intrusion of white men, women had played key roles in our government. He asked our people to not turn their backs on their past or their future.

Charlie's help was especially important because I was stricken with my old nemesis, kidney problems, during the final weeks of the campaign.

Finally, just before the election, I had to be hospitalized in Tulsa, but the physicians never determined the exact location of the infection and could not bring it under control. The lengthy infection and hospitalization would nearly cost me not only the election but also my life, since it brought on extensive and irreversible kidney damage. From that point forward, I was repeatedly hospitalized for kidney and urinary-tract infections, until I underwent surgery and had a kidney transplant in 1990.

Wheeler, an unsuccessful candidate for the chief's job against Ross Swimmer in 1983, tried to make my hospitalization a major issue. He waged a vigorous and negative runoff campaign. He publicly stated that I had never been truthful about my health. It all reminded me of the way Swimmer had been attacked when he was battling cancer. Wheeler, whom I can best describe as an old-style politician, also made claims that I had not hired enough Cherokee people for what he called the higher-paying tribal posts.

> *When she [Mankiller] came back here [to Oklahoma], she had a different philosophy. She grew up in a time when the hippie craze was going on.*
>
> *Perry Wheeler,* Tulsa Tribune, *1987*

When all the ballots from thirty-four precincts plus the absentee votes were tallied, the woman who supposedly knew nothing about politics was declared the winner. The night of the runoff election, we went to the Tulsa Powwow, where my daughter Gina was being honored. In a photograph taken that evening, Charlie, Gina, Felicia, and I look very tired and worn, as if we had just been through a battle. Later that night, we returned to Tahlequah to check on the election results. When the votes of the local precincts were counted, it appeared that I had won easily. Everyone around me was celebrating, but I was concerned about the absentee votes. Once that vote was included, I allowed myself to celebrate.

At last, the Cherokee Nation had elected its first woman as principal chief—the first woman chief of a major Native American tribe. I had outpolled Wheeler, and John Ketcher had retained his post as deputy chief. Wheeler conceded victory to me shortly before midnight.

At long last, I had the mandate I had wanted. I had been chosen as principal chief of the Cherokee Nation by my own people. It was a sweet victory. Finally, I felt the question of gender had been put to rest. Today, if anyone asks members of our tribe if it really matters if the chief is male or female, the majority will reply that gender has no bearing on leadership.

Because I have risen to the office of chief, some people erroneously conclude that the role of native women has changed in *every* tribe. That is not so. People jump to that conclusion because they do not really understand native people. There is no universal "Indian language." All of us have our own distinct languages and cultures. In the African-American community, people can rally around a single leader, as they did for a while around Dr. Martin Luther King, Jr. Because Native Americans have our own languages, cultures, art forms, and social systems, our tribes are radically different from one another. Many tribal groups do not have women in titled positions, but in the great majority of those groups, there is some degree of balance and harmony in the roles of men and women. Among the Lakota, there is a very well known saying that "a nation is not defeated until the hearts of the women are on the ground." I think in some ways Rigoberta Menchú, the Nobel Peace Prize winner—a Guatemalan human-rights activist—may be a good rallying force for all of us. She represents to me the very best of what native womanhood is about. I am awestruck by her life and accomplishments, as are many other native people in Central, South, and North America.

In the instance of the Cherokees, we are fortunate to have many strong women. I have attained a leadership position because I am willing to take risks, but at the same time, I am trying to teach other women, both Cherokees and others, to take risks also. I hope more women will gradually emerge in leadership positions. When I ran for deputy chief in 1983, I quit my job and spent every dollar of my personal savings and proceeds from the car-accident settlement to pay for campaign expenses. Friends describe me as someone who likes to dance along the edge of the roof. I try to encourage young women to be willing to take risks, to stand up for the things they believe in, and to step up and accept the challenge of serving in leadership roles.

> *True tribal tradition recognizes the importance of women. Contrary to what you've probably read in history books, not all tribes were controlled by men.*
>
> Wilma Mankiller, Harvard University, 1987

If I am to be remembered, I want it to be because I am fortunate enough to have become my tribe's first female chief. But I also want to be remembered for emphasizing the fact that we have indigenous solutions to our problems. Cherokee values, especially those of helping one another and of our interconnections with the land, can be used to address contemporary issues.

During those first few years of serving as chief, I began to feel an immense responsibility. I would think to myself that if I did not make it to this meeting or to that session, it would reflect poorly on all women. I felt that not only my credibility but also the credibility of any woman who might follow me was on the line.

Gradually, I relaxed. As my comfort level with my position as chief increased with each passing day, I found myself able to accomplish even more for the Cherokee people. I did not even mind some of the publicity that continued to pour in because of my election. I felt that any attention that was being given to me could be diverted to the people of the Cherokee Nation. That was extremely positive.

> *When I look at her, I just see Wilma. But sometimes I think about what she has done . . . and I can't believe it.*
>
> *Irene Mankiller,* Oklahoma Today, *February 1990*

Although my spirits were buoyed by the milestones accomplished by the Cherokee people, I was still troubled by continuing kidney problems. I had been misdiagnosed by doctors in Tulsa, and I sought medical help in Denver. Although I knew I had polycystic kidney disease, I continued to hope that I would not experience total kidney failure, as had been predicted years before by the physicians in California. I even tried some highly experimental procedures to see if I could stave off the disease. Most of those attempts were acts of desperation.

On the advice of a kidney-disease researcher, I traveled to the University of Oregon in the spring of 1989 to undergo yet another procedure. The doctors made a fifteen-inch abdominal incision to expose both kidneys so they could remove the tops of the cysts and bathe the area with antibiotics. At the very minimum, the procedure was believed to lessen the number and severity of the damaging kidney infections, and possibly to slow the progress of the disease. But it did not work. Shortly after returning to Oklahoma, I was again hospitalized with a severe kidney infection.

By the autumn of 1989, I realized that kidney failure was imminent. Again, I was hospitalized. I was told that I would soon have to begin dialysis, and within six months consider the possibility of a kidney transplant. I devoured every bit of written material and research I could find. For a time, I felt very tired. I found myself having to face yet another major health battle to stay alive. Had not the automobile accident, the trauma of Sherry's death, the repeated surgeries, and the bout of myasthenia gravis been enough for one person? I was not certain I could fight so hard again.

While I was lying in yet another hospital bed, one of my doctors came in to speak to me about my various options. I was struck by her youth and vigor. Earlier, she had told me about her marriage plans, and how excited she was about beginning her medical practice. As she spoke, I allowed myself the rare luxury of wondering what it would be like to have her life—a life without constant social and political struggle, without endless battles with disease.

Later that afternoon, after I questioned myself at length about my troubles, I slept. I got through the frustration and sense of helplessness, and I dreamed. When I awoke, I felt refreshed, as if I had come back to a safe place. Once again, I knew I could make it if I tried. I also realized that I would share every step along the way with the public and the Cherokee people.

The transplant team projected that I could wait about six months before the surgery. They wanted to wait until my diseased kidneys totally failed, and then remove them. Then they would place me on dialysis, and put my name on the national waiting list for a donor cadaver kidney. I did not feel good about that plan. I was already weak, and I could not understand how I could possibly survive all the procedures that were ahead of me. During that time, I learned a lot about the great number of people who are on waiting lists for kidneys, hearts, livers, and other organs. Although there has been an increase in awareness of the need for organ donors, the number of donors has not increased. If potential donors could talk with some of the people whose lives have been saved by transplants, they would be convinced that organ donation is the right thing to do.

While I waited, I asked for my close family members to be tested as possible kidney donors. The surgical team agreed. Charlie asked all my brothers and sisters, my mother, and my two daughters if they were interested in donating a kidney. Six relatives immediately signed up—three brothers, two sisters, and my daughter Felicia. After they were all tested, only my sister Frances remained as a viable donor. Most of the others had some form of the genetic kidney disease themselves, although not nearly as severe as mine. Frances, although clear of disease, had slightly elevated blood pressure and blood-sugar level. After further tests, the doctors decided that unless her problems could be eliminated, she would also be struck from the list of potential donors.

I was not very comfortable with much of the medical advice I had been receiving. I told the doctors I was considering getting an opinion from another transplant center. My main physician became very defensive, and told me I could not dictate my treatment.

I was sharing this trauma with my good friend Gloria Steinem. We had become close through our joint work together on the *Ms.* Foundation board. Gloria gave me the name of an excellent physician who she believed would help me. When there was some hesitation on my part, Gloria insisted that I set up a meeting with the doctor at his office in Boston. She was right to persist. Dr. Anthony Monaco, a skilled transplant surgeon affiliated with New England Deaconess Hospital and Harvard Medical School, saved my life.

Only fifteen minutes into our first meeting, I knew I had found the right person. He asked that further tests be conducted on Frances, and although she again appeared to be a good match for the procedure, Dr. Monaco was concerned about her blood-sugar level and blood pressure. He ordered more tests.

Meanwhile, my condition was worsening. I was becoming badly anemic, and I was coping with profound weakness. My kidneys were barely functioning when Frances took the final battery of tests. Charlie and I were at a fund-raiser in New York when we received word that Frances had failed the tests and was definitely eliminated as a donor. We had come full circle and had nowhere else to go.

But then a few days later, Charlie called my last remaining sibling, who had not been tested—my big brother Don in California. Charlie explained the situation, and Don agreed immediately to take blood tests and consider serving as a donor. The results were good—Don was free of any disease and could serve as a donor. The decision to donate one's kidney is difficult. This was especially true for Don, who hates being near hospitals and medical doctors and made it a point to stay healthy so he would not have to get even remotely close to a medical facility.

Don talked with his wife and children about the situation. They were, of course, fearful for his safety. But Don and I went to Boston for a final test to make sure there was a complete match of blood and everything was in order. Everything checked out.

In the spring of 1990, Don agreed to go ahead with the surgery and to give me one of his healthy kidneys. The operation was set for June. I know how hard that decision was for him to make. There are obviously no words to thank him for his sacrifice. As he had been all my life when he worked so hard along with my father to put food on the table and shoes on our feet, my big brother Don was once again a hero. He is indeed my special hero. Without Don, without the diligence of my friend Gloria Steinem, and without the skills of Dr. Monaco, I would not be alive today. One more time, death visited with me, perhaps lingered nearby for a while, and in the end gave me a reprieve.

The surgery took three hours. My brother's kidney was removed and transplanted, and it began to work almost immediately after it was placed in my body. Don experienced incredible postoperative pain, but both of us soon mended, although I suffered much guilt from watching Don go through a painful rehabilitation. But except for a few minor problems, there have been no real complications since the operation. I was back to work in Oklahoma in August, less than two months after having received my new kidney. I am much more respectful of death than to declare myself a clear victor, however. With an illness such as this, even though I feel well most of the time, I am aware that things could go wrong again, that I could experience kidney rejection or other problems related to the transplant.

Since the operation, I have continued to work as hard as possible for my tribe and other Native Americans by adhering to the principles of self-government and by fulfilling as many of my people's needs as possible without the bureaucratic delays of the past. I am proud to watch my people improve their individual lives *on their own* through various educational and employment opportunities. We Cherokees have managed to figure out how to live successfully in a very modern, fast-paced world, while preserving our cultural values and traditions.

There is still much to be done. That is why, in 1991, I decided to run for another four-year term as principal chief of the Cherokee Nation. I wished to continue my work—especially to concentrate on health and housing issues. Although I drew two stalwart opponents, William K. Dew and Art Nave, I won another term by a considerable margin. The newspapers called my victory a landslide because I received 82.7 percent of the votes. I really did not expect to do that well. I was only hoping to avoid another runoff. But by receiving so many votes, I felt that our people were saying the issue of gender and doubts was at last buried.

My inauguration ceremony was held on August 14, 1991. It was another full house. Charlie held the Bible as I again took the oath of office. There were a lot of speeches and warm words. I felt very comfortable at the podium delivering my address. I knew many others were present there that day besides the people gathered in the auditorium. I felt their presence, too.

> It's a fine time for celebration because as we approach the twenty-first century, the Cherokee Nation still has a strong, viable tribal government. Not only do we have a government that has continued to exist, we have a tribal government that's growing and progressing and getting stronger. We've managed not to just barely hang on, we've managed to move forward in a very strong, very affirmative way. Given our history of adversity I think it's a testament to our tenacity, both individually and collectively as a people, that we've been able to keep the Cherokee Nation government going since time immemorial.
>
> Wilma Mankiller, inaugural speech, 1991

Although our tribe has continued to make remarkable progress, we still have much to do. Issues I am working on now include a new education plan, Cherokee language and literacy projects, developing Sequoyah High School into a magnet school, developing a comprehensive health-care system, an extensive array of services for children and youths, settlement of old land claims, taxation, housing initiatives, safeguarding the environment, and economic development.

My family also remains very important to me, and is a great source of joy.

Felicia is quiet, somewhat shy, and expresses little interest in politics. She is content with a nice job at Northeastern State University in Tahlequah. She is tall, and very slender and striking. She has dark brown hair and brown eyes. Felicia has two sons and a daughter, Aaron, Jaron, and Breanna Swake, ages seven, three, and two, respectively.

Gina is very bright and outgoing, and was always on the honor roll. She too is tall and pretty, with thick black hair that she keeps in a wild tumble of curls, even now at twenty-seven. She has inherited my interest in politics. She has one son, Kellen Quinton, who is four years old.

Both of my daughters married men with Cherokee ancestry.

When my girls were growing up, I encouraged them to read, appreciate music, maintain a sense of humor, and dance. We danced to all kinds of songs, but our favorite was Aretha Franklin's "Respect." After the car accident in 1979, I could no longer do that type of dancing. I am always saddened when either of my girls refers to "the time when Mom danced with us." I still do ceremonial dances, but I no longer do very much contemporary dancing.

Charlie's son Winterhawk Soap, who lives with us, is thirteen. Like his father, he is a Plains-style dancer. He attends Cherokee ceremonial dances, and is interested in Cherokee culture. Winterhawk likes art and history, and is a good student at Rocky Mountain School, where my brothers and sisters and I walked down those country roads to school years ago.

Now, at my home at Mankiller Flats, surrounded by my books, my art, my grandchildren, and the natural world, I realize that my journey had indeed brought me to the place where I was always destined to be. As I sit by a winter fire or walk to the spring where my family has gone for generations or rest on the porch where the walkingsticks like to come to munch on redbud leaves, I often think about my past and the history of my people.

I recall the numbers of Cherokees who, in the last two centuries, left behind our traditional ways. Those Cherokee elite, as I call them, adhered to the white ways. I also think of their counterparts, the traditionalists who remained true to our tribe's past. I remember hearing that this division created incredible stress and confusion within our Nation, and in 1811, a large comet blazed across the sky for weeks. There was talk of more war with the British and with the Creeks. I recall the old stories.

It was during that time that our people reached a crossroads. It was a period of great uneasiness, and that year and the next, there were severe earthquakes that caused fear to spread among our people. An indication of this turmoil was conveyed by the Warrior's Nephew to the Moravians. He reported that some native people—led by a man beating a drum—had descended from the sky. The man had warned the Cherokees that the Mother of the Nation was unhappy. She was unhappy that we had given up planting corn. She was unhappy that we had let the whites take over our sacred towns. The Mother of the Nation wanted the Cherokees to return to the old ways.

According to the oral tradition, it was during this time that a great Cherokee prophet called Charley claimed to have received a message from the Great Spirit, the Creator of Life and Breath. Charley emerged from the mountains accompanied by two wolves. Charley told an assembly of Cherokees that the Great Spirit was displeased that we had given up our old ways in favor of the white man's mills, clothing, and culture. He told them that the Great Spirit was angry and wished the Cherokees to take up the old dances and feasts—to return to the time when they listened to the Great Spirit in their dreams. Charley warned that if they ignored the message he delivered, they would face death. However, when death did not overcome those who chose to ignore his prophecy, his power diminished among our people. But some of us realize that the death Charley talked about may not have been physical death, but the death of the spirit.

This is one of my favorite stories. It is a lesson. When it is told well, I can visualize the prophet and his two wolves coming out of the night to warn the Cherokees about the impending loss of our traditions and culture.

Among the artworks I keep in our home are a painting and a wood sculpture. They are depictions of Charley and the wolves appearing before the council of Cherokees. Having Charley in my home reminds me every single day of the need for contemporary Cherokees to be on guard. Having Charley nearby reminds us to be sure to do everything we can to hold onto our language, our ceremonies, our culture. For we are people of today—people of the so-called modern world. But first and foremost, and forever, we are also Cherokees.

CHRONOLOGY

---

at least
18,000 B.C.   Indigenous people are living in the Americas.

A.D. 800   The Spiro culture appears south of the Arkansas River in present eastern Oklahoma during the mound-builder period.

1492   Christopher Columbus lands in the Americas. Contact between Native Americans and the Spanish results in the first permanent American settlement by Europeans.

1500   An estimated seventy-five million indigenous people are living in the Western Hemisphere, including six million in the present United States. The Cherokees are the indigenous holders of more than seventy million acres in present Tennessee, Georgia, Alabama, Kentucky, North Carolina, South Carolina, and Virginia.

1519   Hernán Cortés introduces the horse in Mexico. Half the Santo Domingo Nation is killed by smallpox, a disease new to North America.

1532   The Spanish conclude that the indigenous peoples possess true title to the Americas. To acquire ownership of the New World, the Spanish will be required to conquer the lands in a "just war," or to persuade the native peoples to relinquish ownership of their own volition.

1538   Mapmakers use the term *America* to designate provinces of the New World for the first time.

1540   When the first Europeans in the de Soto expedition venture into the "Province of the Chelaque," the Cherokees are settled along streams and waterways, pursuing trade and navigation.

1541   Coronado journeys onto the Great Plains and introduces horses, mules, pigs, cattle, and sheep to the North American continent.

1609   Santa Fe is settled by whites following missionaries into lands claimed by Spain.

1626   Native Americans sell Manhattan Island to Dutch settlers for approximately twenty-four dollars in trade goods.

1673   Cherokees bargain with itinerant British traders for British use of rivers through Cherokee lands as trade routes.

1680   The Pueblo nations of present New Mexico revolt against the Spanish, driving soldiers and settlers back to Mexico. Europeans do not return to the area until the 1690s, when De Vargas negotiates a peaceful agreement with the Pueblos.

1721   The Cherokees sign a treaty with the colony of South Carolina to establish formal boundaries between Cherokee and South Carolina settlements. The governor of South Carolina requests that a principal chief be appointed to facilitate the whites' dealings with the various groups of Cherokees.

1730   A delegation of six Cherokees visits London to cement the Cherokee Nation's relations with the British Crown. While they are there, the unofficial Treaty of Dover is negotiated, containing provisions for eternal friendship between the two sovereign nations and exclusive British trade rights.

1752   Christian missionaries initiate the first attempts to influence the Cherokees.

1754   Benjamin Franklin proposes a union of American colonies to assure central control over Indian policy and agreements. The French and Indian War begins, pitting Native American nations against one another in the service of Great Britain and France. As a result, the British Crown assumes control over relations with native peoples, taking the responsibility from individual colonial governments.

1760   An ill-fated war between the Cherokees and the British begins. The conflict will last a year, ending with surrender by the Cherokees.

1761   Two successive Cherokee delegations visit London. British-Cherokee relations are improved by creation of two "Indian districts" and appointment of agents to serve them.

1763   Mass migration of settlers onto Native American lands occurs. King George III of Great Britain issues the Proclamation of 1763, setting aside all lands west of the Appalachians as "Indian country" and ordering all British subjects to remove themselves from tribal holdings.

1776   The American colonies declare their independence. Many Native American nations are allied with Great Britain because of agreements made with the Crown.

1776–1777   Successful Revolutionary War raids on Cherokee towns provoke the execution of a peace treaty with the Americans. The treaty cedes to the whites nearly all Cherokee lands in South Carolina and large tracts in North Carolina and Tennessee. Cherokees led by Dragging Canoe refuse to sign the treaty, and they secede from the Cherokee Nation, removing themselves to Chickamauga Creek, where they continue to wage hostilities against the Americans.

1781   The United States adopts the Articles of Confederation, giving the Continental Congress sole power over all Indian affairs providing that no state's legislative rights are infringed.

TREATY OF HOPEWELL — 1 8 3 8

1785   The Treaty of Hopewell, the first between the United States and the Cherokee Nation, is signed. The treaty places the Cherokees under the protection of the United States government and "no other sovereign," and pledges to keep them from oppression.

1787   Congress passes the Northwest Ordinance, which promises that Native American territories "shall never be taken from them without their consent" and that "they shall never be invaded or disturbed, unless in just and lawful wars authorized by Congress."

1789   The United States Constitution is adopted, and one article empowers the president to make treaties, including those with Native American nations, with the consent of the Senate.

1790   The Trade and Intercourse Act is enacted by Congress, restricting whites from entering Indian lands and selling alcoholic beverages there, and establishing standards of justice for crimes by one race against another.

1791   The Treaty of Holston is signed, initiating the first complete peace between the United States and the Cherokee Nation. The treaty states that the United States "solemnly guarantees to the Cherokee Nation, all their lands not hereby ceded." In exchange, the Cherokees officially place themselves "under the protection of the said United States of America, and of no other sovereign whatsoever."

1792   The Cherokee capital is moved from Echota in present Tennessee to Oostanaula in Georgia because of a shift of population farther south.

1794   The Spanish negotiate a treaty with the Choctaws, Chickasaws, Creeks, and Cherokees. The Cherokees cede more land to the United States. A Cherokee group led by Chief Bowl immigrates to present Arkansas.

1801   The first mission school is opened on Cherokee lands. The school had been requested by the Cherokee National Council.

1802   Thomas Jefferson signs the Georgia Compact, which includes support of Indian removal.

1803   The United States doubles in size with the Louisiana Purchase. The pursuit of Manifest Destiny begins. Thomas Jefferson initiates the first removal policy, proposing that all eastern tribes of Native Americans be removed to the newly acquired lands. Congress appropriates funds for the action, which is unpopular with the majority of native nations, including a significant majority of Cherokees. There are already some Cherokee settlements west of the Mississippi.

1804   The Cherokees cede land in Georgia. Lewis and Clark begin their historic expedition to chart the course of the Missouri River.

1805   The Cherokees agree to decrease their tribal holdings. The United States reaffirms its guarantee of protection for the Cherokee Nation.

1806   A treaty in January cedes tracts of Cherokee lands in Tennessee and Alabama to the United States.

1808   The Cherokees adopt a written legal code. Portions of the code have been in use since 1797 and before.

1810   The Supreme Court hears the first case on Indian law. Its decision in *Fletcher vs. Peck* is that states can grant land subject to Indian title. The validity of Indian title is to be based on occupancy.

1812   The War of 1812 begins. When the British withdraw from American soil, native nations lose the option of allying with another nation. Future treaties will become unilateral instruments to advance western expansion of the United States.

1813   The Western Cherokees establish a capital at Tahlonteeskee, near the Illinois River in present Oklahoma. Cherokees ally with Americans during the war in which the Creeks fight against white domination. Seven million acres of Cherokee land between the Verdigris River in present Oklahoma and the boundary of the Western Cherokees is sold to the United States.

1814   A Cherokee soldier saves the life of Andrew Jackson at the Battle of Horseshoe Bend.

1817   The General Crimes Act comes into effect, providing for federal prosecution of crimes by non-Indians against Native Americans on Indian lands. It is the first law to provide for federal criminal jurisdiction over Native Americans on their own lands. U.S. mail service is inaugurated throughout Cherokee lands. The Exchange Treaty sets aside eastern lands for the Cherokees and equal holdings in present Arkansas. A clause pertaining to reservations gives ceded lands to heads of families who become citizens of the United States.

1819   In February, the Old Settler Cherokees agree to a treaty that provides for land-exchange agreements and their removal to Arkansas Territory. A fund is created by Congress for the "civilization of the Indians."

1820   The year marks the beginning of the United States Indian removal policy, which will remain official until 1861. The policy calls for removal of Native American nations beyond states' boundaries and west of the Mississippi River.

1821   Sequoyah (George Guess or Gist) completes the eighty-five-character syllabary of the Cherokee language. Use of the syllabary spreads rapidly throughout the Cherokee Nation and to the Western Cherokees.

1824   The secretary of war creates an Office of Indian Affairs in the U.S. War Department.

1825   The United States begins removal of Native Americans to western lands.

1827   A written Cherokee constitution is adopted by elected delegates at New Echota, Georgia.

1828   The first issue of the *Cherokee Phoenix*, a national, bilingual Cherokee newspaper, appears. Gold is discovered in the eastern portion of the Cherokee Nation. More than ten thousand gold seekers flood the area. The Georgia legislature enacts edicts negating Cherokee sovereignty and extending state authority over the Cherokee Nation's lands.

1830   The Indian Removal Act is passed by Congress, initiating the systematic, forced relocation of native nations in the East to Indian Territory, west of the Mississippi, in an effort to prevent altercations with white settlers.

1831   In a landmark decision in *Cherokee Nation v. Georgia*, the U.S. Supreme Court holds that Indian tribes are not foreign nations but domestic dependent nations.

1832   The U.S. Supreme Court hands down another landmark decision in *Worcester v. Georgia*. A Georgia state lottery parcels out land claimed by the state in Cherokee territory. The Supreme Court holds that the Cherokee Nation is a distinct and independent community that Georgia has no right to enter except with consent of the Cherokees.

1835   Despite overwhelming Cherokee opposition to a treaty intended to facilitate the tribe's removal, members of the Ridge or Treaty Party sign the Treaty of New Echota, giving up title to all Cherokee lands in the Southeast in exchange for land in Indian Territory.

1836   Congress ratifies the treaty of New Echota despite the protests of Cherokee Chief John Ross and thousands of Cherokees.

TRAIL OF TEARS — 1893

1838   The Cherokee Trail of Tears begins. The forced migration will claim the lives of more than four thousand Cherokees.

1839   Treaty Party leaders Major Ridge, John Ridge, and Elias Boudinot are assassinated, partly for having signed the Treaty of New Echota. The Convention of 1839 reunites the Old Settlers, Treaty Party, and Ross Party Cherokees in Indian Territory. A constitutional convention follows.

1849   Congress transfers the Office of Indian Affairs from the War Department to the newly created Department of the Interior.

1861   The Confederacy courts the Cherokee Nation for support of its cause against the Union, despite strenuous attempts by Chief John Ross to keep the Nation neutral. A treaty is signed between the Cherokee Nation and the Confederate government. The Cherokee Nation fields two regiments to fight in the Civil War. A violent struggle will separate Cherokees loyal to the Union from proponents of the Confederacy.

1862   President Abraham Lincoln signs the Homestead Act into law, offering anyone older than twenty-one a free 160-acre tract of land in the West.

1863   In February, the Cherokee Nation abolishes slavery within its boundaries and abrogates its Confederate treaty.

1866   To punish the Five Tribes for having supported the Confederacy, the United States government compels them to accept new treaties surrendering the western half of Indian Territory, where about twenty tribes from Kansas and Nebraska are to be settled on thirteen reservations.

1868   Members of the Cheyenne Nation are massacred by George Custer and his troops in Indian Territory at the Battle of the Washita.

1871   The Appropriations Act provides for the termination of treaty making with Native American nations. The act recognizes all treaties enacted before 1871 as remaining in force.

1872   Wholesale slaughter of the American bison begins. In the next two years, more than four million buffalo will be annihilated.

1876   The U.S. Seventh Cavalry and northern Plains Indians clash in the Battle of the Little Bighorn in present Montana, during the United States' centennial year. The battle, in which the Indians were victorious, will become widely known as "Custer's Last Stand."

1878   Boarding schools are established for Native American children off reservation lands. Students are punished for speaking their native languages and practicing their own religious beliefs.

1883   The practice of traditional Native American religions becomes a federal offense.

1885   The Major Crimes Act provides for federal jurisdiction over seven major criminal acts between Native Americans on reservations. The list will later be expanded to include fourteen crimes.

1887   The Dawes Severalty Act or General Allotment Act comes into effect, preparing Native Americans for eventual termination of tribally held land by granting 160-acre allotments to each male, promoting private farming with the intention of easing "assimilation." Teddy Roosevelt will call the Dawes Act "a mighty pulverizing engine to break up the tribal mass."

1889 "Unassigned lands" in Oklahoma Territory (formed from western Indian Territory) are opened to white settlers.

1890 The Battle or Massacre at Wounded Knee occurs near Wounded Knee Creek in present South Dakota when members of the Seventh Cavalry kill more than 150 members of Big Foot's band of Lakotas. The event draws the Indian wars to a tragic close. The Organic Act officially establishes Oklahoma Territory.

1891 Ethnologist James Mooney arrives in present Oklahoma to study Native American societies and cultures.

DAWES COMMISSION — 1945

1893 Congress establishes the Dawes Commission to work for the negation of tribal title to lands held by the Choctaw, Chickasaw, Cherokee, Seminole, and Creek nations. James Mooney prepares a Native American exhibit for the World's Fair in Chicago. Lands in the Cherokee Outlet in present Oklahoma are opened for white settlement.

1898 The Curtis Act abolishes tribal courts and laws but allows Native American nations to retain mineral rights to their lands, and extends the allotment policy to the Five Tribes in Indian Territory. The Dawes Commission begins to enroll members on tribal rolls.

1901 Congress confers United States citizenship on all Native Americans residing in Indian Territory.

1902 The secretary of the interior authorizes the first oil and gas leases on Indian lands in present Oklahoma.

1903   W. C. Rogers is elected chief of the Cherokees. It will be sixty-eight years before another chief is selected by vote of the people of the tribe.

1905   The Sequoyah Constitutional Convention meets in Muskogee, Indian Territory, in the interest of proposing that Indian Territory become an Indian state.

1907   Oklahoma statehood combines Indian and Oklahoma territories into a single state.

1912   Sac and Fox athlete Jim Thorpe of Oklahoma wins the Olympic pentathlon and decathlon in Stockholm, Sweden.

1924   Congress passes the Indian Citizenship Act, granting voting rights and United States citizenship to all Native Americans born in the country's territorial limits, although indigenous Americans are still considered to be outside the protection of the Bill of Rights. Indians will not receive the right to vote in all states until 1948.

1928   The Merriam Report reveals in detail the massive failure of federal Indian policies since the late nineteenth century.

1934   The Wheeler-Howard Act, sometimes called the "Indian New Deal," replaces the Dawes Act, ending the allotment policy and providing for political and economic development of reservations and creation of autonomous tribal governments, all under increased supervision by the Bureau of Indian Affairs.

1936   The Indian Welfare Act becomes law, allowing Native American nations to adopt constitutions and receive charters of incorporation.

1944   The National Congress of American Indians is established in Denver, Colorado.

MANKILLER'S BIRTH—1993

1945   Wilma Pearl Mankiller, future principal chief of the Cherokee Nation of Oklahoma, is born at Mankiller Flats near Rocky Mountain, Oklahoma.

1946   The Indian Claims Commission is created to deal with Native American claims for compensation. The commission's work will continue until 1978, when the remaining 102 cases will be transferred to the United States Court of Claims.

1948   Cherokee Chief J. B. Milam, a U.S. presidential appointee, calls a Cherokee convention to discuss revitalization of the Cherokee Nation.

1949   The Hoover Commission recommends in its report on Indian affairs that Native Americans be fully assimilated "into the mass of the population as full, tax-paying citizens." W. W. Keeler is appointed chief of the Cherokees by President Harry Truman.

1953   Congress adopts the "termination policy" as the new solution to the "Indian problem" by passing House Concurrent Resolution 108, which is intended to "end [Native Americans'] status as wards of the United States." During the next thirteen years, Congress will enact statutes terminating federal relationships with more than one hundred Native American nations, causing more than eleven thousand people to lose their status as "recognized" Native Americans. More than a million acres of land are removed from trust protection.

1956   The Mankiller family moves from rural Adair County, Oklahoma, to San Francisco, California, as part of the U.S. government's relocation program. The Bureau of Indian Affairs had instituted the program, which relocated thousands of Native Americans in the late 1950s. The program's goal was to abolish native people's ties to their lands and cultures. More than one-third of those who were relocated returned home, marking the program's failure.

1962   Native American nations are made eligible for benefits under the Manpower Development and Training Act.

1964   The Economic Opportunity Act extends benefits to native people for the first time, through the Office of Economic Opportunity Indian desk.

1968   Congress enacts the Indian Civil Rights Act, which extends the Bill of Rights to Native Americans for the first time. Religious freedom will not be legislated until 1978.

1969   Native Americans seize Alcatraz Island in San Francisco Bay, beginning an occupation that will last nineteen months. The group hopes to bring attention to Native American concerns and the growing problems faced by indigenous people in the United States.

1970   The termination era ends and the self-determination era of Indian policy begins. Election of chiefs to lead the Five Tribes replaces the practice of federal appointment of tribal leaders. A U.S. Supreme Court ruling confirms Cherokee, Choctaw, and Chickasaw ownership of bed and banks of a ninety-six-mile segment of the Arkansas River in Oklahoma.

1971   W. W. Keeler becomes the first elected principal chief of the Cherokees since Oklahoma statehood.

1972   Members of the civil-rights organization known as the American Indian Movement occupy BIA offices in Washington, D.C., culminating a march known as the "Trail of Broken Treaties." Their actions are intended to focus national attention on Native American issues.

1973   AIM members take over Wounded Knee, South Dakota, beginning a sixty-nine-day siege. The group demands a full U.S. Senate investigation of conditions on reservations. AIM also demands the return of the Black Hills to the Lakota Nation.

1975   Ross O. Swimmer is elected to the first of three terms as principal chief of the Cherokee Nation. A fifteen-member Cherokee tribal council is seated. Congress passes the Indian Self-Determination and Assistance Act.

1976   Cherokee Nation voters ratify a new constitution.

1978   The American Indian Religious Freedom Act grants Native Americans protection for the exercise of traditional religions and religious practices. The BIA establishes criteria by which Native American nations can be federally acknowledged as tribes.

1983   United States Indian policy recognizes a government-to-government relationship with Native American nations, but emphasizes the need for less reliance on federal support and more development of reservation economies. Ross Swimmer and Wilma Mankiller, a political "odd couple," are elected as principal chief and deputy chief of the Cherokee Nation, respectively.

1984   The first joint council meeting in 146 years occurs at Red Clay, Tennessee, between the Eastern Band of Cherokees and the Cherokee Nation of Oklahoma.

1985   Wilma Mankiller becomes the first woman principal chief of the Cherokees when Ross Swimmer resigns to head the BIA.

1986   Senate Concurrent Resolution 76 reaffirms the constitutionally recognized government-to-government relationship between the United States and Native American nations. The resolution acknowledges the need for utmost good faith in upholding treaties as the legal and moral duty of the United States.

1989   The Brendale opinion of the U.S. Supreme Court states that whenever a piece of land in a reservation passes out of trust, tribal sovereignty is negated.

1990   Chief Mankiller signs the historic self-governance agreement authorizing the Cherokee Nation to assume responsibility for funds formerly administered by the BIA. Tribal courts and tribal police are revitalized, and a Cherokee Nation tax commission is established.

1991   Chief Mankiller wins her third term in office, receiving 82 percent of the vote. The fifteen-member Cherokee tribal council includes six women.

1992   Chief Mankiller is selected by President-elect Bill Clinton to represent Native American nations at a national economic summit in Little Rock, Arkansas.

1993   The United Nations declares this the "Year of the Indigenous People."

BIBLIOGRAPHY AND SUGGESTIONS
FOR FURTHER READING

Ethnologist James Mooney, so prominent in the late nineteenth century, was one of the first European Americans to record and preserve the Cherokee oral tradition, so intelligent and eloquent. Mooney's books, *Myths of the Cherokee* and *Sacred Formulas of the Cherokees*, were based directly on information he collected from Cherokee spiritual leaders and story-tellers. Three-quarters of the tribal stories Mooney published in the late 1800s were collected from Ayunini, or Swimmer, a doctor, spiritual leader, and keeper of Cherokee traditions. Although Swimmer spoke and wrote only in the Cherokee language, he provided Mooney with written texts and skillful recitations.

Many Cherokee storytellers shared their knowledge with Mooney. Itagunahi, or John Ax, provided the ethnologist with a century's worth of experiences in ceremonial traditions. Other Cherokees who spoke through Mooney's accounts include Suyeta, or the Chosen One; Tag-wadihi, also called Catawba-killer; Chief N. J. Smith; Salali; Tsesani, or Jessan; a woman named Ayasta; and James D. Wafford, known as Tsusk-wanunnawata.

Ahern, Wilbert H. "Indian Education and Bureaucracy." *Fort Totten: Military*

Post and Indian School, edited by Larry Remele. State Historical Society of North Dakota, 1986.

Ammon, Solomon R. "History and Present Development of Indian Schools in the United States." Thesis, University of Southern California. Reprint. San Francisco: R and E Research Associates, 1975.

Ballenger, T. L. *Around Tablequah Council Fires*. Oklahoma City: Cherokee Publishing Company, Inc., 1945.

Bean, Walton. *California: An Interpretive History*. New York: McGraw-Hill, Inc., 1978, 1973, 1968.

Bell, George Morrison, Sr. *Genealogy of Old and New Cherokee Indian Families*. Bartlesville, Oklahoma: George Morrison Bell, Sr., 1972.

Bernstein, Barton J., and Allen J. Matusow, eds. *The Truman Administration: A Documentary History*. New York: Harper & Row, 1966.

Brown, John P. *Old Frontiers: The Story of the Cherokee Indians from Earliest Times to the Date of Their Removal to the West, 1838*. 1938. Reprint. Kingsport, Tennessee: Southern Publishers, Inc., 1971.

Burt, Jesse, and Robert B. Ferguson. *Indians of the Southeast: Then and Now*. Nashville and New York: Abingdon Press, 1973.

Campbell, Janet, and Archie Sam. "The Primal Fire Lingers," *The Chronicles of Oklahoma* 53:4 (Winter 1975–76).

Conley, Robert J. *The Witch of Goingsnake and Other Stories*. Norman: University of Oklahoma Press, 1988.

Cotterill, R. S. *The Southern Indians: The Story of the Five Civilized Tribes Before Removal*. Norman: University of Oklahoma Press, 1954.

Cunningham, Frank. *General Stand Watie's Confederate Indians*. San Antonio: The Naylor Co., 1959.

Cunningham, Hugh T. "A History of the Cherokee Indians." *The Chronicles of Oklahoma* 8:3 (September 1930).

Dale, Edward E., and Gaston L. Litton. *Cherokee Cavaliers: Forty Years of Cherokee History as Told in the Correspondence of the Ridge-Watie-Boudinot Family*. Norman: University of Oklahoma Press, 1939.

Dale, Edward Everett, and Jesse Lee Rader. *Readings in Oklahoma History.* Evanston, Illinois: Row, Peterson and Company, 1930.

Debo, Angie. *A History of the Indians of the United States.* Norman: University of Oklahoma Press, 1970.

————. *And Still the Waters Run: The Betrayal of the Five Civilized Tribes.* Princeton, New Jersey: Princeton University Press, 1940. Reprint. Norman: University of Oklahoma Press, 1984.

Deloria, Vine, Jr. *Custer Died for Your Sins.* New York: Avon Books, 1970.

Drinnon, Richard. *Keeper of Concentration Camps: Dillon S. Myer and American Racism.* Berkeley: University of California Press, 1987.

Ehle, John. *Trail of Tears: The Rise and Fall of the Cherokee Nation.* New York: Anchor Books, 1988.

Ellis, Jerry. *Walking the Trail: One Man's Journey along the Cherokee Trail of Tears.* New York: Delacorte Press, 1991.

Everett, Dianna. *The Texas Cherokees: A People Between Two Fires, 1819–1840.* Norman: University of Oklahoma Press, 1990.

Fischer, LeRoy H., ed. *The Civil War Era in Indian Territory.* Los Angeles: Lorrin L. Morrison, 1974.

Forbes, Jack D., ed. *The Indian in America's Past.* Englewood Cliffs, New Jersey: Prentice-Hall, Inc., 1964.

Foreman, Grant. *The Five Civilized Tribes.* 1933. Reprint. Norman: University of Oklahoma Press, 1968.

————. *Indian Removal.* Norman: University of Oklahoma Press, 1953.

Franks, Kenny A. *Stand Watie and the Agony of the Cherokee Nation.* Memphis, Tennessee: Memphis State University Press, 1979.

Gentry, Curt. *The Last Days of the Late, Great State of California.* New York: G. P. Putnam's Sons, 1968.

German, Avis. "Refugee Indians Within and from the Indian Country, 1861–1867." Master's thesis, Wichita State University, 1987.

Gibson, Arrell Morgan. *Oklahoma: A History of Five Centuries.* Norman: University of Oklahoma Press, 1981.

Hausman, Gerald. *Turtle Island Alphabet*. New York: St. Martin's Press, 1992.

Hendrix, Janey B. *Redbird Smith and the Nighthawk Keetoowahs*. Park Hill, Oklahoma: Cross-Cultural Education Center, Inc., 1984.

Holmes, Ruth Bradley, and Betty Sharp Smith. *Beginning Cherokee*. Norman: University of Oklahoma Press, 1977.

Holt, Barry H., and Gary Forester. *Digest of American Indian Law*. Littleton, Colorado: Fred B. Rothman & Co., 1990.

Hudson, Charles. *The Southeastern Indians*. Knoxville: University of Tennessee Press, 1976.

Hunt, David C. "Indian Kings and Councillors." *American Scene* (Tulsa, Oklahoma: Thomas Gilcrease Institute of American History and Art) 13:2 (1972).

Jacobs, Wilbur R. *Dispossessing the American Indian*. New York: Charles Scribner's Sons, 1972.

Josephy, Alvin V., Jr. *Red Power: The American Indians' Fight for Freedom*. Lincoln: University of Nebraska Press, 1971.

―――, ed. *America in 1492: The World of the Indian Peoples Before the Arrival of Columbus*. New York: Alfred A. Knopf, 1992.

Keith, Harold. *Rifles for Watie*. New York: Thomas Y. Crowell Co., 1957.

Kilpatrick, Jack Frederick, and Anna Gritts Kilpatrick. *Run Toward the Nightland: Magic of the Oklahoma Cherokees*. Dallas: Southern Methodist University Press, 1967.

King, Duane H., ed. *The Cherokee Indian Nation: A Troubled History*. Knoxville: University of Tennessee Press, 1979.

Lavender, David. *California: Land of New Beginnings*. New York: Harper & Row, 1972.

―――. *The Great West*. American Heritage, 1965. Reprint. Boston: Houghton Mifflin Company, 1987.

Lyons, Mohawk, et al. *Exiled in the Land of the Free*. Santa Fe, New Mexico: Clearlight Publishing, 1993.

Mathiessen, Peter. *Indian Country.* New York: The Viking Press, 1984.

McLoughlin, William G. *Champions of the Cherokees: Evan and John B. Jones.* Princeton, New Jersey: Princeton University Press, 1990.

————. *The Cherokee Ghost Dance.* Macon, Georgia: Mercer University Press, 1984.

McWilliams, Carey. *The California Revolution.* New York: Grossman Publishers, Inc., 1968.

Meredith, Howard L. *Bartley Milam: Principal Chief of the Cherokee Nation.* Muskogee, Oklahoma: Indian University Press, 1985.

Mooney, James. *Myths of the Cherokee* and *Sacred Formulas of the Cherokees,* from the nineteenth and seventh annual reports, Bureau of American Ethnology. Reprint. Nashville, Tennessee: Elder Booksellers, 1982.

Moulton, Gary E. *John Ross: Cherokee Chief.* Athens: University of Georgia Press, 1978.

Nabokov, Peter, ed. *Native American Testimony.* New York: Viking Penguin, 1991.

O'Brien, Sharon. *American Indian Tribal Governments.* Norman: University of Oklahoma Press, 1989.

Cherokee Nation Records 8, Vol. 251, Laws of 1863 to 1868. Oklahoma Historical Society, Oklahoma City.

Parker, Thomas Valentine. *The Cherokee Indians.* New York: The Grafton Press, 1907.

Pearson, Keith L. *The Indian in American History.* New York: Harcourt Brace Jovanovich, Inc., 1973.

Perdue, Theda. *The Cherokee.* New York: Chelsea House Publishers, 1989.

Rawls, James J. *Indians of California.* Norman: University of Oklahoma Press, 1984.

Remele, Larry, ed. *Fort Totten: Military Post and Indian School.* State Historical Society of North Dakota, 1986.

John Ross Papers. Thomas Gilcrease Institute of American History and Art, Tulsa, Oklahoma.

Rossman, Douglas A. *Where Legends Live: A Pictorial Guide to Cherokee Mythic Places*. Cherokee, North Carolina: Cherokee Publications, 1988.

Smith, Benny. "The Keetoowah Society of the Cherokee Indians." Master's thesis, Northwestern State college, Alva, Oklahoma, 1967.

Starr, Emmet. *Cherokees "West,"* 1794 to 1839. Oklahoma City: Printers Publishing Company, 1910.

———. *History of the Cherokee Indians and Their Legends and Folk Lore*. Oklahoma City: The Warden Co., 1921. Reprint. Tulsa, Oklahoma: Oklahoma Yesterday Publications, 1984.

Strickland, Rennard. *Fire and the Spirits: Cherokee Law from Clan to Court*. Norman: University of Oklahoma Press, 1975.

———. *The Indians in Oklahoma*. Norman: University of Oklahoma Press, 1980.

Thomas, Robert K. "The Origin and Development of the Redbird Smith Movement." Master's thesis, University of Arizona, 1953.

Thornton, Russell. *American Indian Holocaust and Survival: A Population History Since* 1492. Norman: University of Oklahoma Press, 1987.

———. *The Cherokees: A Population History*. Lincoln: University of Nebraska Press, 1990.

Turtle, Eagle/Walking. *Indian America: A Traveler's Companion*. Santa Fe, New Mexico: John Muir Publications, 1989.

Tyner, Howard Q. "The Keetoowah Society in Cherokee History." Master's thesis, University of Tulsa, 1949.

Wardell, Morris L. *A Political History of the Cherokee Nation,* 1838–1907. 1938. Reprint. Norman: University of Oklahoma Press, 1977.

Weatherford, Jack. *Indian Givers: How the Indians of the Americas Transformed the World*. New York: Fawcett Columbine, 1988.

———. *Native Roots: How the Indians Enriched America*. New York: Crown Publishers, Inc., 1991.

Wilkins, Thurman. *Cherokee Tragedy: The Story of the Ridge Family and the Decimation of a People*. New York: The Macmillan Company, 1970.

Woodward, Grace Steele. *The Cherokees*. Norman: University of Oklahoma Press, 1963.

INDEX

Wilma Mankiller continues to serve as principal chief of the Cherokee Nation of Oklahoma. Her other writings include "Keeping Pace with the Rest of the World," published in 1985 in *Southern Exposure*. It will be republished in an anthology entitled *Reinventing the Enemy's Language*, edited by Joy Harjo and others. Mankiller is co-editing, with five other distinguished women, *A Reader's Companion to the History of Women in the U.S.*, soon to be published by Houghton Mifflin Co. Her writings also have appeared in *Native Peoples* magazine and in other native-oriented publications.

Michael Wallis, a biographer and historian of the American West, was born in Missouri in 1945. He is the author of several best-selling books, including the critically acclaimed *Route 66: The Mother Road* (St. Martin's Press, 1990); *Pretty Boy: The Life and Times of Charles Arthur Floyd* (St. Martin's Press, 1992); and a collection of stories and essays entitled *Way Down Yonder in the Indian Nation* (St. Martin's Press, 1993).

Wallis has lived and worked throughout the Southwest and Mexico. He and his wife, Suzanne Fitzgerald Wallis, have lived in Oklahoma since 1982. They also maintain a residence in northern New Mexico.

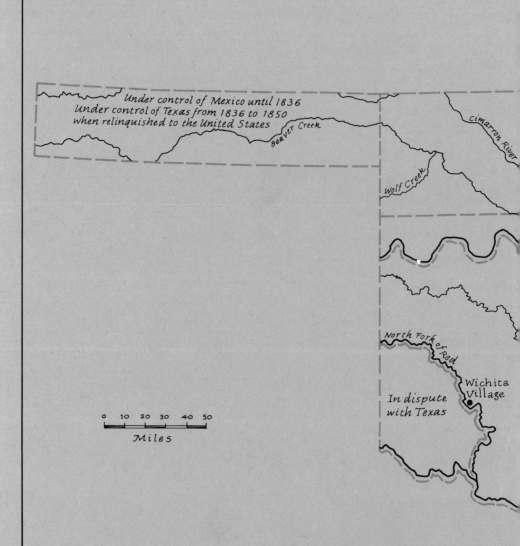

Under control of Mexico until 1836
Under control of Texas from 1836 to 1850
when relinquished to the United States

Beaver Creek

Cimarron River

Wolf Creek

North Fork of Red

Wichita Village

In dispute with Texas

0 10 20 30 40 50

Miles

Indian Territory, 1830-1855